THE CHAMPION SELL

RICHARD RIVERA

THE CHAMPION SELL

The 5 E.L.I.T.E. Sales Habits to Building and Winning with Buyer Champions

RICHARD RIVERA

ISBN: 9798376543924

www.thechampionsell.com

DEDICATION

Kimberly, through all the ups, downs, rounds, and rounds, no one could have supported me more with the love, acceptance, and patience as your mighty heart has. I look up to you as much as our amazing children do. And as an inspiration for this book, you're a pretty badass elite seller yourself!

All my love.

CONTENTS

FOREWORD

JOHN MCMAHON

I n the Sales profession, as in life, we make choices. And, if we are honest, there are only two choices. One, become **elite** at the sales profession by gaining a deep understanding of the game and mastering the required skills to perform at the highest level. Or two, take the easy path, sleep walking through the job, never gaining the knowledge to fully understand "What to do" and never being disciplined to master the skills of "How to do it".

The core of becoming *elite* in sales is the ability to seek and develop an internal **Champion**. Sellers need a Champion because only a Champion has the influence to elevate us in the account to the person that will ultimately approve the deal. That person is the Economic Buyer, or "EB". Elite sales reps know that their deal will eventually land on the desk of the Economic Buyer, the person with discretionary use of funds. The EB has the unique authority to manipulate their budget and is typically a high-level executive with a deep understanding of business operations and the strategic initiatives of the business.

They seek input from key players in their organizations, people they count on to help achieve their vision and goals.

Typically, Champions gained influence with the Economic Buyer because their expertise and credibility on past decisions has helped them develop a positive reputation. They may have gained political power, garnered technical respect, or have specific expertise in a domain, each of which has given them influence in the company. That influence gives them the power to access the Economic Buyer in future critical decisions.

In *The Champion Sell*, Richard Rivera outlines *The 5 E.L.I.T.E. Sales Habits to Building and Winning with Buyer Champions*, where he specifically teaches why we all need Champions to succeed. But what makes this book different from all other sales books in the market is that Richard describes in detail "How to" build everyday selling habits that will lead you to finding and developing powerful Champions. Many companies and books will tell you what a Champion is and how important they are in your selling process, but they don't teach you how to find them, what to look for, what to say, when to say it, build an emotional connection, how to lead them, how to build a trusted relationship, empower them, and what will inspire them to help you gain access to the Economic Buyer.

Let's be real, in many companies it's difficult for a salesperson to become *elite* because they're poorly managed. Salespeople are told by their manager to "Go find a Champion". At the same time, the sales manager is directing the sales reps strictly through *activities*. Send more emails, make more calls, get more meetings, show more demos, do more presentations..."Do more activities!", all in the hope that activity will lead to accomplishment.

To meet their activity goals, reps compliantly work their activities with the first person willing to speak with them in an account. From that point, they try to hurry through the sales process to complete additional activities, more meetings, more demos, more presentations, more validation events. When reps rush through the sales process knowing little-to-nothing about the customer's business and their specific use cases, how can they practically convince the customer that their product or service solves their business issues? They can't. They also can't possibly gain an emotional or business connection with the buyer. So, how are they supposed to find and build a Champion? They can't!

So, the default is to do what they've been trained to do. Talk about the product. They'll talk about the product in feature/function technical terms with a hope and a prayer that; 1 - they get lucky and are speaking to a person that can decide to buy, and 2 - maybe something they said about their product's features/functions resonated and will compel the customer to buy.

However, the odds of 1 and 2 aligning are slim.

In that initial contact, most sales reps perform their activity with the full intention of making their way to the top of the organization. After a few calls with the initial contact, the rep tries to go higher in the account but in many cases, reps get blocked by an insecure manager, a *coach* who doesn't want the rep to go over their head, or worse, an *enemy*. In some instances, they make their way higher in the account but they speak only in technical product terms, not business terms. They get relegated down the organization to the level and person that speaks the same technical language.

If they came late into a buying process, they may be blocked from going higher by the competitor's Champion who wants to control the decision criteria and the decision process in an effort to purchase a different product. Other times, they may be blocked by the Champion of the installed product who is looking to keep the "status-quo", an effort to maintain their own status in the company. These are all ultimately, *enemies* we face in any way you slice it.

The competitor's Champion and even the installed base Champion might pose as a *Fox in Sheep's' Clothing*. They make the rep believe that they're "neutral", saying they will decide to "champion the best product". Sometimes, to maintain control, the installed or competitive Champion may threaten to kick the salesperson out of the account if they go over their head. So the rep, trying to avoid confrontation and believing in the contact, surrenders and rides through the buying process, completely controlled by the supposed Champion.

Other times, the contact may be a well-intentioned *Coach* that wants to buy the product, has the reps' best interests at heart, and even gives the rep inside account information. The rep wants to believe that this Coach could grow into a Champion and can carry them through the buying process to a purchase, only to discover later that the Coach lacks the power and influence in the account to elevate them to higher levels.

When the rep is eventually informed that they lost the deal, the contact finds a way to let the rep down easy. They often use common excuses like, "We decided not to buy now" or "We lost the budget". In most cases, the customer won't have the courage to inform the sales rep of the reality of what occurred. In rare instances, the customer is somewhat honest and says that the competition called much higher in the account and the decision was made at a higher executive level. Of course, that's true. The competition did call higher because they were sponsored by their Champion into the Economic Buyer's office.

When the rep honestly analyzes the lost deal, they realize that they were never in control of the deal. They were being controlled by the competitor's Champion, an installed base Champion, or simply mislead by a manger who lacked influence. In every step of their sales process, they failed to become a "business partner" with the customer. They couldn't affect the buying criteria and had no knowledge of the buying process or how the purchase would ultimately be decided. They were being told what to do, when to do it, and were led by the customer down a one-way dead end street.

On the other hand, *elite* salespeople understand that not everyone on a company organizational chart has the influence to elevate them in the account to the Economic Buyer. So, they take their time to seek out people on the power chart. They seek those with influence and authority because they know that they can build a sales campaign around them, a *Champion!*

They shy away from building a sales campaign around NINA and ANI. Those with No Influence, No Authority. And those with Authority, but No Influence. Elite reps know that spending time with NINA's and ANI's of the organization is not a total waste of time because you may find a *Coach*. A Coach may meet with you, understand the value of your product, give you inside information, want you to win, and *coach* you. But elite sellers are never fooled into thinking that NINA or ANI have the power to elevate their game and provide the control they need.

Elite sales reps understand that Champions are intellectually astute and politically shrewd. Champions are extremely careful not to attach themselves to small pains and certainly not work with unprepared salespeople. They won't jeopardize their standing in the company or their reputation with the Economic Buyer with a salesperson who doesn't understand their business, and certainly not on a rep who is incapable of articulating, in business terms, how they can solve a serious business problem. Champions want to work with a *trusted* business partner to ensure the meeting with the Economic Buyer meets its objectives and the implementation of the *trusted* solution is successful to maintain or enhance their reputation.

So, elite reps find and quantify mission-critical business pain during the initial phases of the sales process because Champions want to attach themselves to the solution of a major business pain. Prior to entering an account, the elite sales rep is armed with open-ended questions and a cold proficiency of the customer's use case, use case pains, how their product differentiators solve the customer pain, the potential value of their solution, and pertinent customer success stories.

Through this process, the elite sales rep can gain an *emotional connection* with the potential Champion by being authentic, having the customer's best interest at heart, and aligning what they sell to what that buyer emotionally cares about most. There's a saying that "People don't care how much you know until they know how much you care".

Being authentic means being *you*, being curious, listening carefully, and thus being able to sense a real perception for what the buyer wants and needs. Once an emotional connection is established, the elite sales rep can now *lead* the customer toward a *vision* for a solution like theirs. At that point, the potential Champion no longer sees a sales rep. They see a potential business partner.

But, is that enough to *champion* a product? No, because Champions have personal aspirations. To realize those aspirations, they need to differentiate themselves within the organization. So, elite sales reps target crucial business problems that directly effects one of the Champion's job measures, a major strategic initiative, or a significant company objective like revenue, cost, productivity, or risk. The potential solution will show the

Champion's added value to the company and, in return, they obtain a personal win by being recognized for their efforts. This allows the elite sales rep to *inspire* the Champion to *commit* to the buying journey and to being their active sponsor.

The work is far from done. Elite sales reps understand that they need to *empower* the Champion by developing their necessary knowledge, while seeking out and partnering through any pending hurdles in the remaining buying process. Together, they must prepare for the Economic Buyer meeting, the upcoming battle with the competitor's Champion, build the cost justification, and plan for product implementation and training needs. As they do this work for their Champion, they also have to ensure and help with the alignment of all other relevant stakeholders. Elite sellers know that Champions value being empowered because they want to eliminate risk in the buying process and implementation. They understand that the EB will hold them personally accountable for a successful outcome.

The difference between elite sales reps and everyone else is clear. In almost all companies, eighty percent of the revenue is generated by twenty percent of the sales reps. How is that possible? Is it magic? No. Do the *twenty percent* know something the *eighty percent* don't know? Rarely. It's actually what they do that's different.

The *twenty percent* have discovered and work to master their *elite* selling habits of finding and building their sales campaigns around people with influence and authority in accounts. They think BIG! They know they need get to the Economic Buyer and solve major business problems because that's where the big money lies. And to get there, they know and believe that they'll never do it without a **Champion!**

You can get there. Make the choice and discover the *5 E.L.I.T.E. Sales Habits to Building and Winning with Buyer Champions* in Richard Rivera's, **The Champion Sell**.

John McMahon was the Chief Revenue Officer at 5 public software companies: PTC, GeoTel, Ariba, BladeLogic, and BMC. He currently is on the board of directors for Snowflake, MongoDB, Lacework, Sigma, and Observe, and has been an advisor and on the board for Hubspot, Glassdoor, Sprinklr, SumoLogic, and AppDynamics. John is also the author of the best-selling book, *The Qualified Sales Leader* and is co-host of the popular podcast *Revenue Builders*.

THE CHAMPION SELL

INTRODUCTION

THE CHAMPION SELL

W e don't sell to companies. We sell to people.

When I got into sales, I never expected how intimidated and nervous I'd feel just before the potential buyer answered my phone call or even when I was about to walk into their office for the first time. It wasn't that I wasn't confident in the product I sold. I'd been trained well, was fully bought in to my differentiation and business value. For me, it was just so different than what I was used to.

Before I sold, I was a schoolteacher, coached football. Those kids didn't intimidate me. I just wanted them to be successful, and most of them really wanted the same thing. But, sales wasn't like that. I mean, when I'd prospect back in the day, when you actually picked up a phone and called a buyer directly, they would be so disappointed to hear a salesperson on the other end. No matter how noble my intentions, I always felt like I was paying a tax for all of the other sales knuckleheads who came before me. I just wanted to help and I had an amazing product to tell them about.

Even when I could get them engaged in learning about my product, I really struggled more than I thought I would to get them to understand it. It didn't make sense to me. I knew my message down cold. I'd studied it, practiced it, and I knew what I was talking about. Yet, time and again, I would somehow be failing to make the right connection with the buyer.

But what was a far more painful journey in my sales career was when I started finding deals to work but just couldn't control any level of urgency or predictability of when they would close. I would take a deal loss over a deal *push* or *no decision* any day.

When you lost a deal, you could at least learn from why you lost it. That painful memory would become a valuable instinct for you in the future that would prevent you from ever making that mistake again. But a *push*? Man, when a deal moved from quarter to quarter, eventually ending up in some *no decision*, that was beyond frustrating. For me, it was mentally crushing.

I've always been someone who put learning and growth ahead of financial outcomes. As an athlete, I was always taught not to focus on the scoreboard. If we did the right things on the field, the wins would come. And they did, just like coach said.

But, in sales, in this *push* or *no decision* deal, you're left pretty clueless as to what happened, what went wrong. Why didn't they buy? I know some of you are probably thinking, "Dude, sales isn't that intimidating." Well, I agree and I eventually figured some things out and was able to be consistently successful.

But, there's no doubt that when I started managing other sellers, I saw all the same feelings. What I observed with my teams, as well as what I figured out with myself, was that the fear and uncertainty we sellers experience is rarely about what we sell or our competition. Sales uncertainty, caution, and lack of confidence usually lies between the seller and the buyer. People selling. People buying.

More compelling was the realization that when I was able to master a true understanding of those people, the buyers, how they thought, their actions, and why they'd ever want to put their reputation on the line to sponsor what I sold, my career turned into one of the most successful parts of my life. I discovered financial freedom.

But more importantly, I uncovered the source of that turnaround. I learned how to build **Buyer Champions**, people who had power and influence in an organization, with access to an economic buyer. I began building emotional and intellectual connections with them, formed real trust. I found the repeatable and instinctual path to lead their vision, inspire their commitment, and empower those Champions to successfully sell for me when I wasn't there.

Many things are necessary to become a good seller. So much knowledge and skills have to be learned over time. But, for myself and in study of what I would call **Elite Sellers**, nothing is more important and game-changing than building Buyer Champions. We don't sell to companies. We sell to people.

If you're reading or listening to this book, *The Champion Sell*, because you'd like to learn how to manipulate buyers more in your secret scheming ways of selling, you should probably close the book or audio file and ask for your money back.

In fact, sellers who are motivated by the challenge of manipulating someone else to prefer your product are really missing out on the amazing greater purpose of selling for a living. If you've been *not so successful* in trying to *challenge* your buyers more, maybe by doing it the wrong way or at the wrong time, there's a good chance this book will show you the reasons why.

Now, that fulfilling purpose of sales will be different for everyone. I think about our time on this earth as having no greater reward than what comes from our relationships and interactions with people.

At our core, even the most introverted personalities like me are social creatures who want to be surrounded by other like-minded people who make us feel good, loved, and significant. We want assurances that we're making an impact, like we're contributing. We need to know that we're being stimulated and challenged to grow. No one wants to struggle. We all want to thrive. But this sales profession and investing in its *craft of selling* affords us the opportunity to impact all those innate core needs we have. Yet, those of us who have chosen this *sales calling* know how hard it is to maximize that opportunity.

Sometimes, the imperfections of the products and services we sell can really get in the way of our success. But what I've observed over twenty-plus years in this business, leading hundreds of sellers and managers, is that too often, *we* are the ones getting in our own way, sabotaging our success. We do this in our communication habits and through our behaviors with buyers.

No, this book is not about relationships. It's certainly not teaching yet another methodology or sales process. If this book is going to impact your craft and help you grow as a seller, it'll be through the strength and confidence around two things.

Buyer Empathy. How often do you feel like you're struggling to build an emotional connection with your buyer, either with you or with what you sell?

So much of that struggle is because no matter how smart we are or how in-depth our training was, most of us have never actually done the job of who we're selling to.

Empathy is a mindset. It's the chosen intentional consideration of someone else's point of view or experience, even if we haven't experienced it ourselves. In sales, regardless of how strong our product or domain knowledge is, if we can't crack that code of connecting what we sell to the unique perspectives and experiences of *who* we're selling to, the *individual person*, then our careers will be frustrating and inconsistent for years.

Ultimately, empathy must be a choice. If you're not so certain how important an empathetic mindset is, one thing *The Champion Sell* will give you is a simple but detailed understanding of why empathy is one of the most critical mindsets of selling. Some of that clarity will stem from basic science, but much of it will come from an intellectually honest self-awareness that you'll gain.

This book will challenge your own selling mindsets and habits which might be preventing you from building those emotional connections with your buyers. Are you someone who sincerely cares about and respects your buyers, but you still struggle to understand the disconnects you have? When you find yourself in misalignment with either their buying criteria or decision processes, do you find it hard to overcome that conflict, pull them toward your point of view and reach compromises?

Empathy is the most powerful overcoming asset we can have in selling to another human being. The good news is that *empathy* can be learned or strengthened. This book will be a great foundation for your empathy mindset.

The second expectation of growth from *The Champion Sell* is **Buyer Intuitiveness.** What is being intuitive in the way we sell to people? How much of your sales activity, the prospecting, presenting your message, negotiating process and price, all feel like such a guess too often?

As conversations start, are you usually pretty confident that the magic words you'll use and natural charm you'll possess will have your buyer in the palm of your hands in no time? Or do you sometimes feel uneasy and accidentally wandering into more uncomfortable higher conflict discussions than you'd like?

These are all examples of lacking *sales intuitiveness*. Most salespeople are not that different in our intelligence or aptitude to do the job. Some are clearly more driven and hungrier than others. Some are armed with the grit and resiliency needed to be great.

But typically, the mistakes we make in sales, if not in life, come from an honest baseline of ignorance. That's not a failure. It's just something we need to know that's important for us to do our job well, and yet we don't.

Hopefully this book will give you a clear understanding of the mind and behaviors of the people you sell to, an *intuitiveness* that guides your sales instincts. When we lack confidence in what we need to know or the expectations of what might happen between buyers and sellers, we either pause and stop, preventing ourselves from finding failure, or we go in hesitantly and cautiously.

Conversely, I've also led those sellers who just say, "What the hell!" and go in *guns ablazing*, led by the blinding light of their own ignorance. Being *intuitive* means having natural involuntary intuition. When we're *intuitive* with the people we sell to, we operate more on instincts and less on thinking. We become efficient sellers, more *naturally* responsive in the moment. Or better, we're instinctual enough to prevent and avoid problems and conflicts all together.

Have you ever heard a buyer say, "Wow, you read my mind," or "It's like you've been sitting in on our staff meetings"? Instincts usually develop from our own personal experiences. So, if you feel like you often lack sales instincts with your buyers, just keep selling for around ten to twenty years to the same exact buyer in the same industry, with the same product, and you should eventually become a superstar. Well, if that's normal, I say *Normal is Overrated.*

If you're invested in this book, it's because you don't want to wait years to finally figure out this human mystery called your *Buyer.* You might be fairly strong in your empathy and instincts for selling, but you'd sure like to reach the next level, go from good to great. Some of you want to become more *consciously competent* and be more consistent with the different buyer interactions and selling situations you're encountering. Maybe you feel like one of those frustrated sellers earlier in your career who can't seem to figure out why your product knowledge and passion just aren't paying dues for you.

You see, while there may be all kinds of different technologies and services that are out there to sell, even different types of sales roles and jobs to consider, if your craft is selling, then the center of your existence must be that human being on the other side of that phone, video conference, or room your sitting in. What we all need to better understand is just who is this person that we're selling to? Why do they react to us the way they do? How do they think and come to make decisions?

So you're clear, this book will not be another academic sales or psychology lesson either. I believe that we sellers need to know *how* to apply that *empathy* and *intuition* in the real sales situations we encounter. In order to get a buyer engaged, attracted to our message, and begin trusting us, we need to know how to lead their vision and gain a commitment and bias for action. What I'll offer as our ultimate mission is that we need our Champions selling on our behalf. Well, what I've observed is that for them to put their own credibility and political capital on the line for us, they need to reach levels of connection and commitment that many of us aren't very sensitive to. If they do reach those connected and committed levels, many of them will need to be *empowered* by us to win the deals we work. If any of this matters to you, I think you'll enjoy *The Champion Sell*. There's no reason anyone should wait years to become an elite seller. It's all about you and that human buyer you're selling to.

What I've tried to do for you in this book is break down just how to master selling to people, in particular those who have the most power and influence in our sales process. We'll define them as our **Buyer Champions.** We'll answer questions like, *What is a Buyer Champion? How are they any different from anyone else I sell to? What do they really need from sellers?* And, *how can we attract, inspire, and empower them to take action for us?*

What I've learned is that the way we motivate a buyer to take action, to commit, isn't by our messaging, sales processes, or methodologies. We either positively or negatively connect with buyers through our **Selling Habits**. Those habits are formed from our mindset. My approach will be to use simple but thoughtful concepts and practical applications focused on the *how* behind elite selling.

Be prepared. This book will go deep into some very detailed but simply applied situational sales learnings from years of experience. Inspired by the ultimate mission of **_Building Buyer Champions_**, this book is about *how to become an elite seller.* It's about winning! I'll spend time trying to guide your mindset, which should lead you to consider some real habit change. Hopefully, I'll relate to the very real and familiar challenges that you and your teams are having with your buyers. I want to simplify sales for you.

The Champion Sell will answer three essential questions: *How can we better understand our buyers,* from their emotions to how they think and make decisions? Then, *how should we communicate with buyers* in a way that disarms them, earns their trust, and influences their vision and commitment? Finally, but maybe most importantly, *how do we empower the most powerful and influential buyers* to sell on our behalf and accomplish both their interests and ours? To avoid making this merely a philosophical exercise, I've focused on **Elite** sellers from intentional observations of what makes the very top performers so consistently great.

As I've considered the focus, the intention is to speak to really any industry or domain of seller. These lessons won't just be helpful in traditional, complex, or enterprise sales. In fact, the more commodity your products or services are, or the more phone or web-based your sale is, I'd argue the more challenging it can be to disarm, engage, and motivate human buyers.

Observed from how truly Elite Sellers consistently perform, I'll walk you through *five critical selling habits* that most of them possess. My examination has come from decades of experience in the most complex high-tech sales to the world's largest enterprises, as well as from sellers and leaders in areas like biotech, medical, industrials, financial, and government sales.

The concepts I'll share have come from my personal experiences in the field, as both a very successful top individual seller and from years serving as a sales and go-to-market executive leader. These concepts are born from thousands of sales calls in most major countries, working with hundreds of buyers with unique personalities and cultural differences. And, sometimes painfully, I've also observed and worked with every level and style of seller under the sun. I've taken all those experiences and analyzed them with a deep psychological study into human behavior and decision making. However, while I'll occasionally refer to the science behind some of the concepts in this book, it's important that you understand that this book is about real selling. My focus is on *how to sell at an elite level*.

ELITE SELLER

To help you get to know me a bit, I'll share a little of my journey. But understand, I want you to know that I, like many of you, had more than my share of struggles and took some time to figure things out.

As a seller I started later in my professional career. I had some sales trials for a few years and certainly with all the things I'll cover in this book. But I was eventually pretty successful. Consistently, I was a top 5 percent performer and multiple times, broke company records closing software deals for tens of millions of dollars.

Even as my career moved into sales leadership roles, my focus was always on selling innovative and disruptive technology, usually at some unicorn startup with a target audience from small to mid to large companies. Trust me, if you've ever sold at a startup, you know how incredibly hard it is to just get someone to take a phone call with you. Most people have never heard of your company or even sometimes, what your product does. Even if what you sell makes a huge impact on a business and you deserve to sell it at a premium price, it's so unbelievably hard to get a buyer to put their neck on the line and sponsor you. In fact, there's an old saying in technology sales that, "No one ever got fired for buying IBM." I'm sure you have similar safe standards in your industry.

Well, that statement actually says a lot about people. I think selling in a startup really illuminates the true psychology of the buyers we sell to. On the surface, it's a pretty big risk for a person to spend their political capital on a company or technology that may not appear to be the safe decision. Thus, you become challenged with disarming those fears and finding that common driver that you can connect them to. Conversely, if you've ever managed a long-term account, selling for a well-known brand, a huge bureaucratic company, or maybe the market leading product that everyone knows about, you've faced your own sets of fears and emotions in your buyers. You've had to overcome those and eventually get to a place where some person or group of people were motivated to act on your behalf.

Every type of sale has one common objective. We're asking *people* to take action on what we sell. Frankly, it's the one greatest factor that makes sales so challenging. So, don't ever let anyone convince you that just because your product or service is disruptive or highly differentiated, that you'll be guaranteed success. Those things certainly help if they can last. The opportunity that's in your control is that regardless of the sales environment or situation, *you* can and should be the difference maker. Have you ever heard the saying, "This person can sell a popsicle to an Eskimo!"? Well, hopefully you're about to learn why.

As I got into managing teams of salespeople, the hardest thing to do was figure out just why I and other top sellers were successful, and then find a way to simplify that for others. Frankly, I sold to a lot of really smart buyers who gracefully led me through my mistakes. While I've been through many well-known best-of-breed sales training programs, it was actually those buyers who taught me the most valuable lessons about sales. To truly understand how I could teach others to sell, I looked at the difference between my own first few years, grinding it out trying to find my own way, compared to those years when I was consistently performing at a high level. I studied as many top performers as I could in multiple different types of sales.

What I found was that this whole class of what I'm calling *Elite Sellers* were all good and committed to different things. Some had certain skills that were better than others. They also had clear weaknesses. All had strong work ethic and discipline, but no more than the many who failed. When they'd be introduced to a new sales approach or method, they'd take a little of this and a little of that. But overall, they would usually lean on their natural selling ways.

However, what became clear was that there was an underlying similarity between all of them. I discovered that all Elite Sellers had three selling habits in common:

First, they're **Intuitive.** Their natural tendencies and general mindset is focused on understanding the people they sell to. Usually, with a pretty strong sense of empathy, they look beyond just the myopic inward view of their products and services. This makes them ask better questions and change course in a conversation or deal strategy. Their first instinct and continual priority is to find any way to get a buyer emotionally connected to them or what they sell. They can also see when they're not connected. Their intuition always questions **The 3 Why's:** *Why would they buy? Why now? And, Why us?* So, they don't typically waste too much time on those unqualified opportunities.

Two, they sell a **Vision**. Meaning, beyond just pitching why their product is better or different, they inspire and connect buyers to what a product or service can do *for* them. This isn't usually how their company messages and markets itself. In fact, most Elite Sellers drift away from their standard company messaging. Whether they do it consciously or not, they know that unless a buyer can see themselves in the future in a better state than they are today, there's not much chance that the capabilities or differentiation of a product will do much to get them motivated.

And last, they build **Champions**, identifying and inspiring *the buyers with power and influence* to sell on their behalf. These buyers become their relentless focus, their priority in everything they do. As a part of their maniacal qualifying nature, they know that nothing is more important than getting the people they sell to actively sponsoring what they sell. Realize, this isn't easy for anyone, even Elite Sellers. Like any relationship, it takes effort and time. Trust has to be built and earned. That takes a commitment from a salesperson. However, Elite Sellers know that an investment like that can't be focused on just any buyer. Elite sellers seek out those with power and influence. It doesn't mean that they ignore buyers who are lower on the buying chain. In fact, they'll often work with those levels strategically to help them build consensus and to connect and influence others. They're resilient and determined to build those *power buyers* into willing and active *Champions*, sponsoring and pushing for the deal through whatever they face.

That's basically it. Yes, their *work habits* and personal traits were all strong. They visibly worked hard, disciplined with pipeline generation and follow up. They manically qualify their time on the opportunities that will most likely buy from them. And of course, they have grit and a *never quit* mindset to persevere through challenges. Yet, what stood out was these three selling habits.

For all of us selling, this is great news. Why? Well, all three can be learned. A habit is something we can willingly change. If you're a sales manager tasked with getting your team productive, you should break talent hiring and development decisions down into those things which can be taught and those that can't.

More than any personality trait or skill a seller can possess, when you look at all three of these elite habits, *Intuitiveness*, *Selling Vision*, and *Building Champions*, they're all behaviors that can be trained, observed, and coached across all selling situations. If it's you who wants to grow as a seller, you control your sales habits. But you have to believe that it's those habits, not your territory or your account list, that's going to get you to the success that you want.

Our habits stem from our mindset. So, I'll spend a lot of time helping you choose the right sales mindset for your craft. But as I do, you've got to look at yourself in the mirror. Only you can change your mindset and your habits. It's just a question of how bad you want to be an elite seller. This is **The Champion Sell.**

CHAPTER 1

HOW DID WE GET HERE?

The Evolution of Sales

In my career, I've been an active learner of anything related to sales, but more interestingly, learning about the way we humans think and make decisions. The more I've studied and observed, from psychology and behavioral experts to the legendary sales mentors I've worked with, the more I began to question why what we traditionally focus on in sales seems to be so far removed from what really causes people to *act*, their *Motivation.*

This idea of *Motivation* started to intrigue me. What really gives buyers a *bias for action*? When I first started leading sales teams, I'd spend hundreds of thousands of dollars getting them trained up on their value selling and messaging skills. Yet still, they seemed to perform so inconsistently. I had to figure this out because I knew the messaging and sales approaches were all strong.

One day, attending one of my quarterly board meetings, I took my usual seat next to two of our lead investors. As we waited for the meeting to start, I asked what I usually would when we'd get together: "So, what are you working on these days?" While I've never been one to be that excited about new technologies, I've always been amazed to hear the stories of some of the tech founders. It's the story of why they created something new more than the invention itself that's always interested me. But, when the conversation then turns to how many of the portfolio companies are struggling, especially with their ability to monetize or sell the product, it would become clear that something was always missing. I mean, wouldn't it make sense that if companies were building truly next-generation products, then the buyers in the market would adopt as fast as you could get the sales pitch out?

The common trend I'd see is that investors would put up millions of dollars to fund an exciting new startup with a smart hypothesis, but the technologies were being built with only the competitive *market* in mind. There was always a new way to do something better, faster, or at a lower cost. But, in the effort to determine product -market fit, rarely did the founders or investors take the time to really understand the actual buyer's problems they were solving for or desired outcomes they were needing. Heck, most couldn't even tell you who their *buyer personas* were, much less what they cared about most.

What so many of these new startups didn't realize is that markets don't take sales meetings with you. People do. And, if what you're selling doesn't emotionally connect to your buyers, they're rarely going to take that meeting from the novelty of an innovation. Certainly, no economic buyer cares if a product is next-gen or old-gen, just as long as it addresses what's important to them in the moment. As I've now evaluated many companies over the years, this is the trend I see not only continuing, but getting worse. The product roadmap, the marketing, the sales messaging, and far worse, the sales habits and behaviors, are all so heavily focused on the product.

I know challenging the logic of this kind of focus seems counterintuitive. *Of course, we're focused on the technology. We're a technology company!* Well, remember back to my board investor observation? It's not that the technology ideas don't have potential. The number one challenge of any B2B investor should be to visualize a successful and consistent sales go-to-market. The ultimate question shouldn't be product-market fit. It should simply be, "Why would a buyer take a meeting with my seller?"

As I also experienced the same challenges for consistency within my own teams, sellers who'd received the absolute best training in the industry, I had to look at history to discover the root cause of this growing disconnect between the products we innovate and the buyers we sell to. Sellers have traveled through a few sales evolutions. It seems like every time an external force changes, we either decide we have to change how we sell, or some book tells us to.

It all makes sense when you think about it. We're intelligent creatures wired to survive. When our world evolves, selling would naturally feel harder. So, we adjust . . . or sometimes, over adjust. Yet is it possible that with this hyper-accelerated technology movement we're in today, that we could actually revert back to the basics of selling, where we all started?

THE EVOLUTION OF SALES

The birth of modern technologies all started pre-World War I, during the *Industrial Revolutions*, which went into the early 1900s. This is when we saw the world's greatest companies built, from

General Electric, Lloyd's, US Steel, JP Morgan Chase to Ford, Dupont, Nestle, and Bayer. While early technologies would pick up great momentum as companies and resources matured, the cornerstone of doing business back then, as it still is now, was *Trust* between people.

The sales craft that dominated the times was a people-based approach focused on *emotional selling*. This made sense. If you didn't have a wealth of new high-tech innovations to *wow* the buyer with, then you had to find a way to get them emotionally connected to what you were selling. Even into the early 20th century, this was especially important during the two World Wars and the Great Depression. When people have less money to spend, the art of understanding and positioning what you sell to their greatest fears and desires was the foundation of surviving in the sales game.

Yet, as the 20th century eventually saw the advent of the personal computer, automobiles, antibiotics, and television, we found ourselves thrusted into a *Technology Age*. These new advancements took us from what was predominantly a psychological selling craft, sometimes even manipulating buyers, into an era of presenting the great features, advantages, and benefits of the hot new *inventions of the day.* This is how salesforces were trained at companies like Xerox and IBM. In fact, if you had any of those companies on your resume, based on their legendary sales development programs, you were a near guarantee to get a job interview at new pharmaceutical giants Merck and Bristol-Myers Squibb or tech leaders DEC and Parametric Technologies.

But eventually, the 21st century started seeing all of these early-stage technologies come together to form the world of *Solutions.* You see, this was the first time it had been proven that more new technology can actually make selling harder. Thus, came the era of *Solution Selling*, mastering the ability to simplify the more complex products and services. To compensate for the rapid and sometimes overwhelming evolution of technology, the craft of pain and gain *Discovery* and *Value Selling* became the focus. A seller leading thoughtful questioning structured to take a buyer on a virtual trip through their own agonizing pain, only to navigate their mental journey toward your solution's unique value proposition, became the prescribed path to ultimate success. But trust me, this is easier said than done.

Among hundreds of my own sellers, I've witnessed that while becoming good at *Discovery* should clearly become one of their greatest skill sets, it's easily the hardest thing for many to learn. Even if our questions are strong, structured, and super thoughtful, there's just so many different personalities and situations in selling which often make it tough to know just how to react to the dynamic sales conversation.

I've always likened it to a baseball analogy. The hardest thing to do in baseball is hit a ball. If you're getting on base three out of ten at bats, you're a millionaire *All Star*. So, in *Discovery*, much like batting where every ball comes at you with different movement and speeds, so do a buyer's answers and objections.

It's also hard for sellers to fight against this natural hormone of adrenaline that kicks in. As a manager, I call it the *Oh no, here we go!* moment. There's a trigger that happens on a sales call when a seller gets so excited about something the buyer says that they stop listening and just can't fight the urge to tell you all about the product. As technology solutions evolved, reacting to the buyer's conversation, understanding their needs, and controlling natural urges to sell have only gotten harder.

Now, we find ourselves today in the middle of a radical *Information Age* that's both exciting and full of incredible opportunities. It's also increasingly harder to sell and even *buy* within. As some modern sales books walk us through in great detail, with so much real-time information at our fingertips, across far more resources than we have time to leverage, buyers are in fact in a much different position today. Yes, they do know more about the technology and market when they meet us. They do expect sellers to *get to it* fast by bringing them incremental value and insights. And yes, the most successful sellers are usually the ones who have the intelligence and confidence to engage in conversations that can often challenge a buyer's point of view.

However, are we leading our sellers down the right path? Has the modern world and its excessive amounts of information numbed us to the fact that *we're still selling to people*? I'm certainly not telling you that *challenging* a buyer is wrong or that *Discovery* is too hard, unnecessary, or unwanted from our buyers. What you should at least consider is that as technology innovation and access to information has grown so much in recent years, have we lost focus of what ultimately matters most in selling, **The Buyer?**

What I'll share with you in these chapters is that it's not actually the psychology or mindset of human buyers that have changed over time. What's changed just might be *how we're selling to them*. And, while adjusting with the times is certainly a natural and logical reaction, have we lost sight of our sales mission?

CHAPTER 2

THE BUYER CHAMPION

No Champion, No Deal

Twelve months in and still, no deals closed.

Some called me an elephant hunter. It certainly wasn't intentional. I guess I lived in a territory where a lot of companies were just really big. In my first six months, I had over twenty meetings at one prospect, what had become one of the largest travel reservation companies in the world. Every time I got to reception at their headquarters outside of Dallas, Texas, the folks knew me by name and greeted me with a badge. Anish, their Director of Applications, was interested in our software for their application deployments. I built him a business case, convinced my team to do two Proof of Concepts, and met with whoever he'd want me to, anytime he'd ask. Strange thing I didn't realize at the time, was that in those twenty meetings, Anish was the only one I'd ever really had a one-on-one conversation with. I never met his boss, and I don't think he'd ever bought anything before.

From a partner, I'd heard rumors that my competitors were in there, so I sent in a preemptive proposal with a lower price than I had originally quoted. Two weeks and I didn't hear a thing back from Anish. One frustrating morning from my Regus office, I called our Vice President of Sales, John. He was in a loud taxi in Italy and promised to call me back in fifteen minutes. I waited by the phone, pen in hand, ready for the wisdom of whatever sales strategy he'd recommend. Fourteen minutes later, and two minutes into my explanation, I hear silence on the line.

I said, "John, are you there? Did I lose you?"

"Champion!"

"I'm sorry, what was that?"

"No Champion...You don't have a Champion!"

Click!

Six months, twenty meetings, zero Champions, no deal.

The focus of these next few chapters is to help you realize and master that *Buyer* mission. As the development of technology, information, and thus, our selling approaches have evolved to such a strong degree, this could be exactly the right time for us to take a breath and get back to the basics.

What I see in the field, and the reason I've written this book, is that those basic levels of understanding and foundational selling behaviors just aren't being emphasized enough today, especially when the buyer and seller reach any reasonable point of misalignment. We're leading new sellers into a state of confusion as to how to approach and communicate with buyers. Much of our guidance puts them faced with conflicts and disconnected engagements that are making sales even harder than it already was.

Even worse, we're taking the learned instincts of veteran sellers, built from years of tough lived experiences, and asking them to adopt the new popular *techniques de jour.* The truth is that sales is about *who* we sell to far more than its about *what* we sell. As long as there's a human being in the buyer's seat responsible for making decisions on the products and services that we sell, the sales mission, whether we realize it or not, will always be to find a way to gain a human connection and commitment from that person. When we find ourselves at the destinations of buyer connection and commitment, we're well on our way to our ultimate sales mission in an opportunity, building a **Buyer Champion**.

Because there are often many different people we meet and interact with in a sales engagement, experience has taught us that, while all people are important and should be respected equally, there is one buyer role who will have the most impact on our success. I'll use the term **Champion Target** to define a buyer who we believe fits the profile of someone we'd like to build into our Champion, although they're not a Champion yet.

There are many traits of what makes someone a potential Champion. Do they have political clout? When we look at an *org chart,* do they appear to have a title of authority? Are they seen as a by-the-rules *company man or woman,* or can they tend to be a bit of a rebel? When we meet with them, do they come across as highly intelligent and open to learn? Are they often the alpha personality in the room? When hard questions are asked in the sales meeting, are they the one who everyone tends to defer to? Are they ambitious, trying to make a name for themselves?

I love to see a buyer who has a significant *personal win* at stake. This could be career promotion, getting a specific solution in place, or achieving a bonus for hitting a management objective.

Across all the potential traits of someone who we could identify as a strong Champion Target, it's important to our internal company communication and to the honest self-awareness of our opportunity qualification that we're able to identify them by name and by a shared strategic definition. For us to confidently say that we have identified and then built a Buyer Champion, they will need to meet a minimum of three disciplined criteria.

THE 3 CHAMPION CRITERIA

1. Power and Influence

A Champion is first, a person of power and influence in the organization that we're selling into. What does that mean, *power and influence*? Let's break each word down. As I do, I want you to begin thinking about the people that you're selling to today. Or worse, the people you're not, but perhaps should be.

What does it mean to have *power*? At its most basic understanding, *power* is a measurement of considerable energy, the strength needed to be able to accomplish the objective. In a business or organization, *power is* usually associated with *authority*. In some situations that authority is simply assumed because of a title and someone's place on an org chart of employee hierarchy. However, in all situations, I caution you that *power* must be observed. We need proof that the buyer we're targeting has the authority to set priorities, involve the right stakeholders and ultimately, make the decisions that count.

Influence, however, is less about energy and more about people. We define *influence* as a person's ability to impact the perspectives and decisions of others. Why would anyone have *influence* over others? Are they perceived to have a unique subject matter expertise or special assets like knowledge? Does their role have this defined charter? Or have they just accumulated political leverage due to company dynamics?

With either trait, *power* or *influence*, Elite Sellers know that we need to see evidence of it. An organizational chart or a strong personality in a sales meeting doesn't always show us the truth. Elite sellers seek the truth with intellectual curiosity.

Examples of *evidence: Have they made these decisions before? Are they identified as a person of power when qualifying a decision process?*

And, *have our observations and other buyers confirmed that they have and will continue to have influence over decisions like ours?*

2. Access to an Economic Buyer

Well first, we need to define what an *Economic Buyer* is. This "EB," as I'll call them, is essentially the person who has discretionary authority to say Yes to a purchase. Most salespeople take the short cut of identifying the EB as someone who signs the order.

We also tend to think that the Economic Buyer is the one who owns the budget. Those aren't necessarily the EB. The larger the company, the likelihood that the actual signer of an order is also the Economic Buyer is fairly low. Signers are often role-players in procurement, sourcing, or in finance. The bigger the portion of a budget in a company, the authority to approve spending the larger amounts of monies out of that budget usually gets higher.

Owning a budget versus approving spending from it becomes a separation of power. While a Champion Target must have power and influence for our decision and could say "No", there's usually only one person who has the authority to say "Yes".

Every company has a budget and it's usually pre-allocated to the different groups, functions, and divisions. What happens in the ebbs and flows of a business year is that based on business performance or other competing priorities, there may be times when spending approvals from the budgets get frozen, delayed, or reallocated across sub-budgets. In a large enterprise, an EB could be a financial or group executive. In a medical practice, it might be the owning physician or perhaps the office director. Sometimes, it's even the patients themselves.

We can never really know who the true EB is until we qualify our buyer's *decision process* at a detailed level across the *steps, timelines, and people* involved in doing the deal. When salespeople only qualify the steps and miss who the people are involved in those steps, they usually fail to get to the truth of who the Economic Buyer really is.

The reason we must know the identity of this mysterious EB is because we'll never truly know if the person who we think is our Champion could actually carry out their *Champion duties* for us. The concept of *Access* to an EB means that the Champion is in a position that can get meaningful business conversations and alignment with the Economic Buyer.

Toward reviewing the merits and spend justification of our deal, we must see evidence that they in fact have the organizational alignment and political ability to get access to the ultimate financial authority of our investment, the EB.

My mentor always reminded us, "There's a lot of people who can say "No" to your deal, but only one who can say "Yes." These first two qualifiers are both to help us decide if we have a Champion Target, a buyer who even meets the minimum criteria, and whether they have the potential to act as a true Champion for us. However, to be able to provide proof that we truly do have a Buyer Champion for what we're selling, look to this third criteria in the definition of a *Champion*.

3. A Willingness to Sell for Us When We're Not There

Ahh. So, what you're telling me is that a true Champion isn't just selling to anyone on our behalf, they are selling to the Economic Buyer? And, unless I have proof that they're selling to the EB and the other key stakeholders, the reality is that I just may not know whether or not I've successfully built a Champion?

That's exactly right. What's most important when we say that we want buyers who have a *bias for action*, is realizing that there is no more powerful action than actively selling internally on our behalf.

Later in this book, I'll talk about the key empowerments our Champions will need from us when it's time to go win the deal. One of them will be to help a Champion sell horizontally to other key stakeholders in common decisions of *consensus*, aligning all the people who have a stake in the decision.

But, most certainly what Elite Sellers know is that if we don't have a Champion also selling to the ultimate economic authority, the chances of that *preference* to buy us turning into an actual *commitment* to buy us has immense risk. Naturally, a prerequisite would be a buyer having the second Champion trait I identified, in that they must have access to the Economic Buyer. Otherwise, how could they sell to them?

So then, what does it mean to have a *willingness to sell for us when we're not there*? Truth is, no matter how smart, skilled, and charismatic we sellers think we are, most buying decisions, even in the smallest high-velocity types of sales, come from discussions and often debates made when we're not around. Hopefully, we've done our job at leading the buyer's vision, positioning our value, and gaining their trust and commitment. Reality is, that's just when the selling starts.

Buyers are emotionally risk averse. One day they can be all-in and the next be talked out of making the decision right now. Change is a scary proposition, especially when there's a lot on the line like increasing expenses with large investments, ensuring business continuity, hitting compelling event targets, or even the health and wellbeing of patients. Someone of power and influence with access to an Economic Buyer has to have arrived at a state of certainty, confidence, and conviction that the decision to go with our product is the right one.

Other stakeholders and influencers may not be so sure. If we're not careful, these buyers could become our competition's Champions, or who some would refer to as, our *enemies*. Therefore, Elite Sellers always try to build multiple Champions.

The bottom line is that without knowing that we've done everything in our control to motivate and empower a Buyer Champion to actively sell on our behalf, we just might be taking the biggest shortcut we could ever take toward our goal of winning business. Until we have evidence that our buyers are really selling for us, the truth may be that we don't actually have a Champion and our deal is at risk, far more than we realize. And, as my mentor and inspiration for this book John McMahon shared with every seller he ever led, **"No Champion, No Deal!"**

THE 4 CHAMPION TENDENCIES

With so many sellers lacking a clear and strict definition of a *Champion*, they're often allowed to believe by their managers that they do have a Champion in a deal. Usually at best, they have a collection of *Coaches*. Clearly, having a Coach in an account who likes us, prefers our product, and sometimes gives us helpful information is a valuable asset to have. However, through painful experience, Elite Sellers have learned that Coaches simply can't get the deal done alone, either because they lack power and influence, access to the economic buyer, or merely because they just refuse to sell on our behalf. Some don't or just won't have a *bias for action*.

If our sales mission is to build Buyer Champions, we have to remember that these are human beings who we're asking to put their credibility, reputation, and maybe even more all on the line for us. As I'll cover in an upcoming chapter, all buyers, all human beings for that matter, go through the same mental decision path in their brain. There's an automatic set of mental responses, ruled by our emotions, that lead us to the decisions we make in life and in business.

But there's also another reality I want you to understand and accept. Different people have their own unique tendencies for how they choose to act on their feelings. As our main objective for a Champion is that we see them selling and taking action on our behalf, for some buyers, the most important action of driving a buying process can be far more stressful or undesired than we sellers think. But I don't want you to overthink and try to analyze the *personalities* of buyers. The last thing we need in sales is even more complication. Quite frankly, there's no evidence that someone's personality is a strong indicator as to whether or not they would be someone's Champion.

On a much simpler level, when you think about the Champion Targets that you choose to focus on, I'd rather you consider that decision on two dimensions. The first is what we've already covered. Do they meet the criteria or definition of a Champion?

Do they have power and influence, access to the Economic Buyer and a willingness to sell for us when we're not there?

The second dimension has everything to do with that last criteria, selling for us. After some brief observation in our first few sales interactions, we need to determine their *tendency to take action*. Even if you've led a brilliant sales campaign with mastery of your domain, if the people who you're selling to can't or won't develop a *bias for action*, then you're going to find yourself wasting time in a deal that will never close.

I've always said the biggest killer of a sales year are the deals we work. I know that may not make sense to some of you. But, if you've ever had a bad performance year because you were convinced a deal would close and you were committed to working it, but it never did, you know what I'm talking about. When we spend time on unqualified deals, we not only don't win the deal, but we also don't build pipeline.

So, what exactly is a ***bias for action***? Simply, it's a person's tendency or bias toward doing things. In business, this is a buyer who takes action more than gives lip service. Rather than sit back and watch others, waiting to see how everything works out, they step up and take control. In the discipline of a Champion-based sell, the *bias for action* that's critical for us is that our buyers are actively selling for us, introducing us to other stakeholders, getting us in front of economic decision makers, going beyond or outside their standard buying process for us, and showing advocacy and guidance in a negotiation. Really, any actions that you would define as the most important that your buyers take in a sales opportunity are how you should be defining your ideal *bias for action* in a Champion.

In the spirit of simplicity toward helping you determine how likely an individual person will be willing to act, I want you to consider these **4 Champion Tendencies.** Like anything we cover in this book, think about your sales experiences and the people who you've encountered along the way. In even those earliest of buyer/seller interactions, could you have seen yourself identifying any of these *4 Champion Tendencies?*

The Complacent

First is *The Complacent.* They might be willing to listen to you. Perhaps they took the meeting just to show their team that they're doing their part in helping the business, or just to look busy. However, their mindset has nothing to do with you. A *Complacent* is always in a state of avoidance. They typically got to their position of authority due to long developed relationships, or maybe just being the last one standing. Anything that adds work or unwanted exposure to them will soon be met with rejection. They don't typically have a great argument or logic for their resistance to us and won't generally participate in much discussion about it.

When we meet a *Complacent,* we first have to adjust our message to how we're easy to implement, easy to use, and nondisruptive to their current world. That's always going to be a prerequisite for any of *The Complacent's* decision criteria. When we sense that we're selling to *The Complacent,* realize that the odds for them taking action are pretty low, regardless of our message. The reason is because a *Complacent* is both low on prioritizing innovation value and low on having a bias for action. So, don't make it about them. They're too protective of themselves.

Make your strategy about the company or something external to them that they care about and won't cause risk to them personally. Curiously discover what vision of problems to solve and priority outcomes do they think the *company* would connect to. Then, immediately qualify if there is anything that would motivate their own personal willingness to act. You can always ask a *Complacent* to make introductions to other stakeholders, but they're usually too complacent to do so.

The Teaser

The Teaser just loves to make the seller feel special by asking for more and more meetings. Have you ever experienced the disappointing moment when you come to realize that the considerable amount of time you've spent with an individual buyer has all been a waste? The good thing about *Teasers* is that they'll answer almost any question we ask. They love to discuss smart ideas to improve the business. Sometimes they show an energetic interest in the innovation of our technology.

A *Teaser* is actually the most misleading of all Champion tendencies. They tell us sellers everything we'd want to hear, validating our value proposition, and making us feel extremely good about ourselves. They play right to our own seller egos. But remember, Elite Sellers are maniacal qualifiers who take the emotion out of the sell. They ask themselves; *Will this person be a Champion or not?*

The greatest sign that you're probably working with a *Teaser* is that you're *single-threaded*. You don't ever meet with other people. Every meeting is always just with them. They tell you that there are no other decision makers, and yet your sales process never seems to move forward. In fact, the existence of *The Teaser* is one of the reasons why a *sales process,* with defined stages that align with and lead us through a buying process, is so important.

If I know I'm supposed to be navigating forward into more mature stages in a sales process and yet, I feel like I'm a hamster on a wheel going round and round but not getting anywhere, it's probably because I'm selling to a *Teaser.* They usually reached their level of power and authority in their organization through politics, intellect, and charm. With *The Teaser,* fight the urge to sell and ask as many questions as possible about the problems and desired outcomes that both the company and other potential stakeholders would care about. Qualify the details of their *decision process* with an almost skeptical perspective. Ask for the assumptive close and be direct with them when they push back.

Consider, a *Teaser* is high on prioritizing the value of innovation, but low on a bias for action to do anything about it. Use all that great information they'll share with you to build a powerful case for change and justifying your solution. Then, use that business case to help go build a consensus with the other influencers around the decision. Even if all these people don't meet the power criteria to be a Champion, *The Teaser* is ultimately a political figure. They'll do anything for popularity, and the consensus of this lower-level decision team will minimize any personal exposure for them.

The Protector

The Protector is extremely risk averse, but not for the purpose of avoidance. They simply have a mindset, and probably even a role, focused on mitigating risk for the business. Maybe they're conservative, have been burned by past mistakes, or perhaps they're just really smart and see potential problems and risks that others can't. Remember, it's not about their personalities. We're trying to identify and build sales strategies around a Champion target's tendency to take action. Once we identify their tendency, we want to play to it, use what it and they have to offer.

When we sense a *Protector*, we should immediately adjust our message to focus on what specific problems we solve or help prevent from happening. While they'll understand and possibly validate them, they'll have less of a tendency to prioritize ambitious new outcomes the business could possibly achieve. In their mind, there are too many problems to solve first. Be up front about the perceived potential risks of adopting your product or service, and the success plan you bring to the table. This is called, *owning the objection*. What that means is that if we know someone's probably going to reject a part of our message, we should address it proactively with a strong but respectful counter position. If we don't, *The Protector* will race to their defensive emotional mindset. Once there, that's a hard place to move a *Protector* from.

Rather than sounding like a canned sales pitch, use relatable customer or peer examples that offer proof points to your message. Delegate the selling. Avoid making it all about innovation and transformation. Those ideals will sound too glorious and idealistic to *The Protector*. Focus on what your solution does well while never minimizing the risk-mitigating considerations that they might have. Even though they'll be the most likely Champion tendency to hit you with objections and counter positions, don't get discouraged. Understand that *The Protector*, while perhaps lower on prioritizing innovation, they're usually fairly high on a bias for action. Their definition of value is just more practical for the business. When they see those risk-protecting opportunities, they're more likely to take action on them.

In our conversations with *Protectors*, as opposed to *The Complacent*, if their objections are smart, thoughtful, and interactive, you have a bigger opportunity than you think. While respecting and succinctly addressing the potential risks, trust that they will have many reasons not to do anything. So, curiously seek to learn what specific criteria that would need to be met for them to sponsor a decision to buy what you sell.

Risk mitigation and business protection are the highest-powered value drivers for their buying decisions. So, if your solution delivers this type of value and you're working with a *Protector*, you just might be able to find some of your largest business.

The Transformer

Ah, the wonderful world of selling to a *Transformer*. Caveat. If you're not selling the most innovative or transformative solution, then you may want to dance with *The Protector* or find one to support *The Transformer*. But, if you've ever experienced an almost easy sales process where your buyer connected to your value proposition early on, inspired other stakeholders to prioritize and believe in what you sell, and then drove a highly efficient and effective buying process, you've probably sold to a *Transformer*.

These are usually your favorite deals, experiences that you continue to use as a benchmark for how you'd like all of your customers to be like. However, don't confuse their high interest with you accepting less discipline needed to close your deal. Keep qualifying and driving the decision process.

While salespeople may love *Transformers*, it's not always the case that they're surrounded by like-minded leaders. Remember the coaching point about Champions and Economic Buyers? There may be many Champion Targets who can say "No", but only an Economic Buyer can say "Yes." Be pragmatic and act like a business partner. Ask them questions like: "What part of the decision process will be most challenging?", "Where could this decision go wrong?", "What stakeholders might reject the purchase?"

In other words, if they're such a *Transformative* leader who's both high on valuing innovation and has a high bias for action, that doesn't guarantee that they're an experienced buyer, that others feel the same way, or that they're an effective internal negotiator. Help them in any way they need you to. You, as the seller, should take on *The Protector* mindset and let your *Transformer* do their thing. At the end of the day, if your mission is to build effective Buyer Champions, it's not likely you could have a stronger tendency for action than a *Transformer*.

THE PURPOSE OF BUYER CHAMPIONS

While the mission of our sales career may be to achieve certain financial goals or promotional ambitions, in working the deal, our mission has to focus on the right thing. And by the way, I realize that many of you in different types of sales have your own business vocabulary and go-to-market. Some of you sell to accounts. Some are competing for contracts. Others are strictly upselling and cross-selling customers. Many of you work individual opportunities. For the purpose of simplicity, I'll use the term "deal" to represent all types of desired sales outcomes.

So, when I speak of the mission of a *deal* versus our *career*, those are and should be separate points of view. The *deal*, or whatever your term is for the opportunity to win, needs a purpose to guide our sales behaviors and choices. However, most salespeople just work in the moment, doing whatever seems to make sense at the time. That's the difference between sales as a job and sales as a true profession. A *Win* is merely an outcome. What salesperson wouldn't want to win?

But try to challenge the way you think about the deals you work. While each one has its own personality and context, they're all pretty much the same. We have a limited set of products or services that we're tasked to sell. Usually, that means that we have a targeted and similar segment of customer prospects to call into, some of us far more restricted focus than others.

We basically want the same three things in every deal. *Access*, then *interest*, and then *commitment*. So, if most of what we're doing and trying to accomplish in our deals is the same, then how can we improve our productivity and performance? How can we use each experience of working a deal to get better, more efficient, more consistent? How can we elevate our craft toward a level of sales excellence? It all starts with establishing a greater purpose in working the deal. While a seller may have priorities of surviving the quarter, winning in a more efficient way, making a name for ourselves, or simply maximizing our earnings, there is no greater purpose toward those impacts and winning business than having effective Buyers Champions in every deal we work.

A *mission* is a greater purpose. Being mission-driven means that everything we do works toward one singular focus. We are so centered that we're prepared to ignore all the noise around us, not letting anything distract us from achieving our desired outcome. How we choose our mission or greater purpose in anything should be a thoughtful decision toward what we truly want the most. Most people in life don't really know what they want. But the great thing about a career in sales is that at a minimum, the need to win and earn financial reward is baked into the job description.

If we assume that our career mission is at least related to winning more than we lose and building a reputation as a credible sales performer, there's nothing in the actual deals we work that could lead us to those objectives more than selling with Buyer Champions. If we've been average in some of our sales activities, even performed poorly at times, but then had a powerful and influential buyer who believed in our message and was selling for us, then we would still have a path to win.

When our greater sales purpose isn't fully committed to *Building Buyer Champions*, we'll always be conflicted between our own stress to hit a quota and the goals that our Buyer Champions have for themselves. As human nature goes, guess who we'll choose to protect? In the natural response to ensure that our needs as professional salespeople are being met, our self-focused mindset will actually work against everything we're trying to achieve. You see, we can't serve two masters. Great *Champion Builders* are *selfless sellers*. If our intent and focus is not completely on the *buyers* who we sell to, we'll just simply lack the mentality for a buyer to want to be our Champion.

Don't think that a buyer focus will make you soft or cause you to spend too much time working deals that you shouldn't. It's usually our lack of attention to and awareness of the buyer and their situation that enables us to stay in unqualified deals too long. Conversely, it's the intellectual honesty of knowing that we don't have and can't seem to build a Buyer Champion that ultimately guides us to walk away from working those deals. We have to remind ourselves what it really means to be mission-focused on building Buyer Champions.

A seller whose greater purpose is to *serve* the customer, like a paid consultant, while honorable in their intent, they'll often be liked but fall short of motivating a buyer toward a bias for action.

A seller whose greater purpose is about presenting and teaching technical capability and innovation, they may be believable around the solution due to their passion and credibility, but they'll lack the mindset to build emotional connections or that which qualifies and moves opportunities to close.

However, when our greater sales purpose becomes *Building Buyer Champions*, we naturally become more intuitive with our Champion Targets. We're just naturally paying attention more. When this is our purpose, it doesn't mean that our sales behaviors will be perfect. It means that we have mentally enabled ourselves to effectively lead our buyers toward a state of trust, connection, and a commitment to our value proposition. In any type of sales opportunity, there is no greater purpose than building Buyer Champions.

CHAPTER 3

THE 5 E.L.I.T.E. SALES HABITS TO BUILDING AND WINNING WITH BUYER CHAMPIONS

W hen it eventually was time for me to accept a management role, I'll never forget how the conversation went. I had a meeting scheduled with my boss Kelly. He was a long-time believer and practitioner of our sales playbook.

When we sat down for my one on one, Kelly asked, "Well, are you ready to manage?" I felt this was finally the right time and was fully confident that I knew everything it took to teach people how to sell and deliver strong performance. But, when Kelly heard this confidence, our conversation moved in a direction I hadn't expected it would. Over the last two years I had been selling into a large global account and had a small team of sellers, specialists, and support staff. They were an amazing team and we had great success together closing one massive deal. I'll never forget what he said next.

"Now Richard, you may think you've been managing for a few years, but truth is you've been leading people. Your non-authoritarian leadership has been remarkable as you've had to lead many people who don't technically report to you. You've done that job well and everyone is impressed. This is why we're talking to you about taking on a Regional Manager role. But let's be clear, you have not been managing a sales team. Over the next year, you're going to have to figure out how to teach multiple people to do what you do. But it's not just teaching. You'll have the quota of all of those people rolled up under you. They'll all be on different levels with unique goals, personalities, strengths, and weaknesses. They'll each have different accounts and selling situations that they'll be struggling with."

Kelly then asked, "You're a father to a couple of kids, right?"

He said, "Now imagine raising a family of six kids on your sales team. You'll hear far more complaints, excuses, and neediness than you ever thought you would. If any of those people don't work out and you need to let them go, then the quota stays on your back. So, this job isn't about getting the big deal closed. You're going to have to learn how to get a full team of people, who are all at differing levels of skill and ramp, to become productive, hitting their number."

At first, I really didn't understand what all the fuss was about. To me, it was simple. Just do what he said. Figure out what I've been doing so well and just teach them how I do it. Yet, it was that lack of humility which led to a very tough first year. Yes, we made our number, but it was from a couple of high-risk big deals that covered up for my inability to get every rep producing. It was that frustrating year of learning that ignited my passion and focus to determine *just what is it that separates the best from the rest?*

Many years have passed since that first management experience. When I decided to take the focus off of me and truly observe the different habits and behaviors of the strongest and weakest performers, I began to see what was actually setting them apart. Of course, we all know that to win in sales, you have to possess the traits of intelligence, high character, drive, and disciplined hard work.

Yet, what I observed was baffling. I'd hired sellers with similar backgrounds and profiles, all provided with the same resources, and who all seemed fairly driven. The playing field was level and resources were far more than anything I'd ever received as a seller. However, year after year, I'd see such inconsistency in the performance of what I'd consider equal and capable sales talent.

It wasn't until one Saturday morning in my first sales executive job when I'd been asked for a call from one of our prospects David, a chief information officer at a mid-sized business in Southern California. Now, while Saturday call requests weren't the norm, I've had buyers ask to speak with me many times, so this was no real shock. I was pretty sure what this call would be about.

After decades of salespeople playing the same price discounting games, leveraging the end-of-quarter incentive, holding a strong line while deferring to the sales leader for pricing approval, it wouldn't be uncommon for a seasoned buyer to just want to skip all of the drama and ask for me directly. So, I took the call fully prepared to hear David out. How he started the call and what he shared was not only a surprise, it was enlightening.

David started with, "First, I have a question for you. In your organization, will we be working with this same salesperson after we buy, or do we get assigned some sort of customer service rep?"

I told David that in our model, we'll have the salesperson stay as involved as you feel they're needed, but we had recently implemented a very strong customer success program and that I could introduce him to the new vice president on Monday if he'd like."

"Ok," he said. "That's good. Hey Richard, I really love your product, and I'm going to buy it. I think your price is fair and your references were strong. But would you mind if I shared some candid feedback on your salesperson? I'm not asking for anything in return. But, after managing many employees for years, I'd want to know if there was a problem with any of my people."

Well, David began to share how frustrated he was with our rep. He said, "No matter how many times we'd repeat ourselves, it was clear that he didn't want to listen. He was often rude and always made everything about him." David felt like his team's interests didn't matter. On multiple occasions, he said he had to just drop off the call and hang up as he didn't want to say anything he'd regret. He commented that our salesperson was clearly smart, knew our products and pricing better than anyone probably, but that he just couldn't be more disconnected from the buyer. David didn't trust him and needed reassurance from me on several items, because his natural instincts told him that he was being lied to.

In fact, David had shared that if his team hadn't aggressively talked him into buying our product, that there was no way he would be sponsoring this purchase with us. So, in essence, he wanted me to know that he was going with us in spite of our salesperson and would only ask that he and his team didn't have to interact with our seller moving forward.

The insight I gained on that call wasn't just about that sales rep. He was actually a pretty good person with just really bad EQ, *emotional intelligence*. My enlightenment then and something that has proven itself out time and time again, was that what separated the best from the rest wasn't their messaging, product knowledge, or even personal traits. It was their selling behaviors, or *habits* they had with the *people* they sold to.

When I observed great sellers, it wasn't just their confidence and communication skills, they got their buyers to really engage and connect at an *emotional* level. It wasn't just knowing their message; it was how they delivered it in a way that got buyers excited about a transformational *vision*. They didn't just gain an interest or preference; they got *commitment* from their buyers. They weren't building rapport; they were building *trust.* More than just helping the buyers and asking for their support, they would be intentional at finding ways to *empower* their buyers, getting them all they needed to gain alignment from others and work to close.

If you've ever wondered if it's true that buyers often buy the salesperson as well as the product, then I'll tell you that it is in fact true. A former board member and chairman I worked with, Steve Walske, used to always say that with the right salesforce who had talent, conviction, and commitment, he'd gladly switch out products with our closest competitor and he knew that we'd still win. I couldn't agree more.

Now, I can tell you that in my career in tech startups, I've represented some incredibly disruptive products. While I've never believed this statement that *a product could sell itself,* if you told me that sometimes a buyer makes their purchase decision regardless of their salesperson, I wouldn't argue with that. However, my mission as a sales leader, as with most organizations, has been to build consistently productive, high-growth sales engines.

So, I can tell you that there's no factor that's impacted productivity more than a seller's ability to emotionally connect with a buyer, more importantly, getting their buyer connected with what we sell.

I've seen these points of disconnect on several levels. When I'd observe a seller prospecting, trying to get meetings and thus, build pipeline, I'd often inspect how they were doing it. I'd work with them to read their emails and listen to their calls. Even with the most creative tactics of researching the buyer first and using some familiar ice breaker, the message was still often focused on us, not the buyer. They tried everything: long emails, short emails, direct calls, partner networking. Yet, if they had been prospecting to me, there was no way that I would have stopped, looked, and listened. This continued into sales conversations and presentations. Even when they'd know their technical information down pat, some would come across robotic or nervous. I'd also see tactics like challenging a buyer with a conflicting point of view, using solid market data or business value reports. However, this would all be done prematurely, resulting in a pretty turned off buyer.

Some sellers would just be outright rude in how they'd make the buyer feel ignorant or wrong. Occasionally, I'd actually hear thoughtful discovery questions asked and then really valuable buyer information would follow in response. I'd expect that the seller would then use that information to naturally launch into a great two-way dialogue and tailored demonstration to what they'd heard. Yet, when it was time to position our solution, it was as if they hadn't listened to a word the buyer had said. These sellers, regardless if it was a prospecting touchpoint, presentation, demo, or even a negotiation, were just disconnected.

Even the most enthusiastic passionate reps were simply selling *at* their buyers. As a result, when I would inspect each opportunity in the pipeline, I'd see buyers who consistently lacked an emotional connection, urgency to buy, and clearly any willingness to invest their own political capital to be a Champion for us.

To that end, I continued to learn, observe, and try to determine just how to drive consistency from so many different levels of sellers. It became clear to me that as proud as we could be of our innovative superior products and our strong value message, it was the buyer/seller connection that became the one ultimate difference-maker between an elite seller and one who just kept getting by. How could anything be more important than the person who we're selling to?

THE POWER OF SALES HABITS

The sales habits we'll cover in the rest of this book will help you learn or refocus on the foundational understanding, behaviors, and mental mindset that all sellers should have at their core. I've defined these habits through an acronym, E.L.I.T.E., E-L-I-T-E. Whether you're new to sales and struggling, fairly good but inconsistent, or trying to establish yourself as great, these five E.L.I.T.E. sales habits will help you simplify your journey.

As I walk you through these five areas of elite selling, you'll hear me refer to them as *habits*: **The 5 E.L.I.T.E. Habits to Building and Winning with Buyer Champions.** *Habits* are the routine behaviors that we tend to automatically repeat. I'll be discussing sales habits or behaviors which we routinely and automatically repeat in our different selling situations. There have been many books and studies on human habits. We've learned that they can be changed, especially when we believe they can and with support and accountability from others.

As a seller with a competent manager, as long as we learn what's best in our sales behaviors, there's no excuse for us to not improve and refine our selling habits. I use *habits* to describe these elite sales best practices because, as opposed to *skills* which are more specific to the type of sell or domain that we're in, sales *habits* are the automatic instincts that tend to either drive or prevent our performance. Charles Duhigg's book, *The Power of Habit,* describes a *habit loop* where our *routines* stem from both a *cue* or *trigger* that we get, as well as the *reward* that we at least believe that we'll receive from the routine.

A simple example: Some people, when they get triggered by something or someone specific at work that stresses them out, they go outside and smoke a cigarette. It's both that stress trigger and the perception that the reward from that cigarette will be a feeling of relaxation, that drives the habit of smoking at work.

Our sales routines, or *habits,* get exposed when we face our different sales triggers. This could be the cue of a buyer answering a phone call, logging into a video conference to kick off a meeting or getting an objection from a buyer. There's not a lot we can do to prevent or manipulate most of these sales triggers. What's worse is that our perceptions of what reward we'll achieve from our responses, don't often work out like we'd hope. If you're not liking the quality of reward that you're consistently getting from your buyer interactions, then it's time to evaluate your sales habits. Our focus must be on *how we respond.*

What Duhigg teaches us is that, where we find our ability to change our habits is in the decision to change the *routine response* itself. Some outputs of this book will be concepts, frameworks, and mental coaching points. So, you should think of each as a guide to help change any undesirable routine *sales responses. The Champion Sell* provides you situational guides to more healthy sales routines across the sales engagement, from initial interaction through the close. However, to define what's healthy and what's not, all of what we do in a sales opportunity should be measured against a singular mission. Are we helping or hurting our ability to build Buyer Champions?

I realize that we all want to win and make money. But that's an outcome. We should all be smarter sellers than that. It's proven that if your sales *mission* is to make money or find a way to win deals by any means necessary, while you may find success at times, those aren't mission drivers that will lead to a consistent high performing career. It's because those mission drivers aren't directly linked to any specific sales behaviors that you can control. In other words, your mission in anything that's important to you should be aligned to things you can intentionally do to impact the outcomes you desire, where there is a clear cause and effect. So again, this won't be some philosophical commentary on sales. The concepts and situations we'll cover will be applying these five E.L.I.T.E. habits to real life selling.

Self-Awareness

I wouldn't be surprised if many of you reading this book are already pretty good at sales or sales leadership. I would also assume that you're reading another sales book because you have a *growth mindset* and a thirst to always be improving. But understand, changing or elevating your sales habits won't happen if you go into these chapters trying to find reminders and validations of how great you are. As I walk you through each habit and the different selling examples, it's important that you analyze yourself with a focus on *how your buyers perceive you*. Making a considerable impact toward any performance goal starts with **self-awareness**.

Why is it that, while everyone on a sales team sells the same product, there's always a group who performs inconsistently and a small few who always seem to be on top? We can make all the excuses we want: better accounts, better territory. What I hope you'll learn is that any level of success that you're having or consistent challenges you may be experiencing all stem from your routine sales habits.

Understand that any habit change has to start with a mindset change. That means being open and accepting that only an honest assessment of yourself will free you to grow however you need. For some of these selling habits I'll cover, you may find yourself surprisingly strong already. Use this journey to become more *consciously competent*, realizing your natural talents and instincts to ensure more consistency and efficiency. Some of these may be completely new to your way of thinking, almost in contrast to what you've believed thus far. That's ok too. Just remember, there's one thing that you can't argue with in sales. **We don't sell to companies. We sell to people.**

For all the times that you got the phone slammed in your ear, you presented to an unimpressed audience, or you worked a deal feeling completely in the dark without any buyer supporting you, *The Champion Sell* will give you a chance to learn why, improve your craft, and become the intuitive elite seller you deserve to be.

So, let's dig into those **5 E.L.I.T.E. Sales Habits.**

THE 5 E.L.I.T.E. SALES HABITS TO BUILDING AND WINNING WITH BUYER CHAMPIONS

Ask yourself how you or your teams relate to these common questions where sellers are struggling more and more to answer. *How do I break down walls in order to get a meeting? How do I get buyers to disarm and trust me sooner? How do I message in a way that relates to where they are today, while also leading their vision into what can be in their future? How do I get these deals to move with more urgency? And how can I get a perfect stranger to put their neck on the line and sell on my behalf?*

The answers to all these challenging questions start with how well we know our buyers. Just like we can't expect a buyer to change and go somewhere new until we understand where they are today, we also can't expect them to connect to us until we begin to understand why they'd connect to anything in the first place. The **5 E.L.I.T.E. Sales Habits** are about getting down to the basics of understanding our buyers before we approach or meet with them. As we answer these important questions, we'll be building our *Sales Intuitiveness.*

Before we can be successful with any individual person and selling situation, we need to possess a basic understanding of the humans in the sale itself, why they react and make decisions the way they do. So, as you walk through your own journey during this book, think less about your products and skills and focus simply on your habits, not your work habits but your *selling habits.* What are you doing regularly in how you communicate that's attracting or deflecting the attention of your buyers? How do you think about the purpose of your message? When your buyers fail to commit and move with urgency, what is it that you might be failing to help them with? What's driving your buyer's willingness to believe in, trust, and sponsor you and your products? When your deals have fallen apart at the end, what are the shortcuts that you might be taking?

Moreover, think about your buyer, how they must feel about *you* the first time you reach out or have a conversation. What are the thoughts and emotions in their head when you begin to pitch your product or service? And, for anything you're asking of them to do on your behalf, anything that may assume additional exposure or risk to them, what do they need in order to believe that you and your products will have their back, do what you say you will?

If you want to know what's behind the Elite Sellers I've worked with, it's their mastery of making a human buyer feel clear, comfortable, and confident in making the purchase decision. Toward the purpose of selling, hiring, training, and leading better, in this book I've simplified what I know to be the foundation of our greatest selling habits into this acronym E.L.I.TE.

The next few chapters are structured around each of these five habits, all driving us toward the ultimate mission of building and motivating Buyer Champions. The first "E" in E.L.I.T.E. is **Emotional Connection.** For this foundational habit, you'll learn what it means to need and build an *emotional connection* with a buyer. All the E.L.I.T.E. habits covered in this book will center around what we'll learn about how emotions play a part in business, essentially how the buyer's mind works and makes decisions. You'll also experience the mindsets that you'll need to be successful. You'll learn that regardless how clear a buyer intellectually understands your message, their path to taking action on those understandings starts with forming an *emotional connection* with you and what you sell.

Next, the "L" in E.L.I.T.E. stands for **Leading Vision**. In this habit, you'll learn how to apply that understanding and mindset of *emotional connection* toward how you *position* your message in sales conversations. In our expectation of elite selling, you'll be asked to question the purpose of those sales conversations. The number one question I get from sellers who believe they're selling a high-value solution is, "How do I lead a buyer to something better, while not ignoring or even insulting where their mind is today?" I'll provide a simple framework and teach how to lead buyer vision in a way that disarms them, avoids objections, and thoughtfully considers their current point of view. From a focus on aligning our positioning to how the buyer mind reacts to our communication and messaging, you'll get simple effective guidance on how to sell *transformation* and how to build buyer *certainty* in that vision.

"I" stands for **Inspiring Commitment**. Even if you consider yourself or your organization strong at building pipeline, the biggest challenge I often hear is how to move that pipeline along, how to motivate urgency within a buyer. Too often, we show up with our ROI calculators and in-quarter discounts to incentivize the decision, but deals continue to stall. The buyers have no *bias for action*. This is one of the biggest mysteries of sellers that I'll try to uncover for you. I'll help you understand what drives human motivation and how we sellers can better align to a buyer's natural path toward becoming committed. While you may learn how to avoid spending time in opportunities that aren't going anywhere, you may also find that it's often our own sales behaviors that prevent the buyer from having the comfort and confidence to move forward with a decision of commitment.

"T" is **Trust-Building**. As you evolve from a basic understanding of *emotional connection*, I'll help you learn not only how critical it is to build trust with a buyer, but just how that emotional process happens in their mind, especially at more heightened milestones of *closure*. We'll discuss multiple sales situations where *trust* really comes into play. Most of us in sales have good honest intentions. However, many sellers are challenged with getting buyers to trust them, their companies, products, and services. Yet, trust is everything. So, we'll get into just how a buyer comes to trust a seller and how we should be approaching trust building in the accounts and deals we work. You'll be challenged to assess how your trustworthiness is being perceived. But you could gain a refreshing enlightenment for how to be more intentional in your trust building. You've already heard the statement, "No Champion, No Deal." Well then, *where you have No Trust, there you shall also have No Champion.*

Lastly, the second "E" in E.L.I.T.E. is **Empowering Champions.** You'll continue to hear an underlining theme that our ultimate mission in selling should be having a Buyer Champion selling for us. This last E.L.I.T.E. habit I've observed through the years is in the approach of how the best sellers personally work to impact the Champion's ability to execute on that objective. Some of us have been lucky enough to get buyers who are just experienced and lead us along the purchase process. But, in order to ensure consistent success, after we've spent all this time building our Champions, we must do everything we can to empower them to do what we so desperately need, to win!

We'll cover what it really means for our buyer to be our Champion during this final milestone of getting our business across the finish line. What closing challenges do they experience and what should we be doing to empower them to confidently sell internally and win? Whether we like it or not, most of the selling happens in those closed-circle meetings and discussions when we're not in the building. Too often, we sellers take for granted just what we're asking from a buyer. Being our Champion often means just as much to them as it means to us.

In the later stages of a buying process like business justifications and negotiations, this can be a fairly risky decision for them, from the credibility of their reputation to achieving career success. I'll share real situational examples of how we can work to *empower* our Champions to win.

What's important for you to understand before we walk through these *E.L.I.T.E.* selling habits, is that they all power each other. This ultimate habit of *Empowering Champions* toward the win is only offered up to us as an opportunity, assuming that we performed in our other foundational habits earlier in a buying process. How can we even think about helping and *empowering* some person to sell for us if we haven't first earned their *trust* to do so? How can someone choose *commitment* to something before they've seen and believed a *vision* of how it will help them? And why would anyone invest the time in learning about the impact and transformative benefits of that *vision*, if they didn't first understand how this *connects* to what they *emotionally* care about?

Whether you're in a high-velocity transactional sell or a longer and more complex sales process, you're still selling to people. Connecting with, building trust, and motivating people to take action is most of what this sales profession is about. The more we can master this intuitive understanding of how human buyers think and make decisions, the more efficient we can be in getting them to act on our behalf.

What you're about to learn is that a buying decision is far more emotional than it is intellectual. Whether you're early in your sales career, hungry to accelerate your growth, or just appreciating an opportunity to get stronger, by taking the time to pause and focus on how you or your teams sell to *people*, you could be impacting your success more than at any other time in your development. Why from this book? *The Champion Sell* will help you get down to the root of elite selling, how buyers and sellers connect across the buying process on through the close.

You see, I've been on the hook for forecasting sales revenue for many years, and there's no data point that's clearer or proven to be true than this: Having a person of power and influence choosing to actively be your sponsor, your Champion, is the number one leading indicator in predicting successful business.

For many years, I thought and led my teams to believe that, if they could just simply get to the hearts and minds of a buyer, they would be masters of building Champions. Worse, I taught that this *Champion-building* skill was different than all of the other things I asked of them: messaging, qualification, sales process, negotiation. What I eventually learned and will be sharing with you, is that *everything* we do in sales is but a single step in a journey that ultimately evolves a buyer toward or repels them away from becoming our Champion.

Unfortunately, many sellers seem almost incapable of making this human connection happen. Has our selling culture become mis programmed? Has our modern world of social communication stunted our ability to build business relationships? Is it possible that the passion and appreciation for true *sales craft* has become replaced by our reliance on technical innovation? I don't really know the answers to these sociological questions. I suppose it's different for everyone. What I do know is that the common threads amongst all sellers that can be changed in order to impact performance are our mindsets and our habits.

Here's the good news and why I wrote this book the way I did. Changing a habit is relatively easy. Habits can be learned, broken and relearned again. You just need to pay attention and to *want to*. Strengths like *empathy* and *intuitive understanding* aren't as hard to build as some think. I love the saying, "It's what we remove from our basket that enables us to carry such abundance."

So, as you walk through these *5 E.L.I.T.E. Sales Habits* for yourself or try to lead your own team's habit changes, my hope is that you'll be able to remove, or at least right size the thoughts and mindsets that are keeping you from selling abundance. If you're already a high-performing seller, be intellectually honest in seeking out the real cause of that painful lost deal or that account that you just can't crack. If you're a young and upcoming seller, believe that your path to move from average to good and good to great, could start with just one foundational habit change. For any sales manager seeking to normalize and accelerate the productivity of a diverse sales team, avoid the urge to absolve yourself from your developmental responsibility by telling yourself that these habits are for the advanced overachievers only. The following chapters will be a reminder of the fundamental sales craft that we should all be on a journey to master. These are *The 5 E.L.I.T.E. Sales Habits to Building and Winning with Buyer Champions.*

CHAPTER 4

EMOTIONAL CONNECTION

Survive, Thrive, Think

THE AHA DEAL

At the mid-point of my career, I'd finally been spiritually saved in the sales religion of **MEDDIC**. MEDDIC isn't a sales process. It's a qualification methodology that had been built letter by letter, quarter over quarter, at a high-growth technology company in the 90s called Parametric Technologies, PTC as they're known.

My mentor John McMahon was their VP of sales. At each management QBR, or Quarterly Business Review, John and the other sales leaders would see a trend in deal qualification gaps. PTC was a hot new startup on the manufacturing floor for CAD design. They were hiring a ton of reps and thus had a lot more opportunities working. In the QBR reviews, it became clear that many opportunities lacked any real pain to justify a deal. *We should be Identifying Pain earlier!*

Other deals would push to the next quarter for lack of quantified business value. *Metrics is a qualifier, John!* Another

QBR, several opportunities would continue to lack an executive to sponsor the financial decision. *We need more Economic Buyers!*

As the acronym of MEDDIC eventually came together after a few quarters, *Metrics, Economic Buyer, Decision Criteria, Decision Process, Identify Pain, Champions,* the subsequent years and thousands of deals lost and closed would build a global cult following of salespeople who came to believe, as did I, that nothing in MEDDIC was more important than the "C," having a deal *Champion.*

So, as I was working in a new startup led by John, MEDDIC was our mindset and we all worked with the expected standard to become *maniacal qualifiers!* In my personal sales journey, there was one deal that changed my career, deeply forming my own certainty that building Champions was everything. As I went into this and all deals the rest of my years, I realized quickly that *Building Champions* was just as much an emotional journey as an intellectual one for the buyer.

I look at my sales career as if it was in two parts, before what I'll call the *Aha Deal* and after the *Aha Deal.* I had already built some calluses and scars in selling into large Fortune 500 companies. The bigger they were, the more I enjoyed the challenge and the opportunity for a big commission payoff. This deal was with a huge manufacturing company based in Texas. I don't know about you, but for a lot of sellers like me, there's a struggle that goes on for years where it feels like you're constantly trying to figure it all out as you go. But then, there's this one deal or account you land that's like this bright light that comes to you, where you have this *aha moment* for your career. This was my *Aha Deal.*

The crazy thing is that this account mentally stays with you. In every deal you ever work moving forward, memories and deal experiences just appear into your head like a recurring dream. Closing this *Aha Deal* transformed not only my sales career, but the way I think, make decisions, and ultimately, changed my sales habits. Now, at the time this deal came along, I was a seriously committed student of the game. I started in sales later than most. So, I always felt like I was behind everybody else, as if there was some secret no one was telling me. In each job I took, I would always be told how much potential I had. Yet, I just couldn't find any consistency. Then, on this one crazy, impossible deal, it all became clear.

One of our most respected technical sales engineers named Sean called me up and said, "Hey man, I've got a huge opportunity from a friend of mine, and I want you to be the rep. But I'm warning you. This may be the hardest thing you've ever done, and you probably won't succeed. But, if you want to give it a try, we have a meeting next week."

I gotta say, my ego felt like I was Tom Cruise in a *Mission Impossible* scene: "Should you choose to accept this mission." So, I was all in after the way Sean pitched it. However, what happened over the next nine months changed my career greater than any sales training, methodology, or manager ever could. In July that year, we showed up at their headquarters and walked into a room full of the smartest assholes I'd ever met. And trust me, I say that with the highest level of respect and affection.

I immediately loved those guys. I could feel two things very clearly when I scanned the room: the competitive tension between the people on their team and their child-like anticipation for how they couldn't wait to totally embarrass and chew up yet another poor sales guy. I was lunch and they were starving.

It didn't take a minute before I totally knew what Sean was talking about. These folks were the real deal, the smartest architects and engineers hired to solve the biggest problems and transform the company. The personalities were huge. Some were super arrogant and wanted everyone to know how smart they were. Others were hyper-analytical. You couldn't cough without them asking why or how. Others were more "systems-thinkers," incredibly adept at seeing the consequences and interdependencies of any technical idea. I quickly realized that this wasn't going to be easy, and it probably wouldn't happen fast. They were a young group. But the prep I got was that this was a *special ops* team strategically chosen across all areas of IT, security, and business applications to solve the top problems in the company. That's why we were there.

My product was a data center automation software startup with a growing reputation and these guys were there to rip it and me to shreds. I stood up at the front of the room, armed with a canned PowerPoint presentation our marketing team put together and just took a deep breath. What I said and did over that afternoon, as well as the following months, disarmed this team and created an *emotional connection* that not only affected the deal, but my career.

Once they connected to Sean, me, the rest of my team, and our product, these guys began teaching me how to truly sell. Because they didn't want me to become another sales idiot, embarrassing myself from buyer to buyer, they broke me down and rebuilt my sales mind and body. My mindset was formed for why people buy and how they need us to sell. In that moment, standing pretty nervously in front of this intimidating group, I chose to shut my laptop and empower this team to tell me what good looked like to them.

I asked, "How did they want me to sell to them?", "What did they NOT want to hear from us that day?", "What kind of partner did they expect?" I not only shocked the hell out of the room with these questions, but they could tell that I was sincere.

I didn't know if we could help them because I couldn't understand half the things they were talking about. After we heard them out, what I said then and what my team's actions showed for the rest of that deal, is that the only thing that they were going to get from us was what they just told me they wanted. They said things like, "Don't try to bullshit us! We know what we need and we'll be able to figure out if your product can do it. So, don't even try."

They said, "Be honest. If we catch you in one lie, you're out of here. And, if you don't have real technical chops, we're not going to work with you. We need to be able to trust you. Our jobs are on the line."

They let me know that this was about them, not us, not me and my commissions, not our forecast, not even our product. This was about them, personal reputations, serious problems to solve, and the technology needed to do it. Now, I'd been around high-performance athletes and coaches with big egos long enough to ignore all the bravado. And I was too technically ignorant to understand everything they needed from the product. But what I heard from that team is not only what led us to close the first of nearly $30 million in business with them over the next few years, but it's what became a selling belief system I've taught and executed with hundreds of sellers and managers over my career. *We don't sell to companies; we sell to people.*

Their emotions are what matters and we can't do anything to threaten them. However, if we can sell in a way that emotionally connects to the individual unique people and personalities in front of us, sales will get easier and our careers can thrive. We will consistently build Buyer Champions.

EMOTIONAL CONNECTION: *The Power of Emotions*

We've all experienced it. The shocking surprise that when we positioned something so valuable and helpful for their business, they simply shut it down. Maybe they weren't ready for the message or perhaps they just weren't willing to put any energy into listening to it. I was brought up in a very proven value-based discovery approach to messaging which was pivotal in my personal sales development. I had command of my message.

Yet, even when discovery questions would dig into the biggest pains and concerns of the buyer's current state, what I experienced was that for them to even disarm themselves and choose to engage in the conversation, I needed to get them connected to the topic first. When I didn't, I could see the frustration and discomfort of the discovery conversation all over their face.

I've listened as my sales engineer began demonstrating the rhythmic script of how our solution worked, only to see the audience race to questioning and debating ratholes of why this would never work for them. I also think about buyer reactions that have resulted from a seller trying to be more challenging in their approach. When the buyer chose to engage but then got their perspectives *challenged* by the seller too soon, before they'd earned any trust and learned enough to tailor their message, the friction created was uncomfortable to watch. Not even an elite seller can easily recover from an emotional conflict in a first impression. No human buyer wants to be told they're wrong. They certainly won't be giving us multiple chances to make up for that rough introduction.

What's the root cause of all this frustrating buyer/seller conflict? **Buyer Emotions**. The power of emotion in sales is not a touchy-feely thing. Think about our biggest sales concerns. *Why would a prospect stop what they're doing and engage with me? How can I get a buyer bought in before they can actually use the product? Why are they so defensive if I challenge them and then annoyed if I ask too many questions?*

We think, *"I just don't understand buyers and they don't understand me."* Most of the time sellers struggle with buyers, it's not their messaging, it's the *positioning* of their messaging, the way they communicate. Sales savant Zig Zigler said it, "People don't buy for logical reasons. They buy for emotional reasons." Let's face it. Sponsoring a purchase, which is typically committing to change something that they're doing today, feels like a risk for any buyer. The reputation of their competencies and expertise means everything toward their credibility. Often, their bonuses, job security, or even career path is on the line with what we sell. So, *emotions* should be at the foundation of how we sell. Why? Because we sell to human beings and emotions are at our core. Determining how buyers feel, and more importantly how we can find a way to connect to those feelings, should always be the first objective we're trying to get to in our mission toward building a Buyer Champion. Our willingness to understand and accept this will guide our sales intuition. We'll be able to predict, react to, and manage buyer emotions in any selling situation from prospecting through the close. The selling will get easier.

Now, it's important we understand what *managing emotions* means. There's a big difference between *manipulating* and *managing*. When we *manage* something in business, we control it before it controls us. Whatever challenge is in front of us, how do we understand it, react, and *win* despite it? Managing something is thoughtful and purpose driven. *Manipulation* has much less of a moral aspiration and exposes a low level of integrity, so I'd rather we just avoid that as an objective.

Manipulators try to influence the buyer with clever, misleading, or unscrupulous tactics and tricks. However, Elite Sellers are intentional and proactive managers of the potential buyer/seller conflict. They understand that a buyer's emotions will always be a challenge they can't ignore. Most of what they'll be asking of their buyer won't be emotionally easy or relieving. In order to build a Buyer Champion, they know they'll need to *manage* a buyer's *emotional state*. So, they take it on directly.

Start with prospecting. There isn't anything more intrusive we can do than to try and interrupt a person's stressful busy day, just so we can make our sales pitch. What I learned personally is that if we're even lucky enough to get a buyer to talk with us, most sellers are just guessing at what they'd be interested in and why. When I was prospecting heavily in my early years, it felt like every time I got a new person on the phone, they acted so threatened and defensive, some outright angry to hear from me.

It wasn't just in prospecting. Even when we did get a scheduled sales meeting, usually including some discovery questions and initial solution discussions, it was crazy how it sometimes felt as intrusive and annoying as a cold call. For years, I was pretty insulted. I mean, I was a professional too. Why was it only me who had to respect their time? It took some time for me to get past my own ego and resentment to realize that maybe, while everything I was taught about my product and our differentiation was true, it was possible that I just didn't know enough about the people I was selling to.

Just what is our ultimate objective when we first meet a potential buyer? Ask yourself if any of these belief systems fit the training or expectations you've received.

Differentiation: *"With every email you write and as soon as you get them on the phone, make sure they clearly know and understand our differentiation. Anyone who has pain will appreciate our differentiators. And whoever doesn't just isn't a qualified customer for us!"*

Value: *"No one cares about our features. No buyer will take action unless they hear our value metrics. ROI is king!"*

Data: *"We've spent tons of money on getting this expert scientific analysis of our product and every conversation you have has to start and end with this data! Show them the study!"*

Any of these sound familiar? Now, I know that these may sound like extreme examples. I also know that there's a bit of truth in all of them. Believe it or not, none of these beliefs are allowed to work and flourish if the buyer is disconnected to us or the message we own. What matters now is that you take this time to pause and really ask yourself, *what do you believe?* What is your ultimate objective when you first meet a potential buyer? If you cringed at all when you heard some of those examples, why is that? Clearly, you've experienced how a buyer can often react.

Here's a few examples I've witnessed:

Buyer Threatened – *Sounds like risk. I don't want anything to do with what they have going on.*

Buyer Disinterested – *I don't understand what this has to do with me. Why in the world would I care about that?*

Buyer Overwhelmed – *Too much information. What is this all about? I don't have time for this.*

Buyer Annoyed – *I'm not answering their questions. Who said I was interested in the first place?*

For twenty-plus years, with messaging perfectly customized for what we sold, I've seen sellers trained in the mastery of leading discovery, value-based selling, maniacal deal qualification, and negotiating on value. Yet, year after year I'd watch far too many sellers come out of those trainings, just like I did in the years before, still lacking confidence. Some felt nerves that would overwhelm them. Others experienced intimidation of the people they'd meet with and fear of the unknown conversation about to happen. Many were the opposite, so overconfident that they would minimize the complexity of the potential challenge ahead. Yet, many of those would still fail miserably.

Seller after seller, meeting after meeting, I'd observe and try to figure out just what was the cause of so much inconsistency. Time and time again, one common theme would present itself. There was always a disconnect between the seller and the buyer, an *emotional disconnect.*

Maybe you've worked in a company that's built messaging tailored for your products and services. Hopefully, that messaging helped you define the pain the buyer might be experiencing, your differentiation they could care about, and the value they'd probably desire. But does messaging actively connect the buyer to anything? Messaging is just content, words.

Connecting the buyer to our message is where our job as sellers gets real. Even the best discovery approaches, the intelligent questions we ask our buyers, while they may be great at getting us the information we need and illuminating pain for the buyer, they won't be effective in attracting an *emotional connection* unless that's our mindset and intention going in. As I continued to lead sales teams, my biggest curiosity grew. *Could it be possible that a prerequisite for a buyer to engage in any intellectual sales conversation was that they first had to begin forming an emotional connection to us?*

The most common problem I saw across every personality, skill level, and experience of seller was simply an inability to understand the buyer and create that bridge between the buyer's emotions and what we sold. Without that *connection* first being built, it was almost like clockwork. Seller would talk, then I'd see common predictable buyer reactions.

First, **The Runaway** – When the buyer felt like the product was actually a threat to their peaceful risk-avoidant job, they'd throw all the ways our product could ruin their lives in our face, and then run. Or they'd just ignore us until we were done with our beautiful pitch. Then, there was...

The Shutdown – When the buyer would minimize the problem and didn't want to hear another word about our product or the topic, conversation over! And of course .

The Counter-Attack – When the buyer used their mighty **power of objection** to weaken the soul of even the toughest high IQ sales reps.

So, I began to study these dynamics. I learned that the problem wasn't always our message or the quality of our discovery questions. There was just a fundamental gap in a seller's understanding of how people are wired, feeding their inability to connect the buyer to whatever they sold. However, in those Elite Sellers I've observed, they all lead a buyer with this first and foundational E.L.I.T.E. habit of building **Emotional Connection**. They may not do it intentionally. Remember, some great sellers are *unconsciously competent*. But any elite seller, no matter how convicted they are in their product's strength and differentiation, how passionate they may be in the value they deliver for their customers, they always seek out the signs of whether the human being they're selling to has made that *emotional connection* for themselves. They're intuitive.

When experienced Elite Sellers have mastered forming *emotional connections*, their instincts predict the potential feelings of the buyer before they escalate or dissipate. They pay attention, looking to confirm that their message is connecting. They don't need to be told by the buyer that there's a disconnect. They already see it and adjust. Hopefully, you're about to get a bit closer to that level of *sales instinct*. So, just what is an *emotional connection* and how do we get it?

Emotional and Intellectual Connections

Simply, there are two primary types of connections any seller must work toward in their selling objectives: **Emotional Connections** and **Intellectual Connections**.

The latter, an *Intellectual Connection*, is simply the mind's ability to understand the logical parts of the message. Some examples of *intellectual connection* would be: understanding what we do, how we work, our capabilities, differentiators, pricing and terms, the process to implement, or the value metrics they should expect in return.

Most sellers are well trained in these knowledge-based areas. It's their ability to clearly explain this information and ensure that a buyer understands that gains them this more *intellectual connection*. Any confusion or disconnect here isn't emotional. It's just a result of ineffective sales communication. The purpose of *emotional connection* is to help a buyer feel emotionally aligned enough with our value proposition so that they choose to *intellectually connect* to what we sell.

However, the foundational *E.L.I.T.E.* habit of forming *Emotional Connection* is not as easy to find a direct path for a seller. *Emotional connection*, in a sales context, means that a buyer has made a positive connection to what our product or service could do *for them*. They feel relatability and familiarity to the potential problem it could solve or outcome it could deliver. An *emotional connection* is this state where a buyer relates to the *purpose* of what we sell. They make this connection as a result of how we sellers have positioned our message. For clarity's sake, we're not talking about what our products and services do. This is about what we sell does *for* a buyer.

Breaking that down, what are these buyer *emotions* that need to get connected to us sellers? During the 1970s, psychologist Paul Eckman identified six basic emotions that he described as universally experienced in all human cultures. The emotions he identified were *joy (or happiness), sadness, disgust, fear, surprise, and anger.* Eckman also studied many sub-emotions and since, other categories of emotions have been discovered.

But the two emotions that exist and matter most in a buyer/seller engagement are **Fear** and **Joy**. What's most important for us to understand in the concept of forming *emotional connections* in sales, is knowing how these emotions drive the natural ways that buyers make their decisions. What we'll cover in depth relates to the *Human Decision Path*. That path, applied to sales, is what I'll call **The Buyer Decision Path**.

As I'll soon explain in more detail, a buyer's mental decision path starts with a very emotional and involuntary reaction to protect itself, **Survival**. In our understanding of emotions, the main one behind survival is **Fear**. Yet with all humans, we don't want to stay in a state of **Fear**. Our brain's subconscious would much prefer to be in a state of **Joy**, positive experiences, and opportunistic thoughts of the things that would make us the most happy. In business, a buyer finds **Joy** in a fulfilling job and their **Vision** for the future, which are both delivered by achieving their

Most Desired Positive Outcomes. Arriving at this destination in a buyer's communication and interactions with a seller, related to what we sell, is what we call an **Emotional Connection**.

Thus, as a seller who's trying to form an *emotional connection,* if the first challenge we'll face is to overcome a buyer's survival-driven *Fears,* then we must disarm and subdue those fears before anything else. If we want to get a buyer to a state of *Joy* in our discussions and opportunities, then we need to connect to their most desired outcomes and positive future vision. In order to meet those objectives, we should have an idea of what our typical buyer's common fears and desired outcomes are going in, as well as how to connect what we sell to them during our sales engagements. This understanding and routine adoption is at the core of our *E.L.I.T.E.* habit of *Emotional Connection*. When we can begin to master this habit, we will have laid a foundation for all other necessary habits needed to consistently succeed in selling to people.

EMPATHY MINDSET

Forming a new habit, like intentionally creating *connections* with buyers, will only happen if we have the right mindset. It's the *Law of Attraction.* Our thoughts become things. Our actions are the result of our attitudes and perspectives, our *mindset.* In the habitual journey to forming *emotional connections,* there is no more necessary mindset than **Empathy**. This is a nonnegotiable in elite sales. Meaning, if we don't possess *empathy* for our buyers, we won't build *emotional connections*.

As this is a foundational habit toward all the other habits we'll cover in mastering the building of a Champion, *empathy* is as critical as it gets. So, I believe you deserve at least a brief but complete understanding of *empathy* and the influence it should hold in a seller's overall mindset. All the facts and data that support the strengths and value of what we sell serve a great purpose to provide credibility, legitimacy, and evidence of everything we've promised. However, this information is only accepted and acted upon after the buyer has already made an *emotional connection* to what we sell. Our navigation to this destination of buyer connection is enabled by our level of *empathy*. So, what is *empathy* and why does it play such a large role?

By definition, **Empathy** is simply the ability to sense other people's emotions, coupled with the awareness to imagine what someone else might be experiencing. Let's break that down. How can we *sense other people's emotions?* Well, just think about the most common emotions: fear, anger, sadness, joy. Aren't they all emotions that we've personally experienced? Sensing those emotions in another person isn't the problem. It's the fact that when we're selling, we're often just not paying attention. Again, if our mindset is fixed on ourselves, the message we need to get out, the industry data they should know, the differentiation we must pitch, the behaviors we lead will all be focused on ourselves.

However, to really listen, take time to observe, and learn about the buyer in the sales moment, this takes an *empathetic mindset*. Now, if the second part of the definition is coupled with the *ability to imagine what someone else might be experiencing*, this must mean that we need to have enough *empathy* to first, even care about the buyer. I can tell you that if you don't care about what your buyers are experiencing, you not only won't ever form a *connection*, but you'll probably have much bigger problems like your buyers just won't like you. You won't even be able to make your own connections to the real value and outcomes that your solution can deliver. And certainly, you won't build buyers into Champions.

When our mindset is first and primarily focused on the buyer, what they're experiencing, the problems they're surviving, the positive outcomes they most desire, we'll naturally find ourselves much closer to our goal of attracting their *connection*. To understand *empathy's* impact on that objective, look at what we're asking ourselves to do in building *emotional connections*. When we're initially crafting our sales message, our focus and awareness has to intently be on the buyer. Even if we've never been in their shoes or met them before, we must structure and restructure our message around what they care about and how they uniquely need our help. We can't do that without *empathy*.

In how we position our message in the sales conversation, rather than leading with our differentiation, strengths, and complex data, we focus on first, disarming fear-driven survival impulses. We can't even consider what those impulses would be without being *empathetic* to what the buyer might be facing in that moment. How could we be able to position ourselves to a buyer's greatest problems and desires if we weren't *empathetic* enough to first consider what they might be in their current state? In the process to truly learn about and understand the environments, situations, and challenges our buyers are currently facing, wouldn't we need to have a mindset that cared in the first place? This mindset of consideration and caring is called *Empathy.*

The *5 E.L.I.T.E. Habits* I'll teach are really all about training your *sales empathy* and how to effectively act on it. How does this separate you from the rest? The truth is, possessing *sales empathy* is not the norm amongst our growing sales fraternity. The typical seller is far more motivated by their product and how transformative it is, especially as technology continues to evolve faster than at any time in history. That hyper-competitive environment also challenges our *empathetic intentions*, how we act on our empathy. In our own survival mode, many sellers revert to an impulse to defend ourselves, proactively fighting off competitive FUD (Fear, Uncertainty, and Doubt). Rather than staying in the moment with intellectual curiosity for the buyer conversation, we take a proactive stance against alternative approaches and competitors. I continue to see it daily in our selling habits. Often, those fear-based tactics end up turning buyers off, either because they didn't come to hear about the competition, or they might not even be sure they want to change what they're doing today.

In my observations from hiring, training, and working with many sellers, while some, maybe you, have figured these human buyers out, as a whole we just aren't a truly buyer-minded sales culture. Some are even trained to believe that too much focus on the buyer causes weakness, reduced aggressiveness, and poor qualification. Well, aren't we selling to people? Consider, if all the messaging around the products and services we sell are starting to sound alike, then why wouldn't we want to unlock this *human buyer mystery* in order to gain a competitive advantage?

Elite habits all start with an *elite mindset.* In my hiring over the years, I've used a performance assessment called a Mindscan™, a basic measure of someone's tendencies around empathy, thinking, and their bias for action accordingly. In evaluating both the highest and not-so-highest performers I've interviewed or who've worked with me, the top sales performers' *empathy* scores were always extremely high.

It's fair that imagining what your buyer might be experiencing takes intentional effort, more energy. There's no shortcuts in selling this way and it's not for the lazy seller. Again, any time we want to change our behavior, we must first change our mindset. To apply this for yourself, think about what you sell. Write down what common buyer negative emotions and outcomes exist when they're *not* using your product or service. Most products and services can only address so many problems. So, it's not that it's hard to do. It's just that not enough of us companies and sellers make the effort to prioritize and document our understanding of the buyer's current state in this context, the real problems and desired outcomes that are associated with our value proposition.

I've led messaging workshops to rebuild company messaging for years, and it's always fascinating how several of the folks in the room really struggle to consider the buyer and keep their focus off their products and services. It's not until they feel the comfort of a room full of others successfully doing it that they finally relax their minds and allow themselves to consider and express this level of *empathy*. In all fairness, that mental struggle to think about me versus them is all a function of our own natural survival mind, protecting us, sometimes unnecessarily. This is all the more reason why we need to form our own intentional mindset toward *empathy*. We need empathy in order to drive the right behaviors that set us apart and make us great at building emotionally connected Buyer Champions.

Empathetic Intent

So, what does **Empathetic Intent** applied to sales look like? Simple. First, make the decision that caring about and trying to understand your buyer's current state is fundamental to how you'll approach your job. In other words, choose an *empathy mindset.*

Second, this mindset can't do anything until you prioritize the time it takes to learn about your typical buyer. This includes the specific businesses and roles that you're calling on, the situations that you're selling into. Lacking *empathy* means that you don't really care how what you do affects others. But, even if you did, lacking **Empathetic Intent** means that you don't do anything with that empathy. You don't apply it in the sales engagement.

Yet, by always pausing to thoughtfully consider your buyers first, especially those higher power and influential Champions you're building, you're avoiding so much of the conflict that creates a gap between buyers and sellers. If you're early on in your sales cycle, selling with **Empathetic Intent** means that you prepare as much as you can about your buyer before you meet with them. You study how your messaging applies to their industry, company, or role that they're in. Research the individual people you're meeting with. Ask for information from partners and others in your network.

In ongoing sales meetings, to ensure that your Champions are always prepared and approve of your plan, **Empathetic Intent** means including them in the preparation for meetings or even, deal strategy. This could be a brief review of the meeting objectives and agenda, strategy for the different people in attendance, a short role-play of that executive alignment meeting, or a what-if strategy discussion before a big negotiation with procurement.

Being an empathetic seller is not just having the mindset. Salespeople with **Empathetic Intent** will always look to proactively consider their buyer and the situations they'll face together. They will take action on behalf of their Champion Targets. By starting with an *Empathy Mindset*, we will have the motivation to sell with an **Empathetic Intent.**

The Purpose of Empathy

Now, if empathy hasn't been your strong suit, either in your mindset, behaviors, or both, then making a change to something new involves making a commitment. How do we gain self-commitment to an *Empathy Mindset?* To inspire any type of new commitment, we humans need to be clear about the greater *purpose* of change.

If your normal mindset is singularly driven by a desire to close the deal and make more money, I'll just tell you that it'll be pretty hard for you to focus on your buyer and build Champions. Why? Because your outcomes, your purposes are all about you. Obviously, you're in sales to make money. Just understand, outcomes and purpose don't have to be the same thing. If the ultimate new purpose you set your mind to in your sales mission is building high-powered influential Buyer Champions who are actively selling on your behalf, then your mindset and actions will naturally start navigating toward thoughts and behaviors that build those Champions. If you have Champions, you'll win deals and you'll make your money.

Empathy is the foundational attitude we need to have in order to become master *Champion Builders*. Buyer Champions are just other people. What we're asking of these people is to do something different than they're doing today. Maybe what they're doing isn't perfect or even as good as what our product or service can offer, but is it good enough? This is the question your Champion Targets are asking themselves.

Of course, making a change sounds exciting and opportunistic to you. You get a commission check. But to your buyer, it often sounds like a huge risk. Also, because you're paying a tax for the sins of sellers and other similar solutions before you, that buyer assumes you're only telling them half the truth. They don't trust you yet. When you suggest change, they hear potential disaster, exposure to more problems that they really don't want to deal with. This is how the human beings we call Champion Targets feel in our sales interactions. How in the world could we sellers, who by the way are usually perfect strangers to our buyers, be able to disarm those fears and help them gain the confidence that everything's going to be ok if they move over to what we sell? *Empathy.* We'll never get there without it.

Now, having a greater purpose for building Buyer Champions will also strengthen our *empathy instincts* over time. Mindset change drives behavior change. Thoughts become things. These two dynamics working together are the simplest example of the *purpose* of empathy.

Notice, I haven't been using the word, **Sympathy**. The definition of *sympathy,* as an action verb, is an emotion or feeling that we've shared with someone, an expression of loyalty or unity. *If you hurt, I hurt. If you're struggling, I'm struggling.* Well in sales, sympathy can often create such a misdirected emotional focus that a seller's control in an opportunity can easily be lost. The quickest path to staying in deals too long, wasting cycles with buyers, and getting outsold, is selling through *sympathy.*

In a more complex sale, one which involves gaining alignment from multiple buying stakeholders and thus demanding more of our time, we're also asked to be strong *qualifiers.* Yes, we're there to understand their pain and position our solution in a way that builds *connection.* Yet in parallel, we're also asked to qualify just how bad that pain is, what they're willing to do about it, and whether we should stay in the deal or walk away.

In Spanish, being in *simpatico* means being sympathetic, having shared attributes or interests, being likeable and easy to get along with. So, being a sympathetic-minded seller means your focus is more on compatibility, commonality, relating to one another. *Simpatico.* Acting in sympathy, especially in sales, gets you and the buyer to a more *comfortable* state. That's why sellers stay in unqualified deals too long. They like feeling comfortable.

Unfortunately, *comfortable* usually means *complacent* in business. And it doesn't equate to *winning*. Sure, we want to disarm and relax a buyer's mindset, but we don't want to let them off the hook from what they need to do to help their business. We need them to take action, assuming we're the right solution for them.

Realize, *empathy* is the driver that serves both of our two main early sales objectives. We want buyers to form *emotional connections* to us, while we also want to *qualify* the business. The key path to this honest awareness of both the buyer's feelings, as well as their likelihood to buy something, is through *empathy*. If empathy is the ability to relate to someone else's situation as if we're experiencing it ourselves, then this *empathy mindset* will also enable us to get closer to uncovering **The 3 Why's**, where we should be seeking to qualify the opportunity: ***Why do they really need this? Why would they need it from us? And, Why do they need it now?***

As a sales qualifier, when we can empathetically understand and relate to the buyer's situation, it becomes fairly clear just how likely that Champion Target will be willing or even able to take action on sponsoring our purchase. I'm not saying that as humans we should absolve ourselves from the good and healthy trait of being sympathetic. It just shouldn't be guiding our sales mindset. Forming the foundational sales habit of building *Emotional Connection* with our buyers begins with a mindset and intent of *Empathy.*

What I'm sharing here is really what this habit of *Emotional Connection* is all about. The foundational mindset and behaviors of creating *emotional connections* will prepare you for high-performance *Champion-based selling*. Winning the deals.

Emotional connection is what makes someone want to invest more time with you in the beginning of your sale. It's what drives the Champion to introduce you to other people of power and influence. It's what motivates them to sell to their economic authority. But it's also those same buyer emotions that need to be managed to prevent skepticism and hesitation at the end of your sales process. We'll never be able to predict or see those negative emotions appear if we lack *empathy*. More *empathy* causes the focus on building an *emotional connection* to be more instinctual. It becomes easier, a more natural path toward connection. Diving into understanding the buyer's unique experiences and situations will become an involuntary habit. This is *sales empathy*, the mindset and attitude to sense your buyer's most common emotions, coupled with the ability to imagine what they might be experiencing.

SURVIVE–THRIVE–THINK: *The Buyer Decision Path*

The most important and core concept to help us build the buyer connection we desire is what I call **The Buyer Decision Path**. Regardless of buyer personality, level of authority, or functional role, learning this simple *mental path,* that we all humans possess by the way, gives us the basic knowledge we need in any selling situation. We don't have to be psychologists or brain specialists to get this. It's really just an elementary understanding of the human mind and how it makes decisions.

THE BUYER DECISION PATH

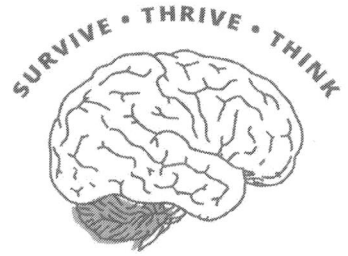

concept based on the work of Dr. John Kotter and associates

Think of this mental decision pathway in the brain: **Survive, Thrive, Think.** This is *The Buyer Decision Path,* a natural sequence or order of how our brain reacts to new people, situations, information, and even the most valuable and impactful business decisions. If we understand this as the *human decision path*, this same sequence illuminates how our buyers will mentally make their different decisions in interacting with us and for our unique products and services. *Survive, Thrive, Think.*

Author and Harvard professor Dr. John Kotter, in his long dedication to studying business and management leadership, speaks of this *Survive and Thrive* dynamic as a *decision-making lens*. Our **Survive Channel**, as Kotter calls it, was the foundational mindset that enabled the original humans to survive amongst far more powerful predators, famines, ice ages, and more. This was our primary decision channel for thousands of years until our **Thrive Channel** developed from the lessening need for outright natural survival. Our mind was allowed to exercise its more positive joy-seeking muscles. As populations grew, our openness to change and opportunity-seeking behavior evolved. Thus, our brains evolved. So, in a way, the highly positive *Thrive* state was also formed from a need for survival. This is why they are both highly emotional parts of our decision making.

Eventually, as time went by and the horizon of modernism began presenting itself, the newest and most impressive part of our brain, the highly intellectual and complex **Thinking Brain** developed to our current levels of cognitive ability. Survive, Thrive, and then, *Think* came along as our post-Neanderthal cognitive brain. But keep in mind this evolution that we'll come back to. This modern logical, or what's referred to as the *Cerebral Brain*, has only been in existence for just over two hundred thousand years. So, as we sellers first strive to learn the basic psychology of how any human buyer makes a decision, especially a higher risk economic or business decision, understanding how this *Survive and Thrive* dynamic is core to our emotional makeup is key.

The first thing we'll cover to develop the habit of *Emotional Connection* is understanding how the buyer's mind naturally works. Think of the brain as a loop that constantly starts these three decision states in order: *Survive, Thrive, Think* and then again, *Survive, Thrive, Think.* This decision loop just keeps running like a recorded loop in an Ed Sheeran song. Whether a seller is prospecting, positioning, demonstrating, or negotiating, the buyer mind asks itself in natural order: *How will this threaten or help my Survival?* Next, *how could it help me Thrive?* And finally, assuming the answers to those first sets of questions are acceptable, *what are the logical rational details that I will now allow myself to Think about?*

Emotional Connection is a *foundational* selling habit because understanding the concept of how human buyers react and make decisions will help a seller in any selling situation or challenge. Now unfortunately, this psychological truth isn't aligned to how sellers are typically programed to interact and negotiate with buyers. We're trained to lead with our differentiation and business value data. When the buyer doesn't get it, we're told to go further, give them more information, push harder! We just lead right into intellectual questions and statements that challenge a buyer's point of view before we've disarmed them and established relevance. Could it be that we're selling backwards to how a buyer thinks and reacts to us?

Basic human psychology proves that when we do this and then get frustrated that buyers aren't connecting, it's because their mind just simply isn't ready to think about us yet. Or perhaps something we've done or said has tripped their *survival wire* and because of us, alarms are now going off in their head.

Many of us need to completely flip the way we approach buyers. Think of this *Survive and Thrive* instinct as a password or a security gate to the intellectual *thinking* part of the brain. How do we help them *Survive* their biggest fears? How could we help them *Thrive* toward their greatest desires?

Unfortunately, that's not how most providers of products and services position themselves. A predominant leading message that overly emphasizes what we do, how we're different, and our value measurement is imbalanced. We make them have to work to discover the answer to, *so what does this have to do with me?* In their most natural state, buyers want to know how what we sell can address what they care about the most, the main problems and challenges they're solving for, and greatest outcomes they desire.

This doesn't sound like a complicated approach, because it isn't. It's just not how most of us sell. You see, once a buyer feels a familiarity to the topic and us, when they begin relating us to themselves, they allow their mind to then, *Think* about our important facts and details. A disarming and freeing feeling comes over their emotions that puts their guard down.

Emotions are the path to connection, trust, and having an inspired vision. Therefore, we get excited about the car or the house we want before we learn all the facts. This is why we think we've fallen in love before taking the time to really get to know someone. We are emotional creatures. Unfortunately for many sellers, we're brainwashed to believe that gaining a connection is all about pitching our capabilities or sharing our new insights and data. While all these things, and much more, will play an important role in the sell, it's the realization that we will never earn the opportunity to drive home our message or challenge the buyer's mindset until we first disarm them and form an *emotional connection*.

You've heard of the *Fight or Flight* instinct? When the way we communicate, how we interact, how buyers perceive our intentions, comes off like a *threat* in any way, buyers will run. This even happens when we push the conversation into discovery questions too early or we're too interrogating. Yes, even the most effective sales technique we can use—intelligent, curious, pain-informing discovery questions—when asked before we've received the buyer's mental decision to participate, can be perceived as a threat. You ask, "How can thoughtful questions trying to help someone be seen as a threat?" Emotions aren't rational.

The SURVIVE Instinct

Understand that one of these three mental states has far more power than the other two. I'm talking Mike Tyson, Ronda Rousey, Wladimir Klitscho pure punching power! You see, the *Survival brain* is always on, always triggered, and always looking to protect. It's both a biological and evolutionary explanation. There are multiple parts to our brain that each serve a different function.

But the parts that make up the *Survival Brain* have just simply been around a whole lot longer than the modern *Cognitive Brain*. Thus, the strength and presence of it is highly active in all the daily decisions we make.

There is a constant push-pull struggle going on within the brain for owning our attention, which has been well studied. Economics Nobel prize winner Daniel Kahneman speaks of this in his 2011 book, *Thinking, Fast and Slow*. With a focus on human decision-making, it rolls up all the complexity of the brain into observations around two fundamental systems. Each of these two systems are in an ongoing fight over who's in charge.

There's the highly *automatic* System 1, the more impulsive, unconscious, effortless part of the brain. Kahneman calls this the FAST brain. It lacks self-awareness or control. Its purpose is to assess the situation and deliver updates to the rest of the brain. This highly emotional FAST brain is in competition with System 2, the *conscious* part of our brain, more aware and considerate. Kahneman calls this our SLOW brain. It's deliberate. It controls our mental processing and rational thinking while it seeks new information and makes decisions. Now you can understand why he calls it the SLOW brain.

The challenge for sellers and the premise for this elite habit of *Emotional Connection*, is that in the human buyer brain, 98 percent of all thinking is coming from the FAST *automatic* brain system. Only 2 percent comes from the SLOW *conscious* mind. How does that happen? Well, our emotional System 1 is constantly sending suggestions to our thoughtful System 2. Thus, that SLOW *conscious* brain is actually a slave to our FAST *automatic* brain. This is why science has labeled them Systems 1 and 2. The fast-reacting automatic brain was developed hundreds of thousands of years before the more modern cerebral brain. Thus, it's longevity and respected elder status has accumulated more power and influence inside that thick skull of ours.

Why is this a challenge for us salespeople? Most sellers have been trained with a mindset geared to prioritize and emphasize leading with the most intellectual tools we have: discovery questions and positioning our philosophies, features, value metrics, and differentiators. Yet, if we ignore or deprioritize the importance of first building *emotional connections* to what we sell, what we're actually doing is selling against the natural current of how the buyer brain thinks and makes decisions.

If you've ever experienced swimming or paddling a boat against a water current, you know how impossible it feels to achieve forward movement. This is what's happening in the buyer's subconscious mind as their resistant emotions continue to take over in our sales communications and solution evaluations. When our buyer may be in a brief moment of intellectual attention to the value or capabilities we're presenting, it's not only normal, but probable that a sudden protective emotional thought will come over them. Even after weeks of opportunistic energy and logical thought to buy our product, those thoughts will eventually be attacked in the buyer's brain by survival nodes trying to keep her from harm. This is why our habits and abilities to build *connections,* despite these powerful survival impulses, are so critical to master. Our first step is gaining awareness and acceptance for how powerful the automatic *Survival Mind* is and how constant this battle is happening between the two systems in the buyer brain.

When we send our first prospecting outreach, join that video conference, and when we walk into their office to meet a buyer for the first time, we will always be greeted by a brain that's in a state of **Survive!** Even those moments in a conversation or sales process when our buyer's mind automatically drifts into a *High Thrive* state, considering positive outcomes and transformations our products and services can deliver, their conscious system sends thoughts of reasonableness and most commonly, risk-avoidance.

Each time the buyer's mind starts to consider logical data about our strengths and potential value, the automatic brain kicks in *fight or flight* and rushes to making objections, just for the sake of objecting. As a seller, we've all been on the other side of those frustrating and often irrational interactions. These involuntary reflexes that will continue to happen during a sales engagement reinforce the importance of intentionally and continually working toward an *emotional connection* with everyone we meet and in each situation we're in.

So, does this mean that building an *emotional connection* is improbable? No, not at all. It just means that our path to developing the habit of consistently building *emotional connections* begins with an awareness of how the brain reacts and makes decisions. We need to realize that we can't be complacent with buyers, that they could always emotionally turn on a dime. When we think that they've changed their mind, most of the time they've just changed their emotions.

The Lazy Brain

Have you ever been cut off mid-sales pitch, totally in the zone saying all the right words that you've been taught in your messaging, only to be abruptly interrupted by your buyer?

"Wait, wait, wait. You lost me."

Or "That's good. You can stop there. I'm not interested and

here's why."

Sometimes you blame yourself, wondering where you went wrong. Most of the time, you blame your buyer. They were either rude or just maybe not smart enough. *How in the world could they have not understood my perfect message?*

Another concept to help you understand these *emotional connections* we strive for is to realize that the brain is also naturally **lazy.** The **Lazy Brain** doesn't want to think and work harder than it must, especially for no reason. This is also a survival instinct.

Put yourself back into the Stone Ages. You're a cave man or woman and this afternoon is your time to rest. You were up early this morning on the hunt. What you killed is now in the camp. Wild animals will be coming around soon, so you to need stand guard rested and ready for a potential fight to protect your kill. And of course, you'll be up early again tomorrow to do it all over again.

You see, the evolution of technology and anything else that makes our lives easier with less to do, has done nothing to inspire our energy. We become lazier as the world gets easier. Why? We just don't see the threat. Yes, that means technological advances create false senses of security that convince us that everything's going to be just fine. I've worked in cybersecurity technology, and it's always blown my mind how some of the most resistant and disinterested buyers are in the security space. The reason is clear. They have a lot of tools at their disposal. And even though they may find all the noisy alerts and signals annoying, they generally believe that they have the answer to their questions in there somewhere.

The more technology we implement, the more complacent we get. It's just the lazy brain at work. Most buyers aren't sitting around thinking questions like, *are there more efficient and comprehensive solutions out there so I can consolidate and optimize my solutions?* Not usually. Their lazy brain is most often content to conclude, *if there hasn't been a known threat or attack in a while, then I'm good.*

We're all basically wired the same way. Unless and until something or someone makes a connection that the brain needs to be activated, the mind will do as little as possible. Unfortunately, this involuntary reaction repeatedly happens in the *Buyer Brain* when we sellers come calling with some new product or service. It may very well solve a problem or address a need in a legitimately powerful way. However, due to all of the other advancements and solutions our buyers have accumulated over the years, they may minimize their pain and think what we sell is just a *nice to have,* or even a threat to their peace and quiet. Now, just because it's natural, doesn't make it right. The brain is lazy because it's protecting itself, even if that's not the right reaction for the situation.

The *Principle of Least Effort* states that our brain uses the minimum amount of energy for each task it can get away with. Why? Well, it just wants to save energy. A seller immediately kicks off a conversation with heavy *discovery* questions on intellectual technical topics and a buyer responds with, "Whoa, slow down. What exactly are we talking about here?" The seller immediately abandons that technique and moves into an overly detailed pitch of all the things that their product does, some big value metric, and how it's so different.

Buyer asks, "So, what is it exactly that you do?" Finally, the seller shoots their last arrow, stating the deep philosophical point of view that their company stands for, followed by the reason why the buyer has it all wrong. This buyer is done. Whether with you or sellers you've observed, have you ever experienced any of these wonderful dynamics?

Maybe one of the more annoying traits of mine that my wife can't stand is when she greets me early on a Saturday morning with a task list of everything we need to get done over the weekend, only for me to bark in response, "Hey, I haven't even had my coffee yet!" Our brains don't want to work until they're ready. This doesn't mean that we sellers need to slow down and always cater to the buyer, only willing to speak when their majesty is ready. It just means that we need to be smarter in our approaches, more intuitive and intentional about connecting to them emotionally.

If a buyer is checked out or annoyed, it could be that we're asking them to work their brain before we've earned the right. The brain's laziness can be so confusing. In some situations, the buyer gets impatient when we don't get right to the pitch. In others, they push back and throw objections for pitching too early. This is a natural conflict that we have to be prepared to face at any time during our sales interactions. When we find ourselves in a conflict or in misalignment, we must first ask, *where have I not emotionally connected with them?* That's the reality of the sensitive, fearful, and lazy brain. Until it knows the purpose for why it should activate, it simply won't.

Have you ever led one of those well-prepared sales presentations, you know the one that starts with the amazing customer reference, then all the accolades your company has won, the core differentiators your product offers and of course, the pièce de résistance final masterpiece closer: your value metrics? You're now feeling adrenaline pumping and anxious nerves as you look out across the room to see how great the reaction was.

Then, to your immediate right, some guy is in a trance reading emails on his iPhone. *Really, bro? You're sitting right next to me! Those emails can't wait?* Minutes later as you continue your monologue, *Oh my God! There's another one doing it at the end of the table. I thought she was cool.*

Of course, you never actually say these things to the buyers, but man do you want to. Lazy brains aren't necessarily someone being rude. That would be a character flaw. Lazy brains are just simply protective. It's the same response when our brains are overloaded with too much information, especially before we've had our mental caffeine jolt.

Have you ever been the recipient of a long email, text message, or a huge book to read? Remember that visceral initial reaction you had. *Holy cow! Is all of this really necessary?* So, when the seven paragraph email with five attachments and three video links gets sent, is it any wonder that the prospect all the sudden goes dark for weeks? What could be a simple solution to their biggest concerns now gets perceived as a much bigger risk than they initially thought. The buyer subconsciously thinks, *if it takes this much information to explain what they do and how they can help me, this must be way too complex for us.* **Lazy brain!**

However, when we sellers become more intuitive, understanding ahead of time that there's going to be a very specific list of problems the buyer is focused on and energy they're saving for something specific, we're able to become so much more efficient and effective at attracting the attention of the buyer.

Getting to THRIVE

Knowing these basic principles of the brain's instinctual survival mode and its tendency toward laziness helps us to realize just how much opportunity is in the **Thrive** part of the brain. The secret sauce to *Survive, Thrive, and Think* is that the brain wants nothing more than to meet its greatest *desires*. That means that the ultimate state we want our buyers to be in for gaining and continuing an *emotional connection*, is the positive-vibes emotional state we call *Thrive*.

If you're someone who's more visual and you need help understanding these responses in the brain, I'll make it simple. Biologically, these *Thrive* emotions come from a totally separate part of the brain as our survival instincts or our cognitive thinking. Think of *Survive-Thrive and Think* as an impulse that travels from the back to the front of the brain. Our initial fear-based survival instincts start in the back of the brain, called our *hindbrain*. Impulses then work their way forward into the mid-brain, where we experience positive emotional stimulus like love and excitement.

As oversimplified as possible, both the hindbrain and mid-brain are collectively our emotional brain system. Finally, traveling into the frontal brain, basically the area behind our forehead, this now serves up our cognitive capacity like memory, rational thinking, and information processing. This is how our brain has physically developed and evolved over the ages. Back to front.

For further visualization, we want to be selling to the middle of the brain. Let's call it the *Connection Sweet Spot*. What's not only interesting, but also really good news, is that this is actually a very easy and natural destination to get to in our communication with buyers. It's our sales training and misdirection over the years that has gotten us all backwards in our approaches. Do you sell back to front, or front to back? Many sellers first go right to the front of the brain's intellectual center before it's ready. Then, to make it worse, we overthink and overcomplicate the communication of what we do, which ironically, prevents us from reaching any buyer connections there. That sends us on a direct launch right back to the protective and lazy survival brain.

You see, while the newer thinking parts of the brain are more complex, the Stone Age emotion-driven system, where we encounter *Survive and Thrive*, was then and still is fairly simple and generalized. Then, why do we sellers fight the urge to keep it simple when we ask questions and position what we sell? It's our own fears taking over. Moreover, it's our ignorance in understanding the human beings who we sell to. We'll worry that, *If I don't make this argument fully with all the supporting facts presented, then this buyer's going to minimize my message.* You see, the problem isn't the buyer. The problem is us.

Well, now you know that a buyer's natural tendency to want to focus on emotionally simple, positive, and happy things are just as, if not more powerful, than our energy-draining *thinking state*. Advertisers have figured out the science. Just look at the best commercials. There's American insurance company Allstate's, "The Mayhem Guy." How many times has he been blown up, set on fire, or thrown onto a moving car, just for the sake of making us laugh?

Pick your favorite drug commercial. Even those conveying the absolute worst events in life: disease, intimacy issues, even tragedy, they all spin the tone to good feelings, the emotional desires we want and deserve with a better quality of life. I've even watched a potato chip commercial on Super Bowl Sunday bring two destined lovers together by the cheesy scent and crispy sound of Doritos.

As sellers, we should also be working toward getting to and staying in this *emotional connection sweet spot*, the *Thrive* state of the buyer decision path. Understanding this human buyer's desire to be in a state of *Thrive*, along with the competing powers of the protective *Survival* and *Thinking* brains, we should also be able to consider the **pace** of our message. I'm referring to the speed with which we move from survival focused problem-solving discussions to positive outcomes and deep-thinking intellectual topics.

While we need to attach to the survival instincts in aligning to the problems we solve, we don't want to stay there too long. Again, think of the buyer's survival mind as a fearful gatekeeper. It's no fun to stand at the security gate. All the good times are when you get inside the party.

But, when the conversations eventually get to those intellectual discussions on our differentiators, value data, and implementation details, that's not a place where we want to stay too long either. We want to avoid that *objections zone*. Our mind should have a mental stopwatch driving our pace to get back into a *high-Thrive* state of the discussion. Get in, get out, and try to stay in the opportunistic *Thrive* state as long as possible. This is where we discuss the positive outcomes that we can deliver, the ones that the buyer cares about the most. Here, we talk proof points from their peers in industry. We tell customer stories all focused on the use cases and outcomes that our buyers relate to. Remember, while we must respect those initial survival instincts that are determining if we're a threat, and it won't make sense when our buyer's brain gets lazy, it doesn't mean that we have to be a victim to these natural responses. We just have to be smart about how we build our buyer *connections*.

The THINK *Danger Zone*

You're probably beginning to wonder, *well, if it's true that the buyer brain works in a sequential decision path, then I'm bound to eventually need to sell to that non-emotional Thinking part of the brain.* That's absolutely correct. Every buyer, in order to complete their self-selecting journey toward becoming your Champion, must form a clear and solid *Intellectual Connection* to what you sell. As a good emotional seller, you've disarmed the buyer's survival instincts by relating what you sell to the biggest problems they need to solve, and you've inspired their emotions by aligning what you do to their most desired outcomes. You've got 'em in a *State of Thrive*.

So where do we go from here? *Survive, Thrive, and NOW,* **Think**. It's time to form an **Intellectual Connection** to what we sell. However, let caution be your guide. The more we've learned about this frontal lobe rational thinking part of the brain, the more we realize that this is a *Sales Danger Zone!* Contrary to what you might believe, the last thing we should ever do is willingly push our way into the *Thinking*, cognitive part of the buyer's brain too soon, too often, or stay too long.

Have you ever heard this response from a buyer: "Just let me think about it"? Well, what does that usually mean for you? What it doesn't mean is that the person doesn't understand you. What "Let me think about it" means is, "I'm just not sure yet. I'm not feeling it." Meaning, "I'm not *emotionally connected*. So, I'll just slow this whole thing down."

While we can learn a lot of things from the complex intellectual part of the brain, the reason that sellers usually get surprised with *objection traps* and counterattacks minimizing our message is that we have all the wrong expectations of what this dangerous place can do for us. All we should expect from the *Thinking* part of the buyer brain is for the buyer to use it to understand our facts and details in order to validate the emotional decision they've already made. Then, as fast as possible, we want to get every bit of our buyer's energy back to the safe and highly motivated state of *Thrive:* outcomes, results, use cases, stories.

In a state of *Thrive*, they're basically seeing themselves in the moment of value, using and benefiting from our product or service. In a state of *Think*, they're only there to understand our concepts as long as the aggressive *Survive* state allows them to. The logical thinking that happens in the third state of the buyer decision path, this tendency that is happy to quarantine itself in the comfortable frontal cortex of the brain, is not *emotional.* Anything that is not emotionally linking the buyer to all the good we can do for them, has a limited shelf life. If you've done your job well as a knowledgeable product and differentiation seller, the buyer may be intellectually *clear, but they may not be connected.*

Far more critical and stickier for you throughout your sales process, is ensuring that you have *emotional connection.* Picture a person standing outside in the face of a strong storm with winds blowing that could rip the roof off a house and throw a car a mile away. But this person is wearing boots that have been cemented into the ground. When those prevailing winds come their way, nothing takes them away from those boots. That buyer's *emotional connection* are the boots cemented in ground, with the storm winds its brutal and protective survival instincts.

Remember, these survival emotions will put a spotlight on the parts of our message that the buyer's intellect will need to spend some time on. So, get in, get out! With this *Lazy Brain* we talked about, if it's not good, then it's bad. If it doesn't sound easy, then it's a threat. *Survival* is the oldest, most engrained, and absolutely most powerful state of the brain's decision path. It always exists, always shows up, and should be respected as our biggest sales adversary.

To understand *how* this emotional survival mind easily takes over the intellectual thinking mind, let me give you this visual. When I used to coach defensive players in American football, their biggest challenge was dropping their head and losing sight of what was in front of them. Their job was to find the ball carrier and tackle them. When they would drop their head, they'd lose visibility, get surprised, and fall behind the ball. So, I used to do this drill I'd call **"The Claw"** drill where, standing behind the player, I'd slap my open hand on the top of their helmet and gently pull their head backwards. As the player felt the tension, I'd ask him to try to pull his head forward. But my hand was strong, and it wouldn't budge. The drill was psychological. I asked the player to always remember how this tension felt and to constantly imagine that hand on the top of their head, like the *claw* of a big monster pulling his head back. Eyes always up. The body will always follow the eyes.

In sales, I want you visualize the buyer's *Survival* state in much the same way. In every conversation you're having with the buyer, especially during the most intellectual ones such as, discussing your capabilities and differentiation, explaining processes, describing commercial terms, negotiating an outcome, always envision this large strong *claw*, just lurking and waiting to reach out from behind the buyer's head at any moment, pulling it back into its safe *Survival* state.

Because of this natural survival pull, just as your smart conversation is starting to make all the sense in the world to the buyer, they'll subconsciously pause and begin thinking about *risk* or *distrust*. Have you ever had a great conversation where you walked away feeling like, "Oh yeah, they're on board. I've got this deal won," but then days go by with no follow up from the buyer? What's often happening is that their *Survival* state is starting to take over again, on guard to fight any potential threats that what you sell might present to them. Our biggest rival in sales is not our competition. It's this *Survival Claw* that can't help itself, constantly reaching out to the frontal thinking part of the buyer's brain, protecting it from *us*.

Again, there's a difference between intellectual *clarity* and intellectual *connection*. We sellers need to raise the standard on where we're trying to get our buyer. Do we stop when we have clarity, or do we more intentionally work toward connection? This is the very prosperous state we can find ourselves once the buyer has internalized our key capabilities and differentiation. They become intellectually connected when our message is no longer about us. We've connected it to them. And, just because it's hard, doesn't mean it's not critical for our success. We have to be aware enough to know that this level of *intellectual connection* must stem from some individual reason that a buyer would want what we sell over their current solution, or our competitors.

If we want to charge a higher value premium, then our buyers need to be connected to the higher impact that value would have on them. This is the opportunity and expectation of striving for *intellectual connection*. Yet, what makes the *Thinking* brain a *Danger Zone* is that it's centuries-long weakness to the power of the *Survival* brain will lead us to an inevitable outcome, if we go there too soon or stay too long with constant, non-succinct, and risk-introducing information that scares them away. As a friend of mine likes to say, "This is Egypt-old!"

Simply, there's only one home for *love* in the brain. The further we lead the buyer away from that emotional *Love Palace*, the colder and more disconnected our sales conversations will get, the more objections we'll face, and the further away our buyer will get from this highly motivating *emotionally connected* state.

Now, trust me. Just because I was a science teacher doesn't mean that I think you need to become some expert in the study of human psychology to be an effective seller. However, it is so important that you understand just why these frustrating dynamics happen in sales so that you or your teams can avoid these conflicts. If we're not gaining *emotional connections* before we work toward *intellectual connections*, it will be very clear to us. Confirmation will come from resistant defensive attitudes we'll get when we position our message, phone calls, and emails that don't get returned, a lack of follow up and urgency in our deals, or the disinterested annoyance we'll feel every time we interact with a person.

But rather than blame our buyer's frustrating brain, we need to realize what *we* may be doing to cause it all. Gaining this level of both buyer and self-awareness will change the dynamics for how we engage with every Champion Target we ever meet. Our acceptance of *Survive, Thrive, Think* will lay the foundation for the *sales intuitiveness* we desire.

Applying EMOTIONAL CONNECTION in the Sales Process

As the next four E.L.I.T.E. sales habits will all include applications of this foundational habit of *Emotional Connection*, some of the examples I'll share here will be repeated throughout the book. But, in those chapters, I'll go much deeper into concepts and actual sales practice, while trying to share any relevant stories.

So, how do we apply the habit of creating *emotional connections* when we sell? First, in reminding ourselves that the buyer's protective survival instincts will bring a constant power of inertia, pulling the more progressive thinking brain back to a state of doing nothing, *Emotional Connection* needs to be built and rebuilt all of the time. This is a full-time job where the objective can never be thought to be met until the deal is signed.

It's another reason why I want you to think of these E.L.I.T.E. practices as *habits*, something we just routinely do. If they're not already defined for you, write out the stages of your sales process in your terms. For each stage you go through, there should be key sales milestones, including the activities and outcomes that are leading indicators of your winning and closing business. Here, in these sales stages, is where you should evaluate where your opportunities and strategies for *emotional connection* might exist.

Prospecting, Discovery, and Presentation Meetings

Most sellers start at the same place: **Prospecting**. This is when we reach out to buyers to try and schedule a meeting. Many sellers have formed muscle memory or learned behaviors that have become automatic. If prospecting is a part of you or your team's weekly activity and your muscle memory is contrary to what I've been sharing, fight that urge to repeat the same counterproductive approaches. With your newfound knowledge, make the prospecting message and tactics all about connecting to buyer emotions.

Here's the secret to prospecting. No one stops, looks, and listens to our prospecting message unless they feel emotionally attracted to it. This attraction only occurs if the buyer can feel disarmed and sensing familiarity and relatability. Consider that for both our message and in connecting to us as an individual. We're not looking for an order here. We just want them to agree to a meeting. Typically, a successful connection will come from two buckets of our prospecting message. The first is a connection to the *Problems or Challenges* that the buyer is trying to address, the *Survive* part of their decision path. Or it could be from a familiar *Positive Outcome* that they're striving toward, the *Thrive* state of their decision path. So, we do our homework.

We should prepare ourselves to lead an **Outcomes-based Prospecting** approach. This all starts with our preparation. If your company hasn't formally provided you with an outcomes-based messaging framework, then just do it yourself on a Monday afternoon with some of your teammates. Before we're able to disarm our prospective buyers, helping them to realize that we're not a threat and that we're associated with their biggest concerns, we'll need to know their common threats and concerns going in. As opposed to just what we do and how we're different, buyers emotionally connect, or at least begin an emotional attraction, when they realize that we might address the biggest relatable fears and desires that they're dealing with.

For each buyer role or persona that we'd want to take a meeting with us, we should define the top *problems* that they're trying to solve and *positive outcomes* they most desire, associated with the solution that we provide. Then, in our outreach, make those potentially relatable *problems* and *positive outcomes* our prospecting message. It's best to keep them short and offer them up in a series of outreaches. But just remember, outcomes-based prospecting messages are the only ones that would relate or create familiarity with a buyer. Any other information or reason a buyer would take a meeting would either be related to our unique situation, or we got lucky.

Also in that prospecting message, sharing brief *Customer Value Proof Points* related to our buyer, such as other companies or credible influencers who use our solutions, is also effective at disarming our buyer, piquing their emotional interest. Associating ourselves to a respected peer of theirs also creates *familiarity*. But what creates a feeling of familiarity the most is the buyer themselves.

So ideally, our prospecting message should include relevant information we've learned about them. Whether through social channels, partners, or team members, we should find out as much as we can about our buyers and the businesses that they work for. We should use these familiar anecdotes, not to appear like we know them well and we're best friends, but to simply disarm them. I've seen sellers learn personal or professional interests about a buyer and send them gifts that relate in order to get their attention, such as a book on a topic they reference in their LinkedIn profile, a ski hat for their favorite hockey team. A seller may have connections to others who went to the same university or post-graduate programs where familiarity can be created. Perhaps something they've professionally published, spoken on, or blogged about creates an opportunity for a disarming connection.

We should also work to create an attraction to ourselves through the introductions and impressions we make in our outreach. Familiarity can breed with the comfort gained over time with us, the seller who's working so hard to get their attention and gain access to their time. This is where approaches matter in attracting an *emotional connection*. Get creative. Is there something you can do to help them get more familiar with you and eventually the solution you sell? Many of my sellers have found success creating short videos. The reason many of us prefer watching YouTube videos to written word is because the human component gives us familiarity and the story offers entertainment. But guidance, don't make it so serious or too lengthy. Whatever our creative approach, we should be like the advertisers and connect to the *Thrive* state of the mind. Loosen up. Make our videos funny, relaxing, or emotionally driven. We just need to be genuine with a concise valuable emotionally connecting message. Remember that we're prospecting to the *lazy brain,* and we just want to be distinguished in a positive way. Attracting *emotional connections* in *Prospecting* all comes down to building relatability and familiarity.

Emotional connection also builds in the **Discovery and Presentation Meetings** we lead. If we get scheduled calls and the meeting matters, try to make it in person. If it must be virtual, get a commitment for the use of video during the call and offer up a reason for how much you think it matters. When we start to engage with our buyers, we should know their *current state* as best we can before we meet with them. Our mindset for these meetings should be that we're *preparing for connection.* We make the time to plan and prepare by writing down what we believe the buyer is experiencing and focused on, what would be familiar and relatable to them, and how we can bridge that connection.

Depending on where we are in our sales engagement, this could be a *tailored presentation* that talks to their relatable business model, use cases, or circumstances. In technology, it could be a *customized demonstration plan* that considers their unique environment or situation. Always use their vocabulary and present personalized examples and experiences that they'll *connect to.*

In preparing to connect, other good information to search for and align with are the initiatives they're facing. I've had sellers who sold to the retail industry. Before every first meeting or presentation, they would walk into a store and document their experience relative to what we sold. That would then reflect in a tailored and emotionally connecting discussion or presentation. Those buyers were impressed and that attracted their emotions.

We should seek to uncover as much familiarity and relatability as possible before and at the beginning of our meetings. Whether it's what we learn about the company, a specific person, or what our typical customers would care about most, we need to internalize this going in so that we can be agile in working our way to a state of connection. In *Discovery* conversations, we should frame those discussions around the problems and outcomes that they care about most. Buyers need to participate in their connection.

However, the biggest caution I can offer in positioning our solutions is to be as relevant and concise as possible in order to make it easy for buyers to connect to what makes our value proposition *unique and better for them*. Simply, a buyer shouldn't have to work so hard to figure it all out. Remember that *lazy brain*. A buyer won't sit around too long trying to solve our sales puzzle. If they can't understand our message, they'll dismiss it. They'll become emotionally disconnected. The bottom line for us sellers is to remember that when we're leading conversations and positioning our solutions, we must connect to the buyer's emotions before their intellect every time.

SUMMARY: *Emotional Connection*

In the coming chapters, I'll help you use this foundational awareness of the human buyers that you sell to and apply it to sales conversations, gaining buyer commitment and urgency, building trust, and the execution of winning the deal. Regardless of the application, with every human being we meet along the course of our sales process, we have to be intentional about both building *Emotional Connections* with them, as well as not doing anything that detracts from the connections we've already made.

Where we all tend to think that we're rational human beings who think about what we do and the decisions we make, science proves that we're almost completely irrational. We choose relationships solely built on emotion and realize far too late that we're not even compatible. We form a bias driven by some recent memory or historical experience. We put people and things into categories, fueled by judgement and prejudice. We snip at someone because we assumed they were saying something totally different than they actually were. Have you ever experienced your buyers doing any of these things with you? While our mind has incredible and nearly limitless capacity, it's not naturally wired to use that capacity, especially when feeling the threats that many salespeople present. Thus, there is no more foundational habit than connecting to the emotions of our buyers.

These emotional *Survive and Thrive* states of the buyer mind are where most of the activity and decisioning happens. We do this by learning about and knowing what our buyers fear the most before and during our sales interactions. These mindsets and habits lead us toward disarming their protective survival instincts by meeting them where they are in their *Survive* state. This allows us the permission to start spending the majority of our time in their highly opportunistic *Thrive* state, while maximizing the short opportunities we get to connect in their intellectual *Think* state. This *emotional connection* becomes a grounded foundation that enables our buyers to want to intellectually learn about and truly invest in becoming a Champion for the high priority positive outcomes that we can deliver for them. *Emotional Connection.*

CHAPTER 5

LEADING VISION

Vision-Based Positioning

THE AUDITORS IN THE HALL

I was once invited to attend a meeting by one of my reps with a large international credit services company. The technical team that my rep had been working with were all excited about our product's automation, the ability to enable over 60 percent faster releases of application changes, a huge productivity gain for the company. After all, their applications were how they did business online with consumers.

This meeting I was attending was the first with their vice president of operations. Everyone on their team, even their most analytical engineers, were convinced that my meeting with the VP would put this purchase over the line for approval. My rep had come prepared with a strong business case, with more than just productivity gains. He and some on their team had quite creatively correlated the faster application release times to increased revenue and loss-avoidance for the company. He'd prepared me well with all the most important discovery questions I could ask, and I was ready. We'd assumed their team had prepped their boss just as well.

So, I kicked off the meeting as I always would, probing, or *trying* to probe into how well he understood the problems in their current release process, while sprinkling the discussion with small value metrics our teams had worked on together. Well, it wasn't two minutes into the meeting where the VP just straight out stuck his hand in my face and said, "Let me stop you there. I have no doubt that across my entire operation there are many opportunities to improve productivity. But I've got problems to solve. We've had two outages this week and damn security auditors are crawling all over this place." He instructed me to wheel my chair back into the door frame of his office and look down the hall.

He said, "You see those guys in khakis with the badges? Those are my auditors. If you can't fix that problem, then this meeting is over."

Well, as a decent sized former college athlete, I wasn't quite used to having someone thrust their hand in my face in a business meeting. But, in the post-meeting debrief with my rep, I listened as he ripped the VP asking, "How in the world could he be so irresponsible to not implement the value that's in a business case that his people built with me?"

I was quick to defend the VP's position. I explained from a basic perspective of human nature. "Simple," I said. "Fight or flight. This guy was emotional toward me because he has other greater problems on his mind. Neither we, nor his team connected to those problems going into this meeting. He was never going to give any energy to learning about our business case or our product unless we could attach ourselves to the emotional problems that he's trying to solve. And we didn't do that."

LEADING VISION: *The Connection Milestone*

Consider that *Emotional Connection* is a foundational habit, a selling behavior that rewards us with the attention and energy of our buyer. If in learning about the very psychology-centric *Emotional Connection* habit, you might have started thinking that this book wasn't going to get into the true mastery of selling, then buckle up as we venture into our second E.L.I.T.E. habit, **Leading Vision**.

This habit of *Leading a Buyer's Vision* will be all about what we should be doing and avoiding in how we position our message in the sales conversation. Because we'll now be thinking about our selling habits across our journey with a buyer, from these initial *vision leading* interactions and eventually on through the close, I want you to think of where we are as a buyer's **Connection Milestone**. It's in these early and paramount sales conversations that the *connection* game is now on! As this book will guide, if they can make a very purposeful and high certainty *connection* here, they'll be prepared to allow themselves to begin working toward further mental milestones of *intellectual commitment, high-trust closure,* and *executing the win.*

However, it's what that buyer *connection* does that matters so much. Gaining an individual connection to what we sell, the relatable potential impact that we can make on a buyer, is the first milestone they'll go through in their journey to becoming our Champion. The power of this *connection milestone* is that it's when a buyer's motivation toward having a *bias for action* begins. What I'll share is that there is no more personal and highly

116

motivated state in a buyer than when we can lead their future *Vision*.

Our buyer will form an *emotional connection* to us when they see how the *purpose* of what we sell is aligned to the positive future state that they desire for themselves. So, what is the *purpose* of your product or service? What does it uniquely do *for* your buyers? How confident and clear are you in that message? How clear is your purpose to the people you sell to? Really think about those self-reflecting questions. In your own sales habits, how often and how intentional are you at positioning the *purpose* of your product or service?

All sellers know that fairly soon in a buyer/seller interaction, we're going to need to position our solution. Some call this a *Sales Pitch*. I don't like to think of it that way and you'll understand more throughout this habit. Essentially, a *pitch* is one-way. Much like the pitcher in baseball who throws the ball to a batter, he hopes for a *swing and a miss*, eventually even a *strike out*.

In my experience, that's how the buyer/seller conversation turns out much too often. But we're the ones who strike out. Seller throws their best pitch, hoping it lands in the strike zone. Only much of the time, it's not only off target, but the result is usually what's called in baseball, a *line drive* right back at the pitcher at a hundred miles an hour. In baseball, statistically this happens less than .001 percent of the time. In sales, I'd bet the percentage would be pretty high. Have you ever thought about that? The moment that we choose to pitch what sell, what we would think is the simplest thing in sales, is actually the highest risk and most dangerous part of our job. That moment is where we potentially attract or completely lose our buyers. I know that sounds a bit dramatic. But as I've shared, after years of developing and leading salespeople, this is the most challenging and low performing area of proficiency that I've observed.

In order to navigate a buyer through the right connections between our unique value proposition and their positive future *vision*, our sales habits will need to be far more intuitive and purposeful than just pitching our solutions or getting our buyers excited. Reaching this aspirational connection to a *vision* that we can uniquely deliver will come from our work toward mastering the craft of how we prepare, listen, learn, and then position our unique message. Gaining a buyer's *certainty* in our solution's ability to reach that *vision* will come from how we strategically lead our buyer to experience the outcomes they desire. Our *E.L.T.I.T.E.* mission during this habit of **Leading Vision** will be to get our buyer to a level of absolute certainty in the impact and value we can deliver toward that future vision they have for themselves. This greater purpose of our *vision leading* conversations should help guide our path to lead a buyer through this *milestone of connection*.

VISION VS. VALUE

If you've been through any modern-day sales training or methodologies, most of them are centered around *value-based* selling. Any strong messaging framework about a product or set of services must absolutely have a *value* component to it. *Value*, in particular *value metrics*, serves as a measurable context for how important we are, validation of our *value proposition*. They provide legitimacy for the price that we want to charge and impactful context for those vision-leading outcomes we can deliver. As the concept of value can sometimes be misused or misunderstood, at the end of the day, a *value* is something that is measured.

Value in business is the measurement of benefit or impact that we can deliver for a customer. In fact, it should be in the *vision* that a buyer wants for themselves where our *value* for them becomes defined. Yet often, this is where value metrics end up falling flat for us sellers when we position them too early and without any learned and aligned context. If a buyer can't make an intellectual connection of the potential *value* we could offer to a positive future vision they've emotionally connected to, then those value metrics mean nothing to them. They're not even interesting.

What makes it even harder in this *value game* is that the competition has all read the same books and taken similar training. As technological innovation has greatly accelerated in the millennium, new competitors have developed more advanced, or at least different approaches, to solve the same problems. Thus, they're all positioning that they can deliver similar business value. Eventually, there's only so many words in our vocabulary to describe the *value* that we can deliver to a specific set of pains. For the buyers, they see the sellers all starting to sound alike with the same value message.

Now, the problem that we sellers will face if we don't get to this awareness of *value* in our message will be in one of three areas. If the outcomes that we can deliver, the positive future vision that our buyer would care about, is not easily differentiated by tangible competencies, then a lack of *value measurement* will **minimize our message**. In other words, a lack of *value in the message* makes it appear that we are one of several providers who can help them achieve their vision. There's no measurable impact that sets us apart. So, because of a lack of differentiating value, we fall into our own trap of commoditization.

The second outcome when we message without a relevant value message is that ***we haven't earned the right to charge the***

price that we'd like to. Perhaps we do have a Champion and they're pushing for the purchase. But, without an aligned potential *value measurement* providing credibility to our price tag, the Champion won't be able to get the deal closed at the price point we desire. The third weakness we create when we fail to sell at a level of measurable value is that when the time comes to question the urgency of making this decision now, we'll lack the ability to defend what the *negative consequences* would be for not moving forward with any level of credibility. Value is intellectual. It's a measurement of how much achieving their *vision* should matter.

So then, just what does it mean to lead a buyer's *Vision? I thought we were supposed to sell on value?* Yes. We certainly should sell on *value*. But this *Leading Vision* habit is about the process in practice of *how we position* our high value message. By definition, *Vision* is simply our ability to see. In having a *vision* for something professionally, that *vision* is either individual to themselves or it's tied to their area of responsibility for the business. Either way, that *vision* is theirs. It's personal. People buy something when they emotionally feel that it will make their future better. They see a *vision* of themselves and then they want it. It's this *personal vision* that motivates them to act. A man buys a nice suit because he sees himself looking successful and respected in it. A couple buys a home because they see their family growing and happy in it. An accomplished woman buys herself a bright red sportscar because she sees herself as powerful and proud when she drives it.

If we think about how our human mind operates, most of its energy is centered around what we emotionally desire. Those emotions could be fear-driven, or they could be opportunistic. What I hope you come to realize is that a buyer's *vision* is like a secret *treasure box*. They either know that they want in or they're actively seeking to find a way. We sometimes meet buyers who feel that they've already found their treasure. With them, we now have an opportunity to expand their *vision* to an even better one. When we sellers can attach to, if not lead a buyer's *vision*, it's like finding this personalized key to unlocking a treasure that our buyer wants.

This applies to anything and everything we sell. If a dermatologist agrees to begin prescribing a new skin treatment, it's because they either envision certain patients living a happier life with an embarrassing condition eliminated, or because they see their business growing from a new revenue stream. A technologist who goes to work daily, frustrated that they don't have time to work on what they were trained and prefer to do, buys a new software solution because they see those mundane tasks being eliminated and their job more fulfilling.

We *lead vision* because it's personal. When we can attach what we sell to an aspirational *vision* of what our buyers want for themselves, we're unlocking a door to a strong *Emotional Connection*. When we then attach *value* to that vision, we motivate buyers to consider a bias for action, the first step toward becoming our Champions.

So, here's the key learning. The *vision* we lead is to a positive future state that our buyer would emotionally connect to. Thus, our real *value* to that buyer will only be in how much we can impact that *vision*.

The buyer's mindset on **vision**. *When you help me see how what you sell could get me to a positive future vision that I desire, I'll start emotionally connecting to you. You've attracted my interest.*

The buyer's mindset on **value**. *Reaching that vision alone would provide value to me. However, if you expect me to take*

121

action on making a purchase with any urgency, I'll need to understand the negative consequences if I delay. And, if you want to charge a higher premium, then I'm going to need to understand just how much value this would be for me.

The Dichotomy of Value

Like with anything that has a high potential of power, *value* has to be handled with caution. *Vision*, which is this personalized fuel to igniting the highly emotional and positive state of *Thrive* in the buyer's brain, is something that we would want to lead and discuss early and often. The brain's state of *Thrive* just can't get enough. However, it's important to realize that there's a bit of a dichotomy in the dynamic of *value* in our positioning, in how it can affect our buyers. On one hand, positioning *value*, attached to the outcomes we discuss and propose as highly quantified results we can deliver, can enhance all of the benefits of emotional and intellectual connection. It can elevate the emotional attraction to our initial messaging, and it can reinforce the value premium and priority of purchasing us later in the decision process.

However, there's a danger to positioning *value* at the wrong time or in the wrong way. Early in our sales conversations, if we've made the nonintuitive mistake of leading with our value metrics as the main reasons a buyer should meet with or consider us, offering up ROI studies, telling customer value stories that don't relate, or just simply positioning value with no context or *emotional connection* formed; we'll be the cause that makes our buyer resist our message. If we've adopted the psyche of *emotional before intellectual connections* and the intention of *leading a buyer's vision*, we should know that aggressively pushing the buyer to be moved by our value metrics should never be done too early before we've begun building *emotional connection* to what the solution could do for them. This is the *dichotomy of value*. A value message can be an asset for buyer attraction, and it can be a turn-off.

THE CERTAINTY LOOP

If we truly desire a Buyer Champion who has a willingness to sell for us, then we should realize that those Champions will need to form a level of *certainty* in order to make that decision. When we start our path toward building an actual Buyer Champion, it's not just about gaining an e*motional connection*, it's really about growing it to a level where the buyer starts to consider just how willing and active an advocate they'll be for us. Depending on the cost or disruption of what we sell, that can often be a sensitive decision for a Champion. When I say that they'll need *certainty*, this means that for them to get to that state of commitment, a Champion will need to develop a deep belief in the outcomes that our solution promises to deliver.

Having *certainty* in any part of our lives means that we have an absolute *belief* in something. Naturally, forming those beliefs comes from our experiences, most importantly, the results that we've experienced. Have you ever heard anybody say, "If I hadn't of seen it for myself, then I wouldn't have believed it!" They witnessed it, saw it with their own eyes. Here's the problem in sales, though. Even if a prospective buyer starts to become fairly connected to what we sell, they're still not a customer yet. This concept of *certainty* starts to frame why it's so important that we have a strategic approach for upselling and cross selling our existing customers. While they may not have experienced all the value we could offer, they are on their way.

So, if certainty in life comes from the results of our experiences, then how are we sellers supposed to build any deep belief in a buyer who hasn't personally experienced our product or service yet? If you're working a deal or an account that has all the traits of one that should be closed already, even if you seem to have a proven Buyer Champion, yet the deal just won't move to close, this could be one of your problems. If a Champion isn't able to experience for themselves what the results and outcomes of that purchase will be, they'll always be hesitant to develop the complete belief needed to be able to sponsor it.

This is all a part of the mastery of *leading a buyer's vision.* And by the way, if we don't lead them to a state of *certainty,* who will? Our competition? If our competition's any good, they'll lead a buyer's vision to a very different and contrary point of view for what the buyer's priority outcomes and criteria should be. And trust me, that vision will be perfectly set up to create *Fear, Uncertainty, and Doubt* in our product or service. What's more realistic, however, is that our competition usually isn't that good.

The most common sales outcome is that our Champions don't buy anything from anyone at all. Nothing makes someone more certain of the outcomes they'll achieve than in the experiences they're already having today. *If it ain't broke, don't fix it.* To a seller, this may sound like insanity, but to a buyer, at least they know what they're dealing with.

If you're beginning to accept that your sales mission is to build a Buyer Champion who will sell on your behalf, then one of the most crucial objectives toward that mission is that we help our buyer form absolute *certainty* in us. Elite sellers know that any level of doubt or hesitation in a buyer's confidence that a) we're the right solution for them and b) that this is the right time to make the change, will derail and stall the buying decision a majority of the time. It's their *survival claw* taking over the intellectual brain.

So, if *buyer certainty* is so vital, then we sellers need to be intuitive enough to know how to help them get there. Like much of what we've covered, for us to choose the right sales strategies, we often need to understand basic buyer psychology. So, I'm going to explain to you just how we develop our *certainty* for things. Once we understand this, it gives even more clarity as to our focus and approach in *leading a buyer's vision*.

I'll share this simple concept I've learned and I call **The Certainty Loop**. First, understand that all humans have a perspective of **Potential**. This becomes our emotional baseline. As you know, the buyers of today will most likely have already developed their own preconceived perspectives of your company or your solution's potential when you walk into the room or join the call.

Potential has been proven to be both the greatest mental liberator and limiter toward us achieving our goals. In 1954, Roger Banister did the impossible and ran a four-minute mile for the first time in history. Running a mile in four minutes was the commonly perceived limitation of our human ability at that time. Within two years after running this four-minute breakthrough, thirty-seven more people ran at least that fast.

As a seller, we must realize that a buyer's perspective of *Potential*, either from their experiences, peers, research, competitors, or possibly from our company's own messaging are in a sense, *limiting beliefs* that need to be overcome. *Potential* is not the critical path to forming a buyer's absolute certainty. It's actually the *limiting belief*.

So, here's how **The Certainty Loop** works. It's simple. And picture me drawing a big circle clockwise. Our perspective of *Potential* drives our *Actions*. Our *Actions* then drive *Results*. Finally, *Results* form our *Beliefs*. And having absolute belief is called **Certainty**.

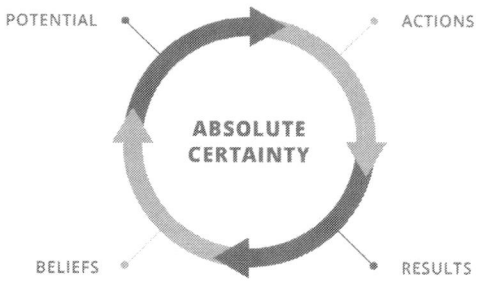

concept based on work from Robbins Research International, Inc.

Perspective of *Potential* drives *Actions*. *Actions* drive *Results*. *Results* lead to Beliefs. The way our brains work, we gain *certainty* when we *experience* results. That's why the rich become richer and the poor become poorer. It's the self-fulfilling prophecy. So, how do we get a buyer to have absolute belief and *certainty* in our product before they even use it? **Vision.** This simple psychological *Certainty Loop* is our guide to a destination we not only should desire, but one for which we are intentional and strategic with every Buyer Champion we target.

To help you internalize this concept of *certainty*, think of yourself and your own experiences. When in your life were you going into some of the bigger decisions you've faced: committing to a relationship or getting married, buying a house, taking the job that you're in today? Think of the decisions where you felt calm and confident. You had absolute conviction and belief that it was the right decision to make. Why exactly did you feel so certain? Were there any previous experiences or results that were present in those decisions? What about the other decisions, where you felt such hesitance and caution? Were those newer situations to you? Did you feel rushed for any reason?

Now, imagine if you were your buyer. How would you ever get to that state of commitment for something or someone such that you'd be willing to go to your peers and economic authority with conviction? What would you need in order to form the intention to convince them that this purchase is the best thing for the business? What would you need to allow your protective risk-averse emotions to subdue and feel empowered enough to take that kind of stand? ***Certainty***.

This knowledge of how *The Certainty Loop* works further clarifies how hard it is to get a buyer to be our Champion. Knowing that we eventually will need to get our buyers to a state of *certainty*, when we begin and continue to position our solution across all of the stakeholders involved in the decision process, we'll need to keep our focus on aligning to and guiding their *vision*. Remember, a buyer understanding our capabilities and differentiation only builds clarity, not connection, and certainly not the level of certainty that we desire. When we feel the muscle memory kick in to turn the messaging spotlight onto all the intellectual facts and details about what we sell, that feeling needs to be a trigger that reminds us of *The Certainty Loop.* Our mindset then needs to get back to leading their vision toward experiences and results that they can see for themselves. For application, consider these *Certainty Strategies* in the context of your type of sale.

Certainty Strategies

Some of these strategies will be applied later in the book. But it's important that we understand that their purpose is to provide the vision of experience that leads to a buyer's certainty. One certainty strategy when a buyer can't directly experience our solution as a customer is using different **Proof Events.** Many companies execute proof of concepts, freemium trials, and pilot strategies. Some industries give free samples of their product. If your company can customize demonstrations or use cases, these also get the buyer closer to the experience.

A more advanced proof strategy is called *Simulation*. If what you sell involves potentially complicated or risky processes such as implementation, migration, a supply chain, a surgery, or any other kind of process, one experience-leading strategy is to offer some type of simulation of that process. This could be a call scheduled to walk-through a tailored process for them using systems that they relate to. A sales team could facilitate a hands-on process workshop. Buyers could be hosted on a customer site visit seeing the solution live in action.

This strategy's related to another called a **Customer Reference**. If it's not realistic for you to get your buyer simulating or experiencing your solution themselves, then offering them a peer testimonial or encounter is one of the most effective ways to provide them some experience of their vision and your value. Companies will get their prospects integrated into customer communities and user groups. Customer and partner events offer opportunities to gain references of positive experience.

Even more effective, connecting them directly to a respected and credible professional peer for a reference call or presentation event can often create *buyer certainty* for several reasons. We find comfort in familiarity. There's nothing on the planet more familiar to a human being than another human. A customer of yours who's an industry peer to your buyer will appear familiar to them. Live references allow for a dialogue that with each question answered, the buyer takes themselves closer and closer to the actual experience of using your product or service. A good reference gets the buyer into the moment of vision and understanding the attribution of value. Often, the interaction itself can be the driver of that certainty and comfort. So, be thoughtful in how you set up these references.

It's critical that we consider context in the connection. Is the reference's situation, industry, environment, or business model aligned as close as possible with your buyer? If not, your buyer will easily dismiss the reference and emotionally lose confidence in you. They might lose trust in you thinking, *If this company isn't aware enough of our situation and our needs, or if they just don't care, then I fear that they may not be a great partner for us.*

Another caution in references is that the personalities and level of knowledge and perspective of each peer need to be aligned. If your buyer is a high-level executive type, then a more functional reference will get into details that don't connect or provide the *vision* your executive needs. That's not really a peer. If your reference has a dry personality, is an uninspiring communicator, or just short on time, and yet you have a buyer who needs a lot of attention and discussion, then this may not build as much certainty as you'd hoped.

Again, sometimes just two people hitting it off, when they establish credibility and trust with one another, can create an *emotional connection* of certainty. Prepared thoughtfully, references and customer events are great strategies for getting prospective buyers as close to the actual experience of vision and value as possible. Great sellers know that the more intimate and familiar they can get a buyer experiencing their solution during a decision process, the more certainty that they can help build. Perhaps these experiential connections can form from the simplest of customer stories and proof points told, to fully involved events and briefings. If a person can experience the positive results of what you sell, even if it's just a limited example, they're far more likely to develop a *vision* for it.

All these approaches are different examples of the greater strategy called **Visualization**. When we can't yet have access to what we want for ourselves, the closest we can get to actually experiencing something is by *visualizing* it. *Visualization* has been studied and proven for decades from sports to public speaking. In basketball, making free throws is one of the most mental aspects of the game. Many players choke at the free throw line, even though they clearly possess the skills to make free throws. Something is mentally getting in the way, some uncertainty. So, the question is, how do you make somebody better who has a mental block interfering with their success?

In 1996, a University of Chicago study by Dr. Judd Biasotto included three groups randomly selected to test their free throw shooting improvement over a thirty-day period. The first was told not to touch a basketball for the full thirty days, no practicing or playing basketball whatsoever. The second group was told to practice shooting free throws every day for thirty minutes a day. The third group was to come to the gym every day for all thirty days and spend a half hour with their eyes closed, simply visualizing hitting every free throw perfectly.

After the thirty days, all three groups were asked to come back and take the same amount of free throw attempts they took at the beginning of the study. The first group, who didn't practice at all, showed no improvement. The second group had practiced every day and showed a 24 percent improvement. The third group, however, the group who had simply visualized success daily, showed a 23 percent improvement.

Visualization of results has been proven over time because the mind is not interrupted by realities. There's no limiting beliefs or perspectives of potential being formed. This emphasis and visualization of results reinforces our beliefs, which powers this ongoing *Certainty Loop*. While hard work can never be substituted, achieving great success in life and in business is mental. When we reach a state of *certainty*, absolute belief in something, it helps us to tap into its full *potential*. This pushes us to take greater *actions* that in turn, get more *results*. Our *beliefs* then become reinforced into a self-fulfilling prophecy from those results.

Elite sellers don't take short cuts, doing the minimum sales activity and tactics. They lead their Buyer Champions through this mental journey toward *certainty*. The progressive building of a buyer's *vision* starts at a personal relatability to problems and desired outcomes that sellers position. Then, if the seller can help their buyer somehow visualize or simulate the experience of results, they can clear a path to forming their buyer's *certainty*. Results drive beliefs, beliefs create *certainty*. It's this *certainty* that gives our Champions the confidence and motivation to act on our behalf. This is by far, the ultimate purpose of *Leading Vision.*

Applying LEADING VISION in the Sales Process

THE VISION-BASED POSITIONING FRAMEWORK

There are many different types of sales professionals reading or listening to this book. While there's differences in the domain

131

or industry that we sell in, our costs and pricing structures, types of sales processes, one thing that all salespeople share in common is experiencing the moment of positioning what we sell. In medical or pharmaceutical sales, you may have had to cater the lunch, bring a speaker, lead some small talk with the staff, just to eventually get your ten minutes of time with the doctor or physician's assistant. Most medical buyers have already formed an opinion about the category of treatment or equipment you offer. As soon as they learn that you fit into that bucket, their emotional mind cuts off any pathway to burning more intellectual calories. In B2B technology, maybe they've heard of your functional area or even your product itself. But chances are, they're far more confused and unclear as to the difference between what seems like dozens of products that all sound alike.

In specialized services, whether what you do is niche or fairly commoditized, the reality is that other firms could deliver the same services as you do. Your value proposition is how you do it so differently. Yet, you have no idea if your buyer knows what they want, how they want to get it, or even if they have a real need in the first place. Every product or service we sell has the attributes of capabilities, or *what it does*, and differentiators, *what it does differently or better.* But where most sellers struggle is understanding just *what it does for the customer.* In all types of sales environments, our buyers are pretty much asking the same four essential questions: *Who are you? What do you do? How are you different? And why should I care?* Then, why is it that salespeople have such a struggle at answering those questions clearly and concisely?

It really starts with the company and its formation of our *sales messaging.* How clear are you in being able to succinctly answer those four essential questions for what you sell? Has your company laid it out well, or are you figuring it out on your own, feeling like you're in a constant state of experimentation? If they have built that messaging, how confident are you that it *hits the mark*? Do you often feel like you sound like everybody else? Is determining how to handle objections and resistance where you spend much of your time and anxiety? Just how easy, efficient, and effective is it to *position* your message?

In our hyper-focus and enthusiasm for the greatness of the products and services we sell, or even for covering up for their shortcomings, it's that personal future *vision* and all its relevant important details where we sellers fail to reach. This becomes the most underlying reason for why we can't build Champions. They may have clarity for what we do. But they don't have a connection to what we can do for them.

All habits stem from a mindset. If our mindset is that it's all about a specific message that every single buyer needs to hear every time, then that's what our habit will be. While the criticality of message may be true, our own fear-driven survival impulses probably won't be patient enough to ask the right questions to inform a *vision-connecting* message for our buyer. We'll just lead with our standard message every time.

Sales mindsets and habits work in all ways that we message. If we don't want to follow someone else's messaging script or format, then chances are that we'll simply form our own instinctual message based on a few successful meetings. We'll often suffer from *recency bias.*

If it worked in that last meeting, I'll use it in this next one.

Conversely, if our mindset is that we should never position what we do until we've completed a set of very rigorous, interrogating questions, then we'll probably find our habits getting challenged by frustrated buyers who don't feel like their time is being valued, that they're not getting what they needed from their meetings with us. The point is that our level of success in the sales conversation isn't about how perfect our messaging has been constructed. If we want to sell with the habits that emotionally and intellectually connect buyers to our products and services, then it's not our message that will attract and form that connection. It's the messenger.

Since *Leading Vision* is a habit that should be practiced at any point in a sales process, with all buyers we encounter, and as often as possible, I'll provide a simple approach to *how* we position that vision in a sales conversation. While I hope you're truly connecting to the mindset and concepts behind how a buyer forms their *emotional connection* and belief in what we sell, I want to help you strengthen your *Vision Leading* habits with an easy-to-follow framework. Due to the dynamic nature of sales, my advice is that a framework should not be implemented as a step-by-step set of instructions to be used with every buyer in the same sequence with the same words. All selling situations and buyer personalities are different, and we need to be able to use our empathy and intuitiveness to adjust and adapt.

However, just as all athletes need a set of rules and coaching points to guide them in the moment of performance, so do salespeople. In our greatest sales conversations, we find ourselves being more *in the moment,* instinctually reacting to what we hear and learn. A good sales framework, when well aligned to the objective, and simple enough to follow, should serve as an impactful mental guide when we are in those common sales moments of our unique sales process. My intention with this framework is to guide how you and your company navigate your messaging and communication with buyers. If your desire is to change some of the bad habits you've had in sales conversations, or perhaps become more intentional at *objection avoidance* and forming *emotional connections*, consider adopting this situational sales conversation guide called **The Vision-Based Positioning Framework**.

Our habits are formed when our responses to triggers become routine. When those responses are rewarded, they reinforce and strengthen the habit. The good news is that it doesn't take long to change a habit. We just need to implement an alternative response to that trigger. So, if you want to evolve your positioning toward a more *vision leading* habit, use this *Vision-Based Positioning Framework* as your alternative response every time you experience the triggers of your sales conversations.

Being a *vision leading* salesperson means that our primary objective is to first align to and then guide the buyer's emotionally-formed *vision*, related to what we sell. Strategically, that vision needs to be aligned to our *unique value proposition*, what we can do differently or better for our customers compared to their current solutions or alternatives in the market.

This *vision leading* mindset does two things for us sellers. One, it drives our sales behaviors to be more in-line with how a buyer reacts to us and makes decisions. Emotion before intellect. *Survive, Thrive, Think.* Secondly, it helps the buyer adopt a similar mindset to ours. We can't expect a buyer to share the same vision as us if we aren't proficient at positioning that vision. When a buyer can see or *envision* their future in a better state than it is today, due to the goodness of what we sell, we have now begun creating an *emotional connection* that enables us to continue toward those *intellectual connections* we desire.

Through *Vision-Based Positioning*, we'll help a buyer discover that positive future vision across two areas. First, what is their vision for the ***problems*** they'd like to solve? A human's primary *survival* response is to solve problems they're facing. Then, what are the positive **outcomes** they'd most envision for their future? Our stronger and older emotional brain wants to remain in a state of *Thrive*. You see, particularly in a more strategic or solution-oriented purchase, a buyer isn't *really* wanting to buy a product or service. Maybe that's what they're saying they want or just what we're hearing. What a buyer wants to invest in is an *outcome*, specifically a positive outcome that they're not confident they could achieve with the solutions they're using today.

Remember, that mental state of a buyer's desired outcome is their *vision*, what they'd like to see in the future for themselves. The reason we sellers need to be *leading* that vision is that too often, our buyers either haven't had the time to research better solutions than they use today or perhaps our competitors or so-called industry experts have already begun to guide their perspectives and point of view. *The Certainty Loop* explains why that's dangerous for us.

Have you ever walked into a purchase process, or heard about one after the fact, where the buyer had made up their mind and bought an alternative solution without any real consideration of what you were selling? A person's perspective of *potential* drives their *actions.* Those buying actions happened without you because their perspective of potential, in the area that you're involved in, had been formed already. Maybe they or someone on their staff had used the alternative solution before and thus, their *experience* had formed their *beliefs*. Maybe some competitive sales pitch or marketing campaign inspired a positive future vision but enabled it in a different way than you do it.

The point is that if we're not leading a buyer's vision, someone or something else will. A *vision* becomes sticky because it's personal. We humans connect, first and foremost, to ourselves. Subconsciously, our survival instincts say, *Look, I feel good about my vision being met, and I'm not going to risk that or the dozen other things I have on my plate by considering something different.* Thus, if when we're trying to sell or market to those buyers and we're only positioning what we do and how we're different, then we're failing to make a connection to what would cause them to take any favorable action toward us. This could be from taking a first meeting through replacing what they use today with us. With *Vision-Based Positioning*, I'll give you some practical discovery and positioning applications that will help simplify your ability to qualify and lead that vision.

Objection Avoidance

Before we go deep into *Vision-Based Positioning*, I think it's important we spend a few minutes on this concept of **Objection Avoidance**, which is at the heart of what we're trying to do in *Leading Vision*. I realize this term *positioning* may or may not be in your normal sales vocabulary, but it should be. If you've ever taken a negotiation course, for example, you learn this idea that often in business, people aren't just sharing opinions and information with you. They're actually taking a *position*, whether you realize it or not. What's often happening in sales conversations is that buyers are perceiving what we sellers are communicating as a *position*.

Wrong or right, our natural survival instinct is to automatically assume that some new information or opportunity being shared with us is a threat. As the buyer hears our sales pitch, their subconscious starts thinking, *So, what exactly are they saying here? I probably don't agree. Does this even have anything to do with me? I've got to avoid this risk. How can I counter their position?*

Why would a buyer sense that a salesperson is taking a threatening position? If the involuntary emotional reaction in our mind is to assume that what comes at us is probably something that we need to protect ourselves against, then we instinctively try to assess the position that the threat is taking. With a traditional sales pitch, the buyer's logical *thinking* state hasn't been set free yet, so they're not necessarily being rational and analyzing every word the salesperson says.

Have you ever delivered your sales pitch only to have the buyer start reacting to things you didn't even think you said, as if they weren't even listening? If you don't feel like you have this problem of conversational buyer conflict, it could just be that you're a naturally gifted and trusting guide in the way that you communicate. However, if you've ever felt like you received an unnecessary and unwarranted defensive response from a buyer, a direct rejection of your message, they were probably reacting to a *position* they perceived you were taking.

So, what happens next? If the buyer senses a threat or doesn't understand how your intended message is for them, they **Counter Position**, or what's often called an **Objection**. Have you ever made a basic unassuming statement about your product and then got torpedoed with buyer objections? You went into the discussion intending to have a healthy intellectual dialogue, only to realize that you're now in the *sales twilight zone* arguing with a buyer who you were hoping to form a great relationship with.

While so much time in traditional sales training is spent on our message and objection-handling to it, if we were to focus on our *positioning*, the better goal would be **Objection Avoidance.** So, if we were to then accept that buyers are simply hardwired to take and react to what we say as a *position*, then we should see this as an opportunity to strengthen our *positioning* habits. There's a difference between our *messaging* and how we *position* that message. I've often found that what truly sets the Elite Sellers apart wasn't their messaging, because that was equal for everyone in the company. The best sellers master the habit of situationally positioning their message to the different buyers they sell to, while avoiding objections.

Problems Solving: *Disarming the Survival State*

While our personalities and action tendencies vary, our brains are all wired the same. When approached by new people and new information, especially in the middle of a typical stressed-out workday, a buyer's emotional inner brain kicks in first and acts as a defense *firewall*. It protects it from anyone or anything that could make its day any worse. When that threat is us sellers, we need to effectively *prove* how we and what we sell are not a threat. What does it even mean to be a *threat* to a buyer? Are we talking about our body language, intimidation, tone of voice? No. In the craft of positioning our message, coming across threatening is much simpler than that. Initially, if buyers don't learn who we are fairly quickly, specifically our credibility, we're seen as a stranger who just walked into their office or popped up on their monitor. When buyers feel that something could be a waste of their time, not related to them, or add risk to their job objectives, they will take it as a threat. Sellers desperately want buyers to hear, understand, and appreciate all their capabilities.

But buyers desperately want to solve their biggest problems. No matter what amazing solution a buyer might find interesting, **solving a problem** is the predominant reason that a buyer would choose to make a purchase, much less take a meeting with us. It's not business. It's human nature.

What many sellers don't realize is that their value starts with a buyer's vision. If we want to immediately disarm a buyer's survival instincts and begin connecting to their personal vision, it all starts with aligning ourselves to the biggest *problems* they need to solve. Yes, buyers want to achieve ambitious and opportunistic outcomes. Yet, that *Thrive* state of their mind won't be available for the conversation until their *survival* state is addressed. For that *Thrive* mind to be truly activated and engaged in the discussion, it will need to feel that it may have found a solution to a priority *problem* that it's facing.

In a *vision-based positioning* mindset, we realize that if we don't first attach to those biggest problems the buyer cares about, their *Survive* state will reject us before the conversation even takes off, whether directly or passively. There's so much we can say in our messaging, and we struggle with our own push and pull impulses to the get the right message out.

However, here's your biggest takeaway. Most of the time, a buyer feeling threatened by us is really about what we don't say. By simply not being clear enough, or just not even trying to communicate how we could solve any of a buyer's main problems, we'll just be seen as a *threat*, regardless of how great our product or service is or how smooth our pitch.

Thus, in the first objective of *Vision-Based Positioning*, in order to disarm our buyer's protective *Survive* impulses, the buyer must first understand the unique **Problems We Solve for**. How could they come to understand that alignment? Again, whether using discovery questions or directly positioning our message, we need to be *in the moment*. This is when we listen and then position. All that matters, whether we get there through strategic thought-provoking discovery questions or from just directly getting to the punch line, if we want to connect to and lead a buyer's vision, we must start with ensuring that they clearly understand what problems we solve for. The conversation may go on, using up the entire hour we had scheduled. Yet, if the buyer walks away from that conversation lacking clarity of what specific problems we attach to, we have no chance at any *emotional connection.*

Again, in the way our minds operate, there is a decision path where disarming our *Survive* mind comes before inspiring our *Thrive* mind. To apply this to a sales conversation, we simply need to be educated as to the unique and most important problems that we solve for our buyers. Then, in both mindset and practice, we need to be intentional in communicating our alignment to those problems that our buyers care most about before we go anywhere else in our messaging.

In starting the sales conversation, we're about to meet an undeniable, yet very controllable human force called *fight or flight.* Remember *Survive, Thrive, Think?* Consider this our *Survival Positioning. How are the unique problems I solve aligned to this buyer? Which ones do they care about and need to hear?*

Just as the sales meeting is about to start, repeat that mantra to yourself. *Survive, Thrive, Think.* Your first objective is straightforward. Disarm any potential survival instincts from your buyer. Until we do, we just won't get their full attention and energy to dive into anything else.

One caution to remind you about the emotional fear-driven *survival* mind. If we sellers were to stay here too long, digging deeper and deeper into the problems that they need to solve, the buyer's mindset just might become even more fearful of change. That sounds crazy but it's truly how our mind works. In the habit of *Leading Vision,* when we think about getting to their state of *Thrive,* this has to be our priority destination, our disciplined line of sight. This place in our mind where we focus on and really start to emotionally connect to positive outcomes and feelings is just naturally where our mind wants to be. This is also where we have more of a tendency to act on something. We don't want to be in a state of fear.

So, what do we do when that fear becomes too present? We avoid it, minimize it, or try to cope with it using false solutions that just seem easier in the moment. Is this walk down our human psychology taking you to any sales memories you have? In a *Vision-Based Positioning* approach, we do need to start with aligning to the biggest *Problems* a buyer is trying to solve. But remember our purpose here. As we immediately work to disarm a buyer's protective emotions, all we're trying to help them do is to subconsciously say to themselves, "Yes, I can relate to these problems. This conversation feels familiar to me. Now, what can you do about it? "

As we master the habit of *leading vision*, we'll learn just how far to go into the problems that we solve, so we can then get to the place where a buyer's vision is truly formed, their *Thrive* state. We'll talk about that in the second part of *Vision-Based Positioning*.

Now, aligning to and positioning the biggest *problems* we solve provides a dual purpose. As stated, it disarms the buyer and activates their mind for the conversation. Think of this as starter fluid to light a fire. But also, Elite Sellers are maniacal qualifiers. So, in this initial effort to start connecting a buyer to the relatable problems we solve, we can begin to qualify them at the same time. Face reality. If a buyer isn't suffering from or willing to prioritize solving the unique problems that we address, then we need to know that as soon as possible. There has to be a real purpose for changing from what they do today, which can sometimes be disruptive to their normal order of doing business. They won't make that decision unless they know that they're solving an important problem that they're not confident they can solve with their current solutions. Maybe we'll need to speak with other stakeholders. It could be that this just isn't the right time for them to address their known problems.

Either way, if we can't find the human source for emotionally connecting to what we sell, then we just won't be able to build a Buyer Champion. As I've said, if there's No Champion, then there's No Deal. So, why not find that out early instead of spending weeks or months on a deal that will never close or that we can't win.

Problem Types: *The Case for Change*

Just what do we mean by *Problems We're Solving*? Because we know that the human mind first reacts to us in a state of protective *survival*, we must start our emotional dance with a buyer by meeting them where they are. When they agreed to take our call or join the meeting, it's predominantly because they have some level of curiosity and potential interest in solving a *problem*. Most salespeople think it's because they're so interested in learning about something new and cool. Usually, that's just not the case. If it's merely the novelty of hearing about what we sell, then the chances of having a real qualified deal are low anyway.

Our ideal dialogue is when a buyer has done their homework, already sees credibility in our solution, and then immediately starts sharing great details about their problems and the need to solve them. However, more often than not, a buyer takes longer to drop their guard and begin to trust us sellers. For those buyers to avoid exposing their situation too much, or even to de-escalate their own emotions, they may use softer language like, *challenges*, *concerns*, or *struggles* they're having. Don't get caught up in the vocabulary. At the end of the day, the human mind views things in two dimensions: *problems* or *opportunities*.

In business, a problem needing to be solved usually falls within these five categories:

1. **Enablement** to accomplish or support a business objective they were otherwise unable to, such as expanding the business or reaching a higher standard. Perhaps your solution could provide a foundational supporting capability to launch a new business service, enable a business to begin operating in a new country or region, or start getting a different result that's desired.

2. **Speed** to deliver something that's time sensitive. This could be internal business services that need to be delivered faster or a timelier customer service that improves their experience. Speed applies when there's some aspect of the business that's just not happening fast enough.

3. **Risk Mitigation** in components of business, such as security, finance, or communications. The company could be challenged with their finance or security controls. A new business service may be higher risk for compliance. Data and technical systems may be vulnerable or having business continuity problems. Or there may just be a recurring negative outcome that needs to be prevented.

4. **Efficiency** in operating the business solutions or services. This could be a part of the business that may need to implement cost controls. An operation and its teams may be struggling with work effort and productivity efficiencies. Where the work, cost, or effort to run or grow the business is too great, *efficiency* could be the problem they need to solve.

5. **Transformation** of a part of the way business is done. Common transformation examples are business services, technology strategy, medical approaches, or in marketing initiatives. Because transformation is often an ambitious initiative, many problems can get in the way of that transformation.

There's a lot of problems in business, but most will sit in one of those five buckets. Think of these five problem types as the **Drivers for Change.** No matter how small the risk or low the investment, most buyers still won't make a change in what they do until there is a **Case for Change**. If you haven't heard or used this term, I want you to really think about what it means and what role it plays in someone choosing to become a Champion.

A *Case for Change* is the purpose for why a buyer would do anything different, and it will be based on one or several of these drivers. On early Discovery calls, this is the number one strategic outcome I'm asking my sellers to get to. Rather than be the sales *entertainer* hearing themselves talk, I want sellers to be the intellectually curious *guide* who tries to put pieces of a puzzle together in seeking out their *Case for Change*. Why would they do anything different? This type of seller thinks, *While I'm going to passionately position how we're so good at solving the problems and delivering the desired outcomes that you care about, I'm also trying to understand just why you'd change from what you're doing today.*

If this two-sided mission sounds hard, it's not because it's that complicated to do both in a sales conversation. It's because most salespeople aren't paying attention, and they're not in the right mindset to accomplish this mission of both qualifying a buyer while also trying to lead their vision. Truth is, if we fully commit to trying to *lead their vision*, we'll usually learn whether we have the vision alignment we need and whether the problems and outcomes they care about are important enough. This is what Elite Sellers are so good at.

Following this *Vision-Based Positioning* guide will provide sellers both the right mindset and conversational approach for this dual-sided mission. When we move from positioning capabilities to positioning and aligning on the unique problems and outcomes we solve for the buyer, we start to *lead vision* . We're more *buyer savvy.* When we evolve from seeing problems as merely opportunities for us to solve, to also questioning them as a potential **case for change**, we now elevate our *business savvy.* Beyond experience alone, this mindset will give us the sales intuitiveness to realize that either we have real problem-alignment that a buyer is willing to solve or perhaps the problems we uncovered don't make for a strong *case for change.*

Problems vs. Pain

Many sellers have been taught a belief that sales is all about *getting to the "pain."* So, you might be wondering, are **Pain** and **Problems** really the same thing?

Early in my career when I received value-based selling and strong qualification training, like many of you, I was told that *I must find the pain.* Where there was pain, there would be a deal. Over time, I began to wonder, *Whose pain is actually going to make someone take a meeting with me? Is it pain the individual buyer is personally experiencing or some pain in the business they're aware of? And, just how bad does the pain have to be?*

I began learning that one person's pain is another person's annoyance. I was a college athlete. In sports, we just learned to cope with pain. You accepted that it was a part of the game and saw it as an opportunity to prove how tough you were, that you could overcome the pain and still perform. Now, an *injury,* well that was serious. An injury was a *problem.* If we didn't treat it, we couldn't do our job, at least not to the standard we expected for ourselves.

What I discovered after years of selling to large companies was that *everybody has pain.* The bigger the company, the more complex its systems and challenges were the more *pain* they had. So, why were so few of them interested in buying, even taking a meeting with me? *Everybody has pain, right?*

We certainly need to know what type of pain we're targeting with our buyers and our solution. Once we understand that pain, instead of thinking that we've arrived at the *qualification finish line,* we should simply find that information interesting. We think, *So, they've got pain that we address. Seems like a bit of an annoyance. What I'd like to know is if this is a serious injury that they need to treat?* I also would assume that a buyer who learns what pain my solution deals with would also find that interesting. However, what we'd both find fascinating is understanding what *problems* we can solve together.

You see, I don't just want to know what pain you have. I want to know how bad it really is and if you're willing to do anything about it. **Problems vs. Pain** is not semantics. The reason we focus on *the Problems that we solve for* in *Vision-Based Positioning,* is that it guides our mindset to the root of why any buyer would have a *bias for action,* not only to make a *case for change,* but to be our Champion. How do we distinguish the difference between a *pain* that may not be fun to deal with versus a real *problem* that they emotionally want to find a solution to?

Think about how a good doctor would diagnose our illnesses. When the doctor starts the medical exam, what are the first questions they ask? "So, what brings you in today? Where does it hurt?" Now, to determine just how much of a problem this pain is, they'll use what we in sales call **Metrics**. "Rate the pain for me. Is it mildly uncomfortable at a three, fairly moderate at a five, or unbearably severe at a ten?" The doctor's trying to figure out if this is an annoyance that you can treat with an inexpensive over-the-counter medicine or if it is a real injury that needs serious attention now, that you're willing to make an investment in healing.

In *Vision-Based Positioning*, we're first seeking out the real *Problems* that you absolutely need to solve for, and then positioning how we uniquely address them. It's this intersection of *Identifying Pain* and the *Metrics* of that *pain*, where we uncover the extent of the *Problem.* Imagine if you went to the doctor and when you told her that your leg hurt, she immediately prescribed surgery. A credible doctor wouldn't do that. So why would we sellers do this in business? This is where we lose our credibility and then buyers don't trust us. Why would we try to lead a buyer toward a vision of a positive future state if their current state wasn't really a clear problem? How could we even determine this if we're not intellectually curious enough going into the conversation? Where the opportunity lies in mastering *Vision-Based Positioning* is that if we learn enough about the *problems* a buyer is needing to solve today, as well as the *desired outcomes* they have for their near future, we can help a buyer see an opportunity to achieve those outcomes through the power of what we sell. This is where the habit of *Leading Vision* begins.

Desired Outcomes: *Inspiring the Thrive State*

You've heard me use the language that *we're looking to create a connection between our buyer and the unique problems that we solve for.* Buying is personal. Their *case for change* doesn't stem from what our products and services do. It's in the drivers behind *why* the buyer would consider doing anything different. So, with a *vision-leading* mindset, our very first question should be, W*hat unique problems could we solve for them?* Let's remind ourselves why attaching to *buyer problems* is so important. One reason is that *no one in business ever buys anything of substantial investment unless it's first solving a problem.* Also, if *emotional connection* is our first objective, we know that in a buyer's mental decision path, their protective survival impulses will have to be respected, addressed, and disarmed straightaway before we can get to their mind's state of *Thrive.* This is the opportunistic, ambitious, *happy state* of making their life better and where we complete the bond of *emotional connection.*

Being in a state of *Thrive* is also where we humans will be more motivated to take action. What are Buyer Champions? They're people of power and influence who have a *bias for action* toward what we sell. We sellers need to be able to lead their vision toward a positive *high-Thrive* state that will motivate them to take action.

After the first step of *Vision-Based Positioning* when we learn and position what relatable *problems* we could address, we're now ready to lead our buyer to their *Thrive* state. This is where they truly want to achieve a vision that we can uniquely deliver. So, our second step in the *Vision-Based Positioning* framework is to align on and position the **Desired Outcomes** that we can deliver for the buyer.

Just think about what you sell today and your current customers. What about your product or service is really behind the reason that they purchased you in the first place? Was it a unique capability or feature you had? Maybe that could have been the case if you're in a highly niche tools space with a relatively low price point. Most of the time a buyer chooses to make a change from what they were doing before, their emotional decision was based on two things.

First, they needed to solve a real *problem*. Second, the reason that they needed to solve that problem was to enable them to reach a positive future *outcome* that was important to them. In our sales conversation, if we've just led a very disarming and enlightening discussion around the relevant problems that our buyer is facing in their current state, and we've begun to help them realize that we uniquely solve those same problems, we should feel this conversational cue that triggers our habit response of positioning the unique *Desired Outcomes* that we can deliver.

The capabilities of a product or service will certainly enable a buyer to do something. However, if that's what we position, before the buyer has an *emotional connection* to us, that's an intellectually high level of effort that we're asking our buyers to make for themselves. *Ok, so you do these things, which sounds like maybe your competitors don't, or maybe they do them differently? Got it. So, why should I care?*

The *Vision-Based Positioning* framework leads us to a focus on *Desired Outcomes* because we intuitively know that our buyers just simply won't care about our very important and hopefully legitimate differentiating capabilities until they're clear in understanding their purpose. They need to answer, *What outcomes are they tied to that I care about?*

Staying in Thrive

This *Thrive* state of the buyer decision path is where we want to lead a conversation that continues expanding around the positive *desired outcomes* that we can deliver. This discipline will provide us with even greater opportunities and alignment to differentiating decision criteria toward us. Sellers, don't be in any rush to uncover the first alignment around a *desired outcome,* and then sprint into your solution pitch, product demonstrations, and scientific studies. Stay focused on the objective. You are here to lead the buyer to remain in this *Thrive* state until you can enable their *emotional connection* to strengthen. The stronger the emotional tie, the more calories they'll be willing to spend on the intellectual facts of what you sell.

When you find yourself riffing in an outcomes-focused discussion, you should pause and remember *The Certainty Loop*. Remind yourself that they already have some level of limiting perspectives of the *potential* around what you sell or the thought of changing anything. Visualize that it's a buyer's *experience of results* that forms their *beliefs* which then gets them into a state of *certainty.* Thus, once here in this *Thrive* part of the buyer's brain, slow down and patiently lead the buyer's vision into discussing multiple experiences and results. Help them visualize themselves in a state of the outcomes you can uniquely deliver with as much personal detail as possible. Unlike the negative feelings associated with lingering in the problems they're trying to solve, the human buyer will feel more motivation and positive connection to you the longer they stay in *a state of Thrive.*

The 4 Outcome Levels

For a buyer, this *Thrive* state takes the appearance of business-critical **Positive Outcomes** that they need to achieve. Like in *the problems we solve for*, the first step is in listening and then crafting our positioning. We should define and document the unique outcomes we can deliver for each of the different types of buyers and/or situations we sell to. Sometimes this is a unique persona or role. In other instances, it's a different industry or vertical application. It could be their maturity level. What's critical is that the purpose of our positioning must be to help our buyers connect to our solution across the various sales situations we find ourselves in. To guide that purpose, when we think of the *Outcomes* that we could potentially deliver for a buyer, they can be thought of across these **4 Outcome Levels.**

First, there are the most basic **User Level** outcomes. For the people who would use or be beneficiaries of what we sell, what outcomes would affect them personally? This is where we can impact their functional abilities, overcome daily challenges, or help them deliver on the desires and objectives associated with their roles and responsibilities. These are especially important in those first interactions and certainly with those who might have less power and authority, but more direct connection to the type of solution we sell.

A second level relates to what those users do for the business, **Operational Level** outcomes. In the businesses' ability to *operate*, there are opportunities for outcomes that make an operation more efficient, go faster, mitigate risk, or produce more results. Operational outcomes can be thought of on three dimensions. First, there's **People**, such as enabling organizational change, team performance, or internal cultural initiatives. Then, there's **Process** outcomes, which could be changes to *process* in order to streamline, innovate, or enable a productivity objective. Lastly, we could impact **Technology** outcomes. These are usually about systems, applications, data to make better decisions, creating less security risk, enabling the business to deliver better services.

A third level, and what some might consider higher in executive priority, are ***Business Level*** outcomes. Think of these as making a macro impact on the financial or **Business Performance** indicators of the business itself, profitability, growth, revenue, asset allocation, competitive differentiation, customer experience. *Business level* outcomes can be internal or external, and they typically have a downstream impact on organizational decision-making or direction. One powerful example is a **Strategic Initiative** that we can impact. When we can associate an *initiative* to the problems and outcomes we discover, we're more likely to find a compelling driver for an actual purchase to happen. I define an *initiative* as *an executive-sponsored outcome with a defined timeline and budget.* Some business *initiatives* are so complex to achieve that if we can clearly align how we uniquely simplify, accelerate, or de-risk the execution of the *initiative*, we become attached to a mission-critical outcome.

However, in the spirit of truly connecting to a buyer's own personal vision, aligned to what can impact the buyer and the business the most, great sellers try to reach the highest and fourth level of desired outcomes, ***Integrated Level Outcomes.*** When we think we've discovered an *emotionally connecting* outcome that we believe we can deliver, we should be thoughtful to how and where we'll fit or can *integrate* into our buyer's unique business. Most sellers tend to ignore or minimize the buyer's current state, their situations, processes, systems, and information. Lacking empathy, a seller often thinks that once our life-changing solution appears in the customer's business, all nonsense and problems that existed before we arrived will disappear in an instant.

153

Well, what we've learned is that if sellers pay attention, we can find great opportunity for our solutions to integrate into that current state. This opportunity could be found in a simple example like integrating into an important business process of a small business, complementing a cornerstone philosophy of a Champion's beliefs, maximizing the potential of an existing investment, or optimizing a complicated system in a large enterprise.

One key to being an elite *vision leading* seller is knowing that once a buyer can visualize our solution in their world, they'll connect easier because it will feel familiar and doable. Thus, they'll be able to visualize it easier, moving them one step closer to a state of *certainty*. So, as you think about what your products or services can do to truly impact your buyers, to lead their vision toward a positive future state, consider what are the specific and unique outcomes that you can deliver.

Buyer Value Proof Points: *Leading Value Certainty*

After discovering and positioning to both the problems that we solve for and unique desired outcomes that we can deliver, the next part of the *Vision-Based Positioning* framework is positioning **Buyer Value Proof Points**. As we've been slowly disarming our buyer's emotional survival instincts and we've worked our way into a state of *Thrive,* those outcomes we've been discussing now deserve some horsepower!

Once our buyer/seller discussion is focused on the most desired positive outcomes that a buyer would care about, the average seller would go right to the intellectual *thinking brain* and start pumping it up with features, facts, and differentiating capabilities. But we want to make that bridge from emotion to intellect, one that drives some buyer momentum in their connection to us. As we've been in this natural two-way conversation, we've been using thoughtful *Discovery* to gain clarity on the problems and outcomes they most desire, as well as positioning outcome-based examples of how our solution could uniquely help them. So, to optimize our growing connection, it's time for us to frame just how positive those outcomes could be. **Value.**

In a *Vision-Based Positioning* approach, we've now earned the right and the attention from our buyer to associate potential *impact* from our solution. Notice, we haven't even talked too much about our solution yet. Going to the *thinking brain* too early and for too long is a dangerous road full of doubting questions and objections. Remaining focused on leading our buyer's vision toward examples of a positive future state that they would connect to, this should lead us to begin thinking how we can build their certainty in what we sell. Here is where we need to get them in a visualized state of *results* and *experiences* we can deliver. Reaching this point in our conversation should be the cue that we need to start positioning relevant **Buyer Value Proof Points**.

As I'll detail a few examples, think of a ***proof point*** as any legitimate example of how our solution has impacted a customer of ours. Remaining in a conversational state, great sellers will make brief but highly aligned points that provide *proof* of the vision and value experience that a buyer could have.

Many sellers position value examples, but how many do so with purpose? It might help sellers to consider ***the purpose of buyer value proof points*** on two levels. One, they're a **Connection Accelerant**. From a well-positioned *buyer value proof point*, it can be like giving a buyer's *Thrive* state a shot of caffeine. The connection gets woken up and just emotionally pays attention more. We can also think of a *buyer-based value proof point* as a **Bridge** that leads a buyer's emotional mind over to its intellectual mind.

When the proof point is relative to the buyer, it's *buyer based*. It's a bridge because it serves both an *emotional purpose* in elevating their attraction, as well as an *intellectual purpose* by associating context and potential importance to the solution. What's key for us to realize is that before our buyer can even put their mental and intellectual focus into learning the details of what our solution is and how it works, we want them as emotionally connected to its purpose as possible.

Great vision-leading sellers are *visual sellers*. In the moment of conversation, as soon as we start learning about the problems and outcomes that a buyer cares about, we should start identifying what *relevant buyer value proof points* we could position that would help them visualize our value. Any messaging framework should serve as a menu of these value proof points organized by their type and category. If you don't have this level of messaging, then go build it yourself by gathering as many of these proof points as you can from your colleagues and customers.

Why **"buyer value"** proof point? Well, this goes to the *relevant* part. The last thing we'd ever want to do in trying to *lead a buyer's vision* is break a connection that's been forming. The connection we're looking to bridge is from our solution to this individual buyer. Our emphasis on *buyer value* has to do with the relevance and relatability to the buyer that our proof point should have. Remember, it's not about our messaging; it's how we position our messaging.

Have you ever attempted to tell a customer story or share a value proof point that missed its mark? It made sense to you in the moment. It was one of the best proof points you'd learned, and it recently spurred on a great discussion with one of your other prospects. Yet this time, it not only didn't connect, it almost turned off your buyer.

Why did they have this reaction? Because you didn't connect yourself to them. The *proof point* you shared wasn't relevant to the buyer. From their point of view, they just took the time to expose to you the biggest problems they're trying to solve for and outcomes they most desire, and then you pitched some story or metric that had nothing to do with what they just shared. This creates buyer frustration, not only because it's not a great sales experience, but because once again, a seller is making them work too hard to figure out if there's a value fit.

Let's go back to that *Certainty Loop*. If we truly want to lead our buyer to a state of *certainty* that we can help them achieve their desired vision, they'll need to start visualizing what their positive experience with our solution could be. Positioning these *buyer value proof points* are habits that Elite Sellers develop a real mastery for. Remember that for *certainty*, our perspectives of *potential* lead to our *actions*, which then drive our *results* or *experiences*, ultimately forming our *belief of certainty*. The challenge for us in selling to prospective buyers is that they usually haven't experienced our product or service yet. Their *certainty* will only form once they have somehow experienced the results of what we sell. To lead them toward that state of *Certainty*, we sellers need to help a buyer visualize those measurable results in the most personal way that we can. Here's two of the most common examples of *Buyer Value Proof Points*.

One that's often mispositioned and misguided is a **Buyer-Based Value Metric**. This should be a proven and legitimate *data point* of a solution's impact, related to the buyer's desired

157

outcomes. Positioning *value metrics* has multiple benefits. Early in the more emotionally centric discussions around positive outcomes that we could deliver, by attaching a measurement of value or *value metric* to those outcomes, we elevate their significance and worth. We're putting a number to the outcome, a valuable percentage or data point that should set our solution apart. Whether the buyer believes us or not, we have them paying attention.

But again, the proof point we're positioning and the context of the metric itself should be thoughtfully aligned to the relevant and relatable problems and outcomes that our specific buyer is concerned with. Put yourself in a sales conversation. When I tell you that I can deliver an outcome that you care about, you emotionally feel good about that opportunity. However, when you also hear a thoughtfully positioned *value metric* that informs you of a higher level of impact you could achieve in that outcome, your *emotional connection* to that potential solution increases. Trust the power of the emotional brain. This connection can strengthen without having a ton of detail about the solution itself yet.

An example of positioning a value metric would be, "Typically, our customers are adopting us because they want to accomplish A, B, and C (the relatable vision outcome). When they do, they often find that they've improved X, Y, Z by over 90 percent (the outcome value or *proof point*)." Have you ever heard the statement, "You've piqued my interest"? That's the buyer's mind verbalizing that they're traveling across the bridge from *emotional* to *intellectual connection*.

I know what you're thinking. *Many sellers are provided value metrics in their messaging and use them often in their positioning. This isn't new information.* Well, if you listen to this now, you'll understand where thousands of those sellers make mistakes every day that disappointingly result in lost credibility and connection with their buyers. The moment we position any value metric or expectation, we sellers think to ourselves, *Oh, they're going to love this!* Then, we throw it out there like some prize fish we caught, waiting for them to show their amazement and jubilation for what we sell. Only, all they see is a big, stinky fish. If the buyer hears our bold value proclamation before they've started to form any *emotional connection* to our solution, their subconscious responds, *Oh yeah. Prove it! And, who cares anyway?*

Unfortunately, many sellers have two poor tendencies when positioning value metrics. First, they position *value metrics* at the **Wrong Time**. When they position their value with strong conviction that their minimum return on investment is something that their buyer should absolutely expect, it's often too early in their sales engagement before they've earned any credibility. They simply haven't learned enough to know what value example to position.

The biggest source of buyer rejection of that *return on investment* or *value metric* is because they haven't formed any *emotional connection* at all with the buyer. This firm impassioned stance, when taken before the buyer is ready for it, at best will just be dismissed. At worst, our buyer emotionally decides that we're just like all the other salespeople. We don't listen, can't be trusted, and we arrogantly assume that every buyer would so desperately need our product.

The second poor tendency that many salespeople lead is in the **Misaligned Content** of the value metrics themselves. The value they present isn't *buyer focused*. Are the value metrics that we or our teams are presenting just simply the biggest ones that a handful of our customers have experienced? Are they metrics that our leadership found to be the easiest to quantify? Are they just the ones in a presentation we were provided with? Those metrics that we add on to our outcomes-based positioning should be the performance indicators that the buyer we're selling to would care about. To aid our discussion, we can typically find that out by just asking how they're measuring value today, or how they would think about measuring value in the future.

If we don't have a metric that relates, it's best not to share one at all. There are other ways to get the buyer visualizing a value experience. There's not much that's more deflating to a seller than blindly positioning their strong value metrics with confidence and swagger, only to have the buyer dismiss their relevance, minimize their importance, or reject their claim all together. If we're going to be great *vision-leading* sellers, we'll need to maintain this *buyer-first* discipline.

Perhaps the most powerful connection bridge that we should use to feed that certainty forming vision in a buyer is a well-crafted **Vision-Based Customer Story**. If relatable, there may not be a more effective way to build *emotional connections* in buyers than well-positioned customer stories. Some value proof points can be shared through a detailed **Customer Case Study** that includes related value metrics.

However, in a sales conversation, there's a real art in capturing the opportunity for *connection* in how we tell a great **Customer Story**. When we mentally listen to a story, we just naturally find ourselves visualizing our potential familiarity and relatability to that story, to the value that's at the core of its storyline. Helping a buyer see results in others, their peers, increases their belief that they could experience those results themselves. But there's a way to tell these stories that effectively connects a buyer and leads their vision. It's simple. A *vision-based customer story* starts with the **problems** the customer was facing, then the **outcomes** they were able to achieve. We then use *a **value metric*** to define the scale of those results, in order to increase the emotional effect. And finally, we state a brief ***differentiated solution statement*** for how they achieved those metrics and outcomes. Make the stories short enough for the *lazy brain* but detailed enough to be entertaining and relatable.

Now, hopefully this all sounds familiar. The simple mental sequence of *Vision-Based Positioning* can be applied to all the situations we encounter in positioning our message. *Vision-based Customer Stories* have another benefit to buyer conversations. They enable us to *delegate the selling*. In a customer story, it's no longer us who's stating a claim. We're an unknown salesperson with little credibility, as we probably haven't done the job of our buyer. We're now enabling our customers, who our buyers are more likely to see as a relatable and credible peer, to become the source of our positioning. *Delegating the selling.* How could a buyer object to a story we're telling about somebody else?

The Differentiating Big Idea: *Simplifying Intellectual Connection*

Now that we're fully engaged in building intellectual connection with our buyer, our next step in *Vision-Based Positioning* is in getting to **The Differentiating Big Idea**. You're the buyer. This salesperson has done a brilliant job of connecting the entire discussion around you. They've led the dialogue with a little give and take. Along with learning a bit about your priority problems and outcomes through some thoughtful questions, they've also shared some short examples of their solution and how it drives impact to those outcomes. That customer story they told really related to what you're going through. This hasn't felt like a one-way discovery interrogation. But it also hasn't been a waste of your time, getting another canned sales pitch about their features and how great everyone thinks they are. It's been a good sales experience. The discussion has gotten you thinking about a vision for a positive future state that you hadn't really had the time to focus on lately. But your intellectual brain can't go much further without, at least conceptually, understanding what exactly their solution does and most importantly, how they're any different.

With an *emotional connection* forming, it's time to lead a buyer to the levels of **Intellectual Connection** that their organizational level, job function, and personality will desire. However, as an intuitive *vision leading* seller, we should now fully accept that the buyer brain wants to be efficient and that staying in the intellectual thinking part of their mind can be a very dangerous place for us. While this is the right time, we must do it in the right way. This is where the protective logical mind rejects us the more information it receives. It makes false assumptions based on mental shortcuts, like assuming it knows what we mean and associating us with incorrect comparisons.

Alternatively, the emotional subconscious part of the mind is where 98 percent of brain activity happens. So, we need to give it love. As the next step of our *Vision-Based Positioning* framework, consider learning and being prepared to tailor your differentiation in the structure of what I call your **Differentiating Big Ideas**.

Being aware of that strong, irrational, shortcut-taking buyer mind, we should lead a habit of *netting out* the most buyer-relevant, highest impact, strongest components of our solution. This is our *Differentiating Big Idea or Ideas*. The **Big Idea** concept has been discussed by several in the investment world, such as venture capitalist Geoffery Moore and capital pitch man Oren

Klaff, author of *Pitch Anything.* When there are so many details and data points to share with a buyer, anything from a software product to biotech treatments or a complex investment package, a seller is often misguided to think, *The more I cover, the more they'll get our value and differentiation.* Nothing could be further than the psychological truth.

Succinctly netting out how we're different enables us to prevent **Cognitive Overload**. This is the first driver of positioning a *Differentiating Big Idea.* Think of *cognitive overload* as an effect of the *lazy brain* dynamic we covered. The human brain has the capacity to process enormous amounts of information. While that processing ability is different for every brain and its unique person, the *lazy brain* is more a function of its emotional protective instincts to reserve its energy if it doesn't feel motivated.

So, *cognitive overload* is basically us salespeople loading up our buyers with too much information at once. This never plays well with the *lazy brain,* and it conflicts with some of the mind's natural responses. One example is what are referred to as mental **Heuristics.** They're really simple to understand. A *heuristic* is a mental shortcut that can work in two ways in our decision-making.

The first is in our ***Associations.*** When we humans hear something, we'll subconsciously take the shortcut of associating it with something else. I'm sure you've experienced that in sales. How many times have you heard the response, "Oh, so you're like this product?" Or "Let me stop you there. You're trying to pitch me one of those types of solutions, and I just simply don't believe in them." This involuntary emotional response makes our decision for us. These aren't logical or probability-driven decisions.

The second way a heuristic can work is in the result of ***Satisfactory Understanding.*** Let's take positioning a

Differentiating Big Idea, one that's relevant to the buyer's experience and relatable in association with a solution that would make sense for them. If we do this, we'll lead the buyer's subconscious mind to decide that our differentiation is *good enough* to get the job done. They will intellectually understand the concept and their mind will typically be satisfied. Have you ever heard a buyer respond, "Oh, I get it"? But you weren't quite sure that they did and wondered how they could *get it* so fast? Maybe you've heard, "Yeah, yeah, yeah, let's move on." This isn't a bad positioning outcome. We're just appeasing the *lazy brain* and how it comes to make decisions.

In these early discussions, a buyer just needs to conceptually understand their basic questions about us. They're more interested in learning how we would relate and align to them. I know you hear "good enough" and you cringe at the thought. But remember, Buyer Champions develop a certainty in what we sell with a *bias for action* because of their belief in the *outcomes* that we can deliver, not our capabilities. To form those beliefs, they either need to personally experience the results or understand the reasonable attribution of how we'll get them there. But, if we want to avoid the rabbit holes and disconnecting effects of going too deep into our solution's attribution, we'd be better off if we just net it out as a *Differentiating Big Idea*.

Another driver of *The Differentiating Big Idea* is **Cognitive Bias**. If the last time I had a similar experience and some strategy worked, my ***recency bias*** emotionally tells me that it will work again this time. That could be completely illogical to the situation. But it's our bias, nonetheless. If I'm a buyer and I hear a salesperson pitch something that sounds related to a negative previous experience I've had, my ***historical bias*** will decide that this pitch is a negative thing. However, if that pitch sounds relevant to a problem that I'm trying to solve and related to a solution I already understand, my ***associative bias*** will decide that it's acceptable.

Differentiation absolutely sets us apart. But ultimately, the buyer needs to learn how our differentiation is a strong *attributing factor* toward the results that they want from us. Differentiation can be a very powerful means to an end. But alone, it doesn't really matter that much to our buyers. I'll say this several times. A buyer won't care how we're different. They'll care how we're different *for them*.

The 3 Differentiation Rules

So, how do we use our differentiation message to help connect to both the intellectual and emotional decision-making of a buyer? Consider following these **3 Differentiation Rules**. The first rule is that a *Differentiating Big Idea* should be ***Succinct***, a brief summary statement of the key concept of our differentiation. Too long and we get ourselves into that *information overload*. The second rule is that it must be ***Relevant***. Buying is personal. The shortcuts of the emotional mind need to easily feel that our *differentiating idea* applies to them and their situation. We find this *relevancy* in the buyer's current state, the problems they're facing, or the desired outcomes they have. The third rule is that the *Differentiating Big Idea* needs to be ***Relatable***. What's the difference between *relevant* and *relatable*? When what we position has *relevance*, it has a direct bearing on the buyer we're selling to, it's pertinent or it matters to them. *Relatability* is found in connecting to an already established association with something or someone else. They *relate* because the situation or context is like what they're facing today.

Too many differentiators lack *relevance* and *relatability*. We either didn't ask or listen for their current state, the problems they're solving for, and the outcomes they desire. Then, when we move to position our differentiation, it's like when my kids throw those slimy blob-shaped toys at our wall. We hope it sticks, but it just may not be *relevant* to what they care about or *relatable* to what they're experiencing.

This is why when companies and sellers choose to position differentiation as something that's so far out there that a buyer can't relate to it, it'll often fall flat. However, incredibly innovative solutions can easily be seen as *relatable* if positioned right, if they're positioned for the right buyer and in the right way. A *Differentiating Big Idea* should be the simple-to-understand concept that our buyer can easily conclude how they would uniquely achieve the outcomes they desire through the power of what we sell. Again, buyers don't care how we're different. They care how we're different *for them*. When they can emotionally connect to this differentiation, just as easily as they can intellectually connect, we've simplified their decision-making.

How will we know if our *Differentiating Big Idea* hits the mark? It'll usually be far less dramatic than we think. When a seller typically hears a response similar to, "Oh, that makes sense. I get it," their tendency is to freak out and assume they undersold their greatness. So, what does the seller then do? They keep talking, going deeper and deeper, waiting to get that *warm and fuzzy* buyer affirmation. Unfortunately for that seller, rarely does it ever come.

What happened was as the seller kept going into more detail, they fed the buyer's natural tendency to question, and then their doubts and concerns grew with every word. The truth is that buyer who says, "That makes sense. I get it," is telling us that we were clear. Responses like that are basically saying, "You've done a good enough job stating how you're different, and I don't have any objections or questions at this time." We should realize that when we hear, "Makes sense," that's a huge win for us. It's only when we start hearing dismissive or debating objection-filled arguments that we should be concerned with how we've positioned ourselves. In those situations, the bigger question we should have is whether we've attracted any *emotional connection* in the first place.

From a strategic selling perspective, this deepening level of detail we position is where we also lead to more normalcy with our competition, less differentiation. In other words, the more information we share, the less we sound different or better. If we're truly differentiated, it's usually due to a small but meaningful list of reasons. We just need to determine which ones apply to our buyer and then state them succinctly and confidently as our *Differentiating Big Ideas*.

SUMMARY: *Leading Vision*

From the execution of **Vision-Based Positioning**, visualize a successful journey that we've just led a buyer through. We initially attracted a positive *Emotional Connection* to us personally, through our own selling approach. Hopefully, we provided an assurance that we were a nonthreatening guide who was genuinely there to help them and deliver value. We immediately disarmed the buyer when we created some relatability with the *problems we solve for*.

Next, rather than pitching a generic solution message of *what we do* or *how we're different*, we took the time to *learn* the very specific outcomes needed from our buyer and then connected them to some unique *positive outcomes* that our solution can deliver. These business-critical outcomes they desire, connected to our solution, seemed to be forming some *buyer vision* that could align to our unique value proposition. When we discussed a few relatable *buyer value proof points*, a great customer story, and proven value metrics, we could tell that our buyer was getting into a "feel-good" *Thrive* state. An *emotional connection* had started to grow toward a *vision* that we both agreed could be truly impactful to their business. They weren't ready to commit to a purchase yet, but they also weren't shutting us down, rejecting our message, or attacking us with objections. In the moment of discussions, our mind stuck to the *Survive, Thrive, Think!* mantra and we can see it working.

We led the buyer's *vision* such that they were ready and curious to start intellectually learning all the details they needed to know about our solution. But, in those important initial conversations, we kept a conceptual understanding of our solution simple with tailored *Differentiated Big Ideas* that were most relevant to them and the impact that they were needing to see. This was good enough for them and our activity and connection started to pick up. We're starting to feel confident that we've led their *vision* to a state that aligns well and our strategic focus moving forward will be in building their absolute certainty in our solution. It just feels like we have a strong Champion forming who seems to really know and believe in our message. We've got work to do in order to get this Champion truly committed, but the connection is there.

The E.L.I.T.E. selling habit of *Leading Vision* is the most frequently required behavior of any seller, as it happens all throughout the sales process and with every individual buyer we encounter. It's the foundation of why anyone would prioritize buying what we sell. So, we need to master it. Sometimes, we meet many different buyers during a sales engagement with unique personalities, buying personas, and organizational roles. But they're all human beings essentially wired the same way. Those buyers will only be willing to take action on a *vision* that aligns to a positive future outcome that they really care about. It's those buyers, not our products and services, that should be the focal point of our sales conversations. When they don't clearly understand how what we sell can help them solve the biggest related problems they're dealing with, as well as achieve the outcomes that they most desire, we just simply won't form their connection to us. We'll fail at trying to lead their vision and they'll never be a Champion for us.

The first step for those buyers to gain the certainty that they'll need to sponsor what we sell is to own a very personal *vision* for the experiences and results that we can enable for them. That *vision* doesn't develop from purely intellectual and generic selling, like leading with a standard sales pitch, all our potential differentiators, and our most proud value metrics. The state of a buyer's *vision* is this distinct place where they can see themselves better off in the future. The E.L.I.T.E. habit of *Leading the Vision* of a human buyer is about connecting what we sell to that individual place. This only happens when we're intuitive and disciplined enough to focus on the buyers that we sell to. Every seller has their own unique strengths. There are those who are very experienced and can communicate the company's messaging with smooth credibility. Others can lead intellectually curious discovery questions. Some are even great at the art of negotiation. Yet, Elite Sellers ultimately build Buyer Champions who do the selling for them. They use the emotional and intellectual connections gained to inspire their buyers to have a *bias for action*. Buyers take action when they are connected to and begin to form certainty in the message of *vision*. Elite sellers *Lead Vision*.

CHAPTER 6

INSPIRING COMMITMENT

Purpose, Plan, Promise

BRICK HOUSE

By the time I'd landed in the St. Louis headquarters of a Fortune 10 telecommunications company, I'd learned my lessons in problems versus pain and outcomes versus capabilities. I knew the importance of Champions and what most of them desired from a salesperson. I'd even closed a few large deals in some pretty complex buying situations. But I had never experienced the complexity that I was about to see.

When I was offered to take this global account over, armed with my own small sales team and a $3 million new business quota, I thought it was an interesting opportunity and I was cautiously optimistic. It wasn't just my previous experience that justified my optimism. Like any situation when you take over a major account, there's an outgoing team who usually briefs you on what they were working on, account plans, org charts, all that jazz. And of course, this exercise includes all their strong opinions of every reason the account is dead, how they tried every strategy to find more revenue, and how the lead executive buyer didn't like our company very much. Their strong negativity just screamed opportunity to me. If any sales team has that much negative belief, then there's no way that their mind would ever be clear enough to see what's in front of them. Negativity kills creative thought. Plus, I just assumed that the account would like me and my new team more.

In this case, "Brick" as everyone affectionally called my SVP target buyer, was advertised as *hard as nails*. The outgoing account rep was even so gracious to provide me with a list of all our products that hadn't been sold to them yet.

I asked him, "What's this?"

He said, "This was our sales plan."

"A list of products?" I asked.

He said, "Yes. That's right. These are the ones that they haven't bought yet. So, we already pitched them all. But maybe you'll get lucky and benefit from all our hard work." Then, in the most gentlemanly fashion I could muster, I ended that call and wished him all the best.

This led me to the office of the main man they just called, "Brick." It was even on a big sign on his door. While I'm always a bit nervous walking in to meet a buyer for the first time, seeing that name on the door, I couldn't help but start hearing that 1977 Commodore's hit, *She's a brick house*. How can you not relax when that gets in your head?

Feeling a bit better as I walked in, Brick was sitting down waiting on me. I expected an image of a cold, terse, all-business buyer who had an axe to grind. But I didn't really get that from

Brick. He was actually a really nice Midwestern family man with a passion for baseball and volunteered every week with his kid's little leagues. Tall, stocky, blonde high-and-tight flat top. His desk was surrounded by pictures of his beautiful kids, and he was kind to me. But, as typical of a very senior executive, I could still tell that he was not a man for chitchat. So, I got us started.

I'd brought along that list of products, and I set it on his desk in front of him. Brick, like me, paused for a second confused and said, "What's this?" Now, he was an exceptionally intelligent and perceptive man. Served him well working thirty-plus years for one of the largest and most politically complicated companies in the world. I didn't answer him immediately. Then, I eventually broke the silence grinning, "This is the list of products I got from your outgoing account rep. If you like, I have a highlighter here. You could pick your favorites and I'll send a quote." Almost as if an accident he regretted, Brick's six-foot-one, two-hundred-and-fifty-pound body let out the loudest laugh until he started coughing. I offered to get him some water.

Face red from the laughter, he smiled and said, "I really needed that after the day I've had. What you got?"

So, I asked him, "In the relatively near term, the next twelve to eighteen months, what are the biggest problems that you need addressed?"

He nodded his head, pondered for a moment, and turned around to reach a presentation he had on his desk. He said, "This is what I presented to my boss and what he's presenting to his boss next week. It has our top objectives and they almost all have to do with this project we call the 'ONE Project.'"

I'd been briefed on this initiative, a massive undertaking, especially in the technology organization. They were finally integrating all the many telecom companies that had come together to form this new evolution of the business. It was essentially a multitude of acquisitions and mergers across four different large multinational businesses. And Brick, well he was large and in charge.

I said, "Thanks for this. I'll read every word tonight and you have my promise that if we can't help solve any of these problems, then you won't hear a word from me or my team pitching any new products." I asked for three months to meet with all the stakeholders over these issues and promised to return with a proposal if I thought we could help.

As I left Brick's office and worked with my team over that next year meeting with executives, architects, and program managers, one glaring challenge we would all face was that if we couldn't solve a problem, mitigate risk, or deliver significant value to a defined objective across the ONE Project, then buyers would have no energy for us. We needed our message and our mission to be about one sole purpose that would be simple and yet impactful enough for buyers to connect and commit to us.

I called our sales plan the ONE Account Strategy. And, we had one purpose: finding opportunities where our technology could uniquely align to any of the objectives on that list. I gathered my team together and we covered the plan with a focus on figuring out where we might be a solution and then learning from and inspiring as many potential Champions as we could.

I had a very smart and experienced team. Everyone brought several things to the table. So, my instruction for the team was simple. "Try as hard as you can to avoid the urge to sell new innovation or transformative opportunities until you've earned their trust that we could solve their problems and you've started building Champions."

We discussed that these people were in a real tough spot. At every single point of this complex mess of technical infrastructure, we quickly learned that it was ONE Project alright: one problem leading to another.

My ask was this: "Focus on our purpose, the mergers. Next, find solutions to the mergers. Build Champions for our solution plans. And finally, we're going to prove the business value to our solutions before we meet with Brick again. I want to be able to look him in the eye and propose a simple and yet compelling purpose in going with us. He'll need to see a clear plan that we've already tested and gained multiple Champions for. I'll need to be able to confidently state a promise of the value that he could expect in return." Everyone was on board, and we got to work.

Eight months later, we finalized a proposal that closed for just under $50 million. My team earned every cent of their large commissions that year. Under every stone we turned over, we found nothing but emotional fear and intellectual focus on the problems they needed solved. Yet, perhaps the biggest surprise at the end of this experience is that we were also able to add those new more innovative and transformative technologies to the contract, even without deep technical validations and long sales cycles. We had already built *emotional connections* and inspired their commitment to us.

INSPIRING COMMITMENT: *The Commitment Milestone*

As I'll later cover in the final E.L.I.T.E. habits, this decision of *commitment* isn't the last milestone we need to overcome. Our Champions will eventually need to execute the purchase process, moving to their steps of *closure* and ultimately, executing the *win*.

Depending on how complex those processes are, we Elite Sellers will need to provide varying levels of *trust building* and *Champion empowerment*.

Yet, contrary to what many sellers believe, we're probably not there yet. At this **Commitment Milestone** in a buyer/seller engagement, we must realize that before they can be ready to move to closure, they must feel and believe in a *commitment* to do so. This just simply isn't as easy for them as most sellers tend to think. Thus, we take shortcuts, often not even realizing where the buyer is in their decision process, nor appreciating what they might need from us. At the point where we believed that we had successfully led a Buyer Champion's *vision* toward a level of *certainty*, we should consider that Champion *Connection*, as the first critical *milestone* in their buying process. In fact, a guidance I'll share as another way to simplify sales is to break down and view your typical sales engagement into a series of *milestones*. As an intuitive people-seller, those milestones should be considered in the context of *the buyer's* decision process.

A milestone is a significant event or stage where something has progressed. If we identify what those milestones are for our buyer's decision process, we're in a more focused mindset to strategically work toward each one. Use whatever language and terms make sense to you. But if the first milestone of a Champion's decision process was one of *connection*, then think of where the buyer is now as a milestone of *commitment*.

Another way I like to think of *commitment* is a buyer milestone of a ***Go/No-go***. Remember, I said that inspiration or becoming inspired is a *process*? Think of this *Go/No-go* milestone as a process, not just a single event. This process is one that should get them closer toward making a formal decision of commitment to either *Go* and do the purchase, or to *not go* forward. This concept of a *Go vs. No-go* decision is where it should start making sense to you how inspiration is a process.

Imagine yourself as the buyer. You've become emotionally attracted and connected to a new solution. You really want to go with it. But you must decide whether to *commit* to purchasing it. For the decision to *go forward* or *not*, while you'd love to follow your emotions and just make it happen, your reality may be that there are *risks* that you'll need to consider committing to. Also, as easy as it would be to selfishly follow your own commitment path, it's possible that you may need a unified commitment with other stakeholders.

They'll need you to commit to some *advocacy* for the purchase. You probably have a higher level of *economic authority* that needs to form their own buying commitment. And of course, there's always that final question of commitment as to how *urgent* this decision needs to be. While it could be true, in a less complex sale, that our buyer is ready and prepared to begin working toward a purchase immediately, the safer and more aware assumption is that they're now at their own mental *Go/No-go.*

When we master the sales habit of *Inspiring Commitment,* we begin to understand what the buyer needs and what they need from us in order to help them in this *Go/No-go* decision process. Moreover, we'll have the insight into what they need to prioritize a level of *urgency* that we ultimately desire for ourselves. Remember, we don't sell to companies. We sell to people. For a person to act on both mentally committing to purchase what we sell and doing so with a highly motivated level of urgency, we sellers need to be sensitive to and aware of what our buyer needs in order to make that commitment.

Connection vs. Commitment

For a Seller, it feels so good, so validating to have high activity, a big pipeline, and buyers who show a real interest in what we have to sell. But have you ever noticed that a forecast call at the beginning of the quarter always sounds just a bit different than one towards the end? There's usually that one seller who loves talking about their amazing opportunity and how "It's ours to lose!"

As the weeks go by, they sound more and more like Chris Farley in *Tommy Boy* as Jo Jo The Indian Circus Boy with a pretty new pet, his possible sell that he just loves so much. Then, as predictable as the last one, we see that opportunity crumble. So, why does this happen?

Too often, I see sellers taking unnatural and desperate actions, all to somehow motivate a buyer to make a decision *now*. It's amazing how everything is just so *unicorns and rainbows*, until it's not. Why is it that deals at one time seemed to have momentum, but then all the sudden, they don't? The team had great meetings, took the buyer out for drinks. They even did a business case with a strong ROI. So, how is it possible that the deal's not moving anymore? Could it be that the deal's just not qualified? Maybe it never was? Maybe it was, but it isn't anymore? How can we explain this mystery of *deal disappearance*?

Let's just think about our *E.L.I.T.E.* selling journey thus far. We prospected and began communicating with a buyer in a way that disarmed them and started attracting some *emotional connection* to what we sell. As sales conversations continued, we began *leading their vision*. We positioned our solution to the most important *problems* they were trying to solve and positive *outcomes* they desired. Then, our solution, its relevant *differentiating big ideas*, and proposed *value* really drove home the *intellectual connection* we needed. They now seem to be at a place where they have a vision that aligns to our unique value proposition. *So, why aren't they ready to buy?*

Emotional and intellectual **connection** is essentially a heightened state of buyer *interest.* It's a very necessary state of attraction that we sellers need in order to begin our path toward a buyer decisively **committing** to buy what we sell. Capturing interest isn't as easy as many sellers think, and its importance can't be minimized. It was hard enough to just get access to the buyer. Then, we had to fight our way through what seemed like a jungle of buyer emotions before we finally made a strong connection. For those Buyer Champions we're now building who have power, influence, and economic access, we must realize that for them to put their credibility on the line and really act on our behalf, it will take more than just being *connected* to our value proposition. Can't that feel hard to believe? After all our work, being highly tuned in to what our buyers need and want to get done, we got them connected. Yet, they still appear hesitant, lacking urgency to do the deal. So, this leads the question, *Is Connection different from a Commitment?*

As there are different definitions and types of opportunity qualification, let's assume in a most basic sense that we have a fairly qualified deal if we've built a strong Champion. Yet, our job and responsibility as an elite seller isn't done yet. Although we've identified them correctly by their defined traits and we led their vision to a level of certainty, we still need to address this challenge of how to **Inspire** a Champion to **Commit** to the purchase.

If it's true that *people* hold the responsibility for committing to a buying decision, then the awareness we must all be in search of is, *What exactly motivates a person to do anything?* Is it my vision and value message? My customer stories and references? A big return on investment? I've been on two decades of opportunity reviews and forecast calls. What's clear is that, while it's always a good result if we can conclude that a deal's unqualified, it's far better when we can strategize just how to speed one up.

In this chapter on the third E.L.I.T.E. selling habit, **Inspiring Commitment**, the awareness you'll gain will help you build strategies that influence buyer motivation and drive urgency. A saying you've heard from me, and one I've always loved, is that we need buyers who have a *bias for action*. But what does a *bias for action* really mean? What's the standard that we're looking for?

In the habit of ***Inspiring Commitment***, I'll share concepts that address questions like, *What is real commitment? What does a buyer need to become committed?* And finally, *How can I inspire it?* There *is* a difference between *connection* and *commitment*. Like anything in sales, the more intuitive we are as to why and how buyers make the decisions they do, the more efficient and effective we can be at aligning to and inspiring those decisions. *Inspiring Commitment* within a buyer is a habit that is targeting the ultimate mental buyer decision: to *commit* to purchasing what we sell.

For simplicity of terminology, when I use the term *purchase*, allow that to represent whatever your relative act of formalizing business is, whether it's entering into or renewing a long-term contract, gaining commitment to your service or treatment, or executing a traditional purchase agreement.

After a buyer is *connected* to our value and before they make whatever type of *purchase* there is, they will need to intellectually *commit* to this formal decision. This is our purpose in mastering a habit of *Inspiring Commitment*. It's as simple as this. A buyer needing to choose to become committed to doing business with us is a mental step that happens in every buying decision. Our

179

selling habits, the routines that we thoughtfully repeat, must be aligned to the common needs of our Buyer Champions. Unfortunately, either because we were guided toward an oversimplified buying expectation or because we only view buying as a business process versus a people process, many sellers become victims of their buyers *not* owning a commitment.

Think of the word *commitment*. It should bring other words to mind like *dedication*, *obligation*, *agreement* to do something in the future. The *commitment* that I'm referring to is a noun. It's a mental state that exists, a destination where a buyer has arrived. What I'll help explain is that in business, buyer *commitment* is a crucial state that has to be in place in the Champions who we sell to before they will actively sell on our behalf and work toward a purchase. Without that mental *commitment*, even if we sellers feel that we've done everything possible to ensure closing this customer, why would a buyer ever do anything if they lacked dedication, obligation, or agreement? Are you a seller who *hopes* for this level of commitment, *assumes* it, *expects* it from the intellectual power of your value message? Or do you make it a priority to gain your buyer's *commitment*? Is it a habit?

For a Buyer Champion, because this careful and decisive pledge is mental, this is why our E.L.I.T.E. habit is about *inspiring* that commitment state. *Inspiration* is a process, and one in which we are being mentally stimulated. The stimulation that we sellers desire is for our buyers to take action for us. At this post-connection stage, it's the action of *commitment* that we can't afford to hope that it magically appears, assume that it's already happening, or arrogantly expect that any intelligent buyer would just have it.

Thus, it's critical that we intentionally and routinely work to *inspire* that commitment. Yet often, we sellers aren't aware, experienced, or empathetic enough to know just what all our Champions are having to commit to. Is it as easy as we think? As we'll also cover in this chapter, an elite seller knows that we need to qualify and inspire the *urgency* of that commitment. This is where I'll walk you through what *motivation* is. When a buyer feels *motivated*, they tend to act on what inspires them. So, when what we desire is for a buyer to become our Champion, just what are we asking them to commit to?

THE 4 BUYER COMMITMENTS

Have you or your sellers ever felt this way? *We've done all we can do to convince you buyers that you should make this decision and go with us. So why don't you just make the decision already!*

So intent on responding to our own professional fears, our perspective and mindset can often be blinded to the real challenges that our Champions have in order to get fully committed. In the habit of *Inspiring Commitment*, we must fully invest in the attention to and appreciation for the different forms and levels of commitments we're asking our Champions to make. Across any type of buying process, from straightforward transactions to strategic small business products and services, and through the matrixed decision trails of larger enterprise complex solutions, all buyers will need to face multiple types of *commitments*.

For whatever reason, sellers and their management tend to oversimplify the buyer's journey toward gaining *commitment.* We minimize the liability of risks involved. We're unconcerned with their challenges of gaining consensus, and we trust that they have everything they need to gain economic authority commitments. To make it all worse, some of us behave intolerantly to any resistance toward urgency.

The level of tolerance and understanding we need will come from a real appreciation for these **4 Buyer Commitments**: *Risk, Advocacy, Economic Authority,* and **Urgency**. It's in these different considerations of commitment that our Champions must provide an answer to.

To understand these **4 Buyer Commitments**, let's start with the *Commitment of Risk*. As we covered, any decision to purchase something new is a commitment of *change* in some form or fashion. With some change, we face great opportunity. But in all change, we take on a level of risk. Every buyer who chooses to become our Champion and commits to sponsoring a purchase of what we sell will be committing to some anatomy of *risk*. What does this mean for us? No matter how much we wish it away, our Buyer Champions will have to commit to the very real possibility that this decision to sponsor us will introduce new risk to them or their business. As buyers aren't always seasoned at purchase decisions, nor candid about their own personal challenges to overcome, we sellers must be intent on discovering all the areas of risk that purchasing our solution may place on our buyer. If a Champion is supposed to have our back, we need to have theirs.

Those risks could take shape as *internal or personal risks*, from their own experience with the usability of what we sell to their reputations and organizational credibility. A Champion's risks could also be *external*, such as additive pressures to or conflicts within the business that this purchase could create. Any seller who desires and expects a buyer to become their Champion, willing to actively put their name on the line and sell on their behalf, mustn't be selfish.

Selfless selling is observed when we positively and proactively identify the risks that our Champion will need to commit to in order to support this decision with us. When we take on this selfless mindset, we can work toward creative and purposeful solutions to reduce or mitigate a buyer's risk. That's when real Champions get formed. Rather than taking the typical sales route of trying to hide and mislead the buyer around our potential risks, Elite Sellers carefully, but intelligently, own the objection professionally. Showing this level of both integrity and high-value partnership tends to increase the trust and strength of our Champions. We need to show them that we care. Equally, we should take these risks seriously and work hard to ensure that they don't come to fruition.

We should also consider a Champion's **Commitment of Advocacy.** Even in the smallest of businesses, there is usually a degree of consensus that needs to form for our Champion to gain full commitment to move forward. If we have adequately qualified their decision process, we'll know if there are other key stakeholders who will need to get aligned to this decision. Intuitively understanding that these different people will all have their own *path to commitment*, as well as empathetically acknowledging that our Champion will have to put in a little extra work to sell to each one of them, this should elicit a concerning response from us to help in any way we can.

Our heightened awareness should see that when our Champion is advocating for something to their peers or authorities, they're putting something very personal on the line: their reputation and credibility. You've also heard me refer to this as their *political capital.* In most businesses, decisions and directions are often a theatre of internal politics, gives and gets, asks and concessions. Everyone of authority has a bit of influence and sway that they can place on others. That influence, however, is not unlimited. Everyone has a finite amount of capital to spend in their organizations. Most just don't know how much they have until it's all been spent. So, buyers will be cautious and prudent with where and why they spend their political capital. Becoming a seller's Champion, a choice that they will actively sell on our behalf within their organization, is an example of spending political capital. But, even in that relationship with us, they'll have limits that we need to proactively and selflessly be sensitive to. With some purchases, they feel so certain that they could care less about any risk to their own political capital.

However, if we don't get our Champion to a confident level of conviction, while they may believe in our cause, there will be moments of hesitation as they message within their own organization. The problem with that is if our Champions don't believe, *the consensus* won't believe. Now, keep in mind at this *milestone of commitment*, we're not necessarily in the final days of the purchase process. The buyer has come out of our series of sales conversations, and they're at this mental *Go/No-go* inflection point. They're deciding whether they want to take this *emotional connection* they've formed and now get themselves and others committed to move forward and with urgency. This realization makes it important for us to consider in their *Commitment of Advocacy*, that not every Buyer Champion is a great salesperson.

This should make us even more concerned with supporting the *commitment message* for our Champion, reinforcing their feelings of conviction. In parallel, we should be questioning what each of the other key influencer's decision criteria, priorities, and reluctance would be toward making any commitments. If our Champion is going to need to commit to *advocating* for a consensus to support a solution like ours, then for every individual involved, we should be asking how we can help our Champion overcome their fears and anxieties associated with this commitment.

Unless the buyer we're selling to is also the ultimate financial decision maker, a common requirement from our Champion is in the **Commitment of Economic Authority**. In the realm of people involved in a buying decision, just consider these varying degrees. As a Champion, I first think about and feel the need to address my personal concerns of commitment. How will this decision affect me? Then, there's attention to the business and other groups or teams related to this solution. However, there is no degree of commitment that is more formal, often process-oriented, and inclusive of all aspects of business consideration than that of *Economic Authority*.

When our Champions are faced with this *Go/No-go* milestone with their economic buyer, that typically executive-level constituent has a perspective that's more informed and often broader than our Champion. Not to mention, they inherently possess a level of authority above that of our Champion. Elite sellers realize that they need to intentionally get those preliminary commitment needs of Economic Authority met as early in their sales process as possible. However, most sellers presume an extension of trust that our Champions will just, *figure it out. Based on our awesome value proposition, it can't be that hard for the economic executive to fall in line.*

Well, *fall in line* is what our Champions usually end up doing if their meetings with *Economic Authority* aren't effective at inspiring a commitment. *Economic Authority*, or what I've referred to as Economic Buyers, don't only bring discretionary authority over the spending of company funds, but they often represent the broader risks and concerns of business disruption and productivity. We sellers should recognize the jurisdiction of authority and brevity of message needed to *net out* the justification of commitment to an economic buyer.

If our Champions are selling to an external economic authority, such as a partner, patient, or client who is ultimately accountable for the investment, then the same, and sometimes far more complicated commitment exists. If possible, it's often in both our best interests if we and our Champions can join these Economic Buyer commitment meetings together. After all, no one can explain our unique commitment message with more conviction and credibility than us.

In any case, whether we're there or our Champions want to address this challenge of commitment without us, we need to be sensitive to the discretion and examination of business or personal rationale in our Champion's *Commitment of Economic Authority.*

Finally, every decision of *commitment* includes one dimension that all salespeople crave, and all buyers show the most caution and prudence toward, **The Commitment of Urgency**. Yes, we'd all like our Champions to escalate our solution purchase to the top of the urgency list. In fact, it's not uncommon for our Champions to confidently proclaim that addressing the purpose that we serve is of the utmost priority, complete with compelling events, initiative timelines, and must-meet deadlines.

Unfortunately, *Urgency* is the most disappointment-rich component of deals that we work and Champions who sponsor us. I'll say this. So much of the time that we're frustrated in the absence of deal urgency, it isn't because our Champion is failing in their role. Most sellers don't maniacally qualify the *decision process* and its natural steps, timing, and people involved. Most of us don't really investigate what the criterion of Economic Authority truly is. We also tend to minimize the critical nature of gaining commitments from all the stakeholders involved in these commitments. Thus, it's not our Champions who are letting us down. It's our false expectations. We'll find ourselves and our sales leaders not showing enough educated tolerance for the true commitment path that's needed in an organization.

However, it is the case that these *urgency* conflicts and indecisions can be due to unexperienced or idealistic buyers who don't fully understand their own types, levels, and complexities of commitment. The understanding that's necessary for a seller is to realize that by asking a Champion to accelerate a decision and buying process with an acute degree of *urgency*, we're asking them to accept a higher level of exposure, risk, and intensity for themselves. This doesn't mean that our Champions shouldn't make their decisions and push our commitments with urgency. We just need to be more informed and perceptive as to how *urgency* forms.

The Urgency Threshold: *What Motivates Buyers to Act*

What would help is if we sellers all better understood what motivates action and drives urgency in a human buyer. Consider this concept I call **The Urgency Threshold**. In studying the science of *motivation*, this is the tendency we have to take action, which is different from *inspiration*, an influence of someone's mental or emotional state. How urgent our buying process is will depend on how *motivated* our Champions are, either for themselves or the business situation.

The way our mind works is that we're *motivated* according to two dimensions of perception, **Fear** and **Desire.** Remember, our perceptions and perspectives drive our actions in life. So, to understand our **Urgency Threshold**, picture a *seesaw*, which you might have played on at your elementary or primary school playground. A seesaw works like a simple lever. It consists of a long plank of wood or metal attached to some fixed center point on which the plank moves as a fulcrum, up on one side, down on the other. Now visualize two children sitting on each far end of the plank. When one pushes up with their legs, the other goes down until they're sitting on ground level. The two children go back and forth, up and down. Now inevitably, as one of the cruelest of childhood games played around the world, the ground-level child quickly jumps off the seesaw, leaving the other kid to crash down to the ground in a painful surprise that will hurt their whole body the rest of the day. As the biggest kid in school, kids did this to me a lot, so I have a very personal visual.

This visualization is much like how our *Urgency Threshold* works. On one end of our *mental seesaw* is the emotion of **Fear.** On the other is **Desire**. In a decision of how *urgently* we should act on something, our mind responds to the degree of perceived *Fear* or *Desire* that we see in front of us. If our *Fear* is incredibly high for something, then we become **hesitant**, protectively still to avoid any uncontrollable risks or threats to our well-being. If our *Desires* are low, then we become **complacent**, void of any motivation to expend any unnecessary energy.

THE URGENCY THRESHOLD

So, think about what can often happen in sales. Let's say that a buyer's *desire was high*, but their *fears were low*. They took several meetings with us and led us on that there was a serious opportunity for us here, but there just wasn't much of a negative consequence to not making a new solution decision. In this case, while we may have found a buyer who was emotionally excited and interested in what we sold, they lacked the motivation to take any action on those emotions. Another scenario that's just as common in business is when a buyer's *desires are high*, but their *fears are even higher*. This can often cause their reluctance and hesitancy to escalate into outright resistance to taking the risk that our solutions present. This prevents their commitment.

As sellers, we should be seeking out a state where our buyers are meeting their *Urgency Threshold*. This is the mental conclusion buyers make where their *fears* for the problems we solve and *desires* for the outcomes that we address are in **balance**. Like a seesaw evenly balanced parallel to the ground, our Champion's *fears* on one side and *desires* on the other are both at a similar level. Like most things in business, we sellers can't make our buyers have a need for what we sell. However, in our efforts to be intuitive guides that try to help inspire buyers toward highly convicted *commitments*, we should know that this *Commitment of Urgency* is just as much a psychological balance as it is some existence of logical facts and details such as events and deadlines.

If you've ever had those supposed compelling events and initiative deadlines committed to you in your deals, only to see them *push* and *no decision*, maybe this helps you understand why. People make decisions. If their psychology isn't in balance between their perception of the desires and fears of making this commitment urgently, then the decision probably won't go the way we want. If urgency is what we desire, especially if we share that interest with our Champion, if we are aware enough as to what would cause a buyer to act urgently, we'll be more likely to affect it or unfortunately, qualify it out. Either way, *urgency* is a sensitive and sometimes high-stakes commitment that our Champions will often discern if it's worth it to push organizationally. That urgency will come far more naturally when our buyers are experiencing a balance of their related *fears and desires* meeting their personal *Urgency Thresholds*.

Applying INSPIRING COMMITMENT in the Sales Process

JANE IS TARZAN

I once supported a rep named Jane, who was one of the absolute best salespeople I've ever worked with. She had a great internal reputation. In a quarterly management meeting where we'd review the sales forecast, one of our board members referred to Jane as *Tarzan*. He had worked with her at two previous companies. We were an early-stage startup going through our productivity growth pains of trying to build enough deal pipeline for all the salespeople we'd just hired. Just like with us, at her previous companies Jane would consistently be the one saving the company's quarter with a well-qualified, pristinely worked deal that was sure to close. Once again like *Tarzan*, I was forecasting Jane to save my quarter.

Having a strong personality, some people thought her close rate was because of her aggressiveness or *whatever it takes* mindset to win the business. But it was actually Jane's intelligence, attention to detail, and overall ability to build trust and *commitment* with the people that she sold to. She was an elite seller who had the intuition that when the customer needed something important like a decision of consensus or a validation event, she knew that it was just as important a step to her Champion's internal credibility as it was to ours. Jane built Champions better than anyone because buyers knew that she truly cared, and she made their success personal. But Jane also brought a lot of credibility to the table.

Our company was helping some of the largest retailers, hotels, and brands transform how they approached customer experience. These types of progressive programs and technologies like ours were new to most organizations. They didn't have the knowledge of where to start and what highest impact strategies to implement. Jane did. She'd learn their business better than some of their own employees. But it was in those higher intensity evaluation stages where she'd truly earn *commitment* from even the most unlikely buyers.

Jane had been selling to big enterprises for almost two decades. She understood their inner workings. When the world's largest money transfer company started feeling the pressures of new lower cost regional competitors, they believed that customer experience could potentially be their best strategy to differentiate. Jane confidently led them toward a vision that, because most money transfer customers use their service fairly regularly, sometimes weekly paycheck to paycheck, that her prospect had a real opportunity to change the game and make their business model about loyal customer relationships. While Jane's conviction for this vision was inspiring to her Champion Beth, she was new in her role and other stakeholders in *the consensus* group had far more political capital and leverage than Beth did. Most of them had been at the company for over twenty years, and they didn't want to implement anything that would cause more work, expose more problems to solve, and spend more money. Ours was a $2 million investment that would tell the business what their problems were on an hourly basis, so Beth had a lot riding on this.

Jane knew that each one of those decision makers had a unique set of decision criteria. She also knew that they all had varying gaps in their willingness to commit. While some weren't fully committed to our solution to deliver results on a global scale for their high-transaction, low-margin business, others just weren't committed to changing anything. Beth wasn't the most experienced buyer, but she was smart and determined, an executive on the rise. She and Jane made a great team. Jane knew that Beth's colleagues would need to see proof of our value promises and that they would not back down easily.

Knowing the power of political leverage and consensus, one afternoon Jane set up a call with Beth to discuss each individual stakeholder in the evaluation process. What she wanted to know was what each considered their priority desires, as well as their biggest fears. Qualifying those concerns of the attributes that they needed to trust most in a solution provider was her focus. Jane knew that those buyers were not going to make this decision because of any differentiating or innovative capabilities we had. We needed to establish credibility and trust with as many of those people as possible. After the call, Jane validated the reassurances that the team needed and gained some evidence that Beth was a true Champion. Jane was confident in the focus of her strategy.

She'd learned that several of the other decision makers were working with and most likely Champions for the low-cost provider. It would all come down to both technical validations that we could work in nearly two hundred countries and in business validations such as crucial customer reference calls. With a focus on building trust and commitment across as much of *the consensus* group as she could, Jane facilitated those validations and every sales milestone with precision. She would go out of her way to first ensure that her Champion was armed with a strong message that could rally as many stakeholders as possible around the purpose of making this change and why they should go with us. Next, she gained full alignment with Beth as to what exact plan for their success needed to be validated. This included proving out the results that mattered most to the business and the different negative influencers. Then, she'd rally anyone and everyone in our company to identify what could go wrong. She was a leader who gained everyone's commitment internally to make this validation event a success. Now that she had learned the buyer's priority criteria, she formed a plan with our engineers that considered our risks and ensured we had the precise path to prove our credibility.

One by one, their detractors would move over to our side. Finally, when Beth and her team were ready for vendor reference calls, Jane ensured that her Champion was well armed with any knowledge they needed about us. But what really cemented their commitment to us came from an *old school* closing technique. She prepared a simple list of strategic questions and concerns for Beth to discuss with our competitor's customers on their reference calls. This was just one of several Champion tests that Beth would pass.

But the character Jane always projected was selfless and her buyers could see it. The reason she was such a great seller was that she focused on people. As much as she'd want to close a deal fast, she was more intent on learning and executing a strategy around what her individual buyers needed to become committed. I call this *slowing down to go fast*. She wouldn't just work to gain commitment from a lone Champion, but across all the decision makers in a buying process. *Tarzan Jane* built high-trust *commitment* because she aligned a consensus around a common purpose, showed them that we had a plan to enable their success, and proved that our value claims were legitimate. If you asked Beth, she would say that Jane had her back.

THE COMMITMENT PATH: *Purpose, Plan, Promise*

Gaining a buyer's commitment can often feel complicated because all buyers are different: their situations, needs, personalities. Well, like most things, what appears complicated is usually far more basic than we think. So, what do we know about *commitment*, besides the fact that it might have been lacking in our high school romance? One, **commitment is a choice**. It's an intellectual, voluntary, and coherent decision that we make. Two, because it's intellectual, **commitment first needs connection**, especially *emotional connection.* This connection draws our attention in the first place, gets us to a place of emotional interest in what something could do for us, driving a willingness to consider a commitment. Thus, **commitment is also personal**. As we'll discuss, there is often some level of risk associated with committing to something or someone. Yet, in our biggest commitments is where we'll also find our greatest opportunities. While the company a buyer is making a decision for may share some of those risks and opportunities, it's a *person* who's making that decision of commitment. Commitment is always personal.

And last, **commitment is obligation**, a mental promise by which a person feels a sense of duty to do something. It's not intention. It's not interest. While it doesn't mean that the intended outcome is certain, it does represent the state of a person who will stick to the mission, determined to meet their objective, because they feel obligated.

So, if we first have a basic understanding that commitment is personally meaningful, then how can we simplify our ability to inspire it in our Champions? Foundationally, we sellers will need to be *intuitive* enough to understand just why someone would become committed. Then, we'll have to be *empathic* enough to be aware of and then align our strategy to the different types of commitments our buyers are faced with. You see, most sellers convince themselves that the buyer's decision is binary. You either believe or you don't. You're committed or you're not. Truth is, even the simplest of decisions involve multiple commitments that our buyers need to get to.

A good friend John Kaplan coined the statement that a buyer should *participate in their own rescue*. I've always loved this because it represents the ultimate accountability that's associated with buyer commitment. A feeling of *obligation* is an example of that accountability. However, what John also shared is that our stance that a buyer must *participate in their own rescue* will only be justified once we sellers have earned the right. If we haven't inspired their commitment yet, we still have work to do. While it is ultimately the buyer's choice to solve their problems, a salesperson has far more ability to inspire that choice than we think. In fact, when we fully recognize the multiple layers and types of commitments that exist, we realize that it's actually our responsibility to inspire that buyer's commitment. To help you with both this level of intuitiveness and empathy toward how we can *inspire* a Champion's commitment, I'll share with you this simple, yet undeniable path that will explain how all buyers arrive at their *milestone of commitment*.

Have you experienced sales opportunities in the past where a buyer, maybe even a Champion, had reached a high level of connection and intent to buy, but they just couldn't get themselves or others around them fully committed? If you think back, you'll probably find that their mental gaps fell in one or more of these three areas. I call this **The Commitment Path**. If we want a person or a group of people to be committed to something, then they'll first need to understand the **Purpose** of it, then the **Plan** of how they'll achieve success, and finally, the **Promise** of what they should expect to receive in return. *Purpose, Plan,* and *Promise.* This is our mental *Commitment Path.* It's how our buyer minds process the decisions they make, no different than how we and our teams choose to commit to things that we're asked of in our jobs.

THE COMMITMENT PATH

Think about anything in your life or career where you've been challenged to devote far more than just your support, but a real commitment. This could have been a commitment of your time, your money, a commitment to change something personally, or perhaps to make a major life decision. If you were initially hesitant, what was your immediate subconscious reaction to the request? You were probably questioning the *purpose* of *why* you should be making this commitment. I'll walk you through some dimensions that you might have measured that question against. But the bottom line is that no buyer will ever begin to consider committing to purchasing anything until they first understand its *purpose.*

Simon Sinek, author of *Start with Why* shares, "People don't buy what you do; they buy why you do it." Our need to understand *The Why,* or *purpose,* in order to consider taking action, initiates from those same survival impulses in our decision path: *Survive, Thrive, Think.* This initial response is not logical, it's purely emotional. Our instincts are usually causing us to react with the thought, *Now, why would I want to do this?* However, the decision of *commitment* is of much higher magnitude. It forces us to consider whether we should take action, introducing potential exposure to risk or questioning of our credibility. We simply don't want to make a mistake. Thus, from this initial emotional response, our intellect is quickly triggered to search for reasoning as to the *purpose* of this decision.

Go back to thinking about those committed decisions that you've had to make for yourself. If you weren't then clear on the *plan* of exactly how you could make the extra time, find the money to invest, enable any personal changes, or endure a major life decision, then were you able to move forward? Did this concern you enough to pause or delay your decision? Did you first need to get comfortable with how you'd make it happen? Finally, at that last moment before commitment, did you feel an impulse questioning what the big benefit or return would be if you made this investment of your resources? Did you ask yourself, *Is this worth it?* Or did you suppress all of those annoying apprehensions and just went ahead with the decision anyway? How often did regret or a hard lesson soon follow? In our personal life, maybe sometimes those negative consequences are uncomfortable, but recoverable nonetheless.

In business, think about what's on the line for your buyers when they choose to commit to what you sell. Are there unintended consequences to other systems, processes, or performance indicators? Are there costly repercussions of high-risk change? Are serious side effects or complications being considered? If the consequences aren't much, then maybe your challenge to inspire your buyer's commitment is more straightforward, and the effort's not as exhaustive. But just ask yourself. How could your buyer make any commitment to you without answering those three essential commitment questions of: *Why should I be doing this? How will I find success?* And, *how much value should I expect in return?* **Purpose, Plan, Promise.**

While this probably sounds like basic sense, the reality is that perhaps the most common gap in a buyer's information needed to support their decision is clarity around the **Purpose** of what our solution will serve for them. If this was so clear, then why do so many opportunities end in a *no decision*? *Purpose* is the most powerful question of a buyer's commitment path. The reason isn't just because they have to understand *Why*. It's because the investment we're asking our buyer to make has *context*. That decision, whether a small or large investment, will be made in consideration of its *purpose* in *context* of the investment, such as the risk, the size, the effort needed. The success **Plan** and value **Promise** of the purchase are also examined with the same consideration of *context*. If we sellers only see our strong justification in a bubble, failing to associate the buyer's context, then our commitment message will always be shortsighted. Has this misalignment of *context* ever happened to you?

Well, why does this disconnect continue to happen? Often, the longer the sales engagement and the wider the influence spans across multiple decision makers, the less clear and more diminished the actual *purpose* of our purchase becomes. The more information the buyer has received and been asked to process, the harder it is for them to synthesize it all into a clear case for commitment. We also see this when the *plan* to enable success is a bit murky and the value *promise* seems questionable and confusing. After all, the brain is lazy, and it will usually refuse to work too hard to put the pieces of the *commitment puzzle* together. This is why *inspiring commitment* is an absolute core responsibility that should be led with intentional routine.

Much like the driver behind our habit of *Leading Vision*, if we sellers keep our own mental focus on our buyer and the proposed outcomes we can deliver for them, we will begin identifying our Champion's potential *commitment path* and *commitment gaps* early on. Often, we found *purpose* in the initial learning of the biggest problems we could solve and most desired outcomes we could deliver for our buyer. We identified the related differentiating capabilities or traits that they could attribute a *plan* for their success. Value metrics and any other *promises* of value that were discussed with our Champion should have provided insight into the results that they most expect.

Yet, at the *milestone of Champion Commitment*, we fall back to our own self-focused preservation instincts in just the same way that our Champions do. We lose focus and don't even realize that our buyer is at a *milestone of commitment*. This is why the state of *commitment* is such a critical focus and destination for us to inspire in a buyer. We sellers get impatient, uneasy, quick to concede concessions, and determined to control the outcome. Or perhaps, we get complacent because we've had so many good meetings and have several supporters who seem to be fully on board.

At the same juncture, our Champions have just as much on the line to make this meaningful decision of commitment as we do to close our business and earn our commissions. But we unconsciously fail to help our buyer make the business connection to the *purpose, plan,* and *promise* of what we sell. Meanwhile, our Champion's hesitation, fears, and concerns grow. *Inspiring Commitment* needs to be a selfless sales habit. Otherwise, due to our self-focus, we'll often fail to see just what our Champion's path to commitment will be.

The Dimensions of PURPOSE: *Seeking the Big Why*

I've always asked this illuminating and anxiety-forming question to my sellers: *If I called each of your Champions and asked them all to tell me the purpose of making this purchase with us, what would they say?* As the uncertainty and nervousness starts to build, the sellers ask themselves, *What would they say? In fact, what would I say is the purpose?*

For years, my customer teams have been responsible for gaining commitments for their customers to renew their agreements with us. So often, I'd be asked to join a peer-to-peer executive call to discuss the renewal. I'd ask every customer the same question. *What purpose do you think we're serving for your business?* Most of the time, the answer is more around our capabilities or what function we provide in their system or process. *But, why us? What's the purpose of choosing us?* Some just couldn't articulate it. They didn't know. Thus, how could they be *committed?*

Across the *Commitment Path*, there is no more important and powerful question than that of *Purpose*. For us sellers to be able to inspire a Champion to be committed to us and the purchase, we must first attack this question with a voracious curiosity. When we humans make a commitment, we're answering questions in order to make a choice. The first questions that our buyer is answering are *What exactly would be the purpose that would be meaningful enough for us to change what we're doing today? And what purpose does this solution serve for us?* Elite sellers don't rely on buyers to define that purpose alone. Their curiosity seeks to determine not only what greater purpose they would be serving, but also how they could broaden and best define that purpose in a way that distinguishes their unique value proposition.

Commitment Purpose

One way to look at the power of purpose, is to view it as a ***Forcing Function***. If the purpose that sits in our buyer's mind feels like a lower impact potential opportunity, then it will lack the inspiration that informs a need for commitment. However, a *forcing function* is a true catalyst that forces an action to be taken. For a *commitment purpose* to be a *forcing function*, there will typically be a real negative consequence to not doing something, or possibly even an absence of choice. When we seek *The Big Why* behind a commitment purpose, we're looking for leverage, something that serves as a *forcing function* for the buyer to say, *This is a critical purpose that I must address*.

The power of *commitment purpose* is seen because of its multiple **Dimensions of Purpose**. These are both ***Internal*** to our consideration and ***External***. If a buyer determines a purpose that serves an *internal* dimension but not an *external* one, while they may feel emotionally connected to it, they'll usually lack the full justification to become committed. If purpose is only *external*, not personal to them, then they may not feel the inspiration to do anything for it. To help guide this quest for action-driving *purpose*, one that acts as a *forcing function* toward their decision, consider that sellers have to be in search of a *commitment purpose* for a buyer on both dimensions, *Internal Purpose and External Purpose*.

Inspiring *commitment* isn't necessarily complicated. We just have to be in true search for it. We can't check that box just because we have conviction in our solution's purpose. This mindset is core to a Champion-based sell. Our Champion is trying to make a decision here, and we have to see it from their perspective. By looking at *purpose* on both an *internal* and *external* dimension for our buyer, we force our mind to remain fixed on the reality of their experience and gravity of this commitment choice.

Common examples of *internal* purpose will typically fit into the category of **Personal Wins**. These are seen when our solution enables a Champion to accomplish something that they need or desire for themselves like career advancement, political leverage, or meeting a management objective. What we sell could uniquely bring them a financial gain or personal profit, especially if they're the owner of the business or an executive measured on financial performance indicators. Perhaps we offer them personal risk avoidance or protection from a threat that they're seriously concerned about. Or certainly, the purpose we serve could just be eliminating a major issue or trouble that they don't want to be dealing with anymore.

Examples of *external* purpose could be financial benefits to their business. Their company could be challenged with enablement of priority initiatives, limited empowerment, and efficiency of organizational functions. The business could need its risks and threats controlled. Perhaps there's an external *end customer* that the business serves who has an important purpose to be met, a customer, a patient, a partner.

With any related example of *purpose*, the more detailed we look at our solution's direct and unique impact, the more effective we'll be at inspiring our Champion. Finding *purpose*, a *Big Why forcing function*, is rarely hard. It's just an exercise in intellectual curiosity about the buyer's unique *internal and external* drivers and motivations. When the inputs of the buyer's greater purpose and outputs that come from our solution's unique value proposition come together, we enable our buyers to be inspired to a *purpose-driven* reason to begin their path toward commitment.

The Enablement of PLAN: *Attributing the Big How*

Of all three stages of the *commitment path*, the *purpose* of making this purchase, the *plan* for achieving success, and the *promise* of value expected in return, none is more crucial to protecting that connection against competition than the **Enablement of Plan**. We earned that connection, both emotionally and intellectually. Reaching that energy generating state of *Thrive* and leading our buyer's *vision* took our time and intelligence. We have earned this.

The first step is realizing that we're at this *commitment milestone*. The second is to view it as a fragile opportunity that we must execute properly. For our Champion, the *commitment message* of the *purpose* for taking action, *The Big Why*, is now clear. That *purpose* is serving as a *forcing function* for them to intellectually invest more energy into learning how our solution will enable their success. Now, our Champion is ready and needing to understand *The Big How* it will work for them. Their commitment won't form until they fully grasp how they'll be able to attribute their success to our solution. This is the *enablement of plan.*

In psychology, this is called *Attribution Theory*, which is based largely on the work of Austrian psychologist Fritz Heider and his peers in the 1950s. *Attribution* is the involuntary response that all people will subconsciously question *how* they could explain what would cause something to succeed. Said differently, related to a Champion, a human being needs to know how they could attribute the ability of a positive outcome to happen before they'll believe it and be willing to take on any personal risk to achieve it.

Much like trying to push toward an intellectual connection before we've gained an emotional one, *attribution* is one of the main reasons we get buyer objections. It's just an example of our survival instincts in action. In buyer/seller interactions, no matter how much they like or trust us, a buyer is not going to believe or intellectually commit to our proposed value, until they understand just *how* they would attribute their success. When we fail to position attributes to our vision and value message, our buyers will be mentally challenged to consider any true commitment. I'll share some categories and examples of **Success Attributes**. But the key realization for this *commitment path* of *enabling plan,* is that *value attribution* is a buyer dynamic that we're going to need to be aware of.

Attribution Theory also explains that people are basically naive. They tend to see cause and effect relationships, even when there are none. You might have experienced this in sales when buyers either made assumptions that went against your message or became closed off from an unfair or inaccurate conclusion. Now, this can be a great opportunity for us if we make the attribution of our value proposition clear and compelling for our Champion. This involuntary need for attribution is why the *enablement of our plan* to drive buyer success is a necessary habit. Otherwise, we're opening up ourselves up to some pretty great risk. Our risk is in the human nature of decision-making, the buyer brain's natural protective tendency to be as efficient and burn as few calories as possible. This mental dynamic leads many buyers to make false conclusions and incorrect decisions as to what will most enable their needs from a solution.

However, we sellers are just as much to blame. To understand why our *commitment message* of *plan* is such an important component of our competitive strategy, *Attribution Theory* tells us two things. One, the buyer brain will involuntarily need to attribute their success with our solution to some causal factors before they can move forward in any formal sponsorship. Two, a buyer's brain has a high probability of being naive and easily swayed to false claims if we don't get their first. It's not because our buyers aren't intelligent. It's just that all of our brains are wired to take mental shortcuts. This alone justifies why we need to be so deliberate and determined to inspire a buyer's commitment when they reach this decision milestone.

Commitment Plan

Because our messaging objective here is to gain deep intellectual buyer commitment, the message that makes up their **Commitment Plan** will need to be positioned to a much higher strategic standard. Its content will move from *The Big Why*, the purpose to making this commitment, to **The Big How**, the *plan* for just how they will be able to attribute their success. That influential *plan* for how we'll enable our buyer to meet their objectives needs to succinctly meet two minimum non-negotiable requirements. One, to personally inspire our buyer's commitment, the *plan we* message will need to specifically and clearly show how we will help them reach their highest level of **Value Realization**.

Value Realization is a term and a mindset that basically means, rather than merely explaining how our solution will work, *value realization* is when we define how our solution will deliver a specific desired measurable impact. If a buyer can't see evidence of how they'll achieve *value realization*, then all they'll be left with is unknowns and unanswered questions for this new product or service. To lead their mindset from solution understanding to solution commitment, they must clearly appreciate the actual plan for how they will be able to achieve their desired value.

The second higher standard requirement of a *commitment plan* is that it encompasses and highlights a credible aspect of our

Differentiation. Again, think about this *commitment path* that our Champion is mentally going through at this milestone. *Ok, I'm clear on the big purpose of this decision, internally and externally. But, as much as I love and believe in this one solution, I do know that I have other options. They all have their pros and cons, different levels of investment, and risks that I've got to consider.*

That buyer brain is at decision inflection point. Our competitors aren't going to stop selling. *Attribution Theory* tells us that we can't rest on our own Champion comforts. A threat isn't gone until a deal is done. We have to intentionally protect our **Champion Connection** and prevent any competitive threat from challenging the commitment that we've earned. Our *commitment plan* message will effectively inspire our Champion by driving the confidence that our solution provides them a success plan for not only meeting their *value realization* goals, but by doing so in a way that is unique to only us. If they don't associate our *differentiating big ideas* to their plan toward *value realization*, then we could be inspiring their commitment to buy alright, but just not buy us.

Success Attributes

As we make the careful consideration for how we want our Champion to think about our *plan* for their success, the message of our solution needs to be thoughtfully framed around our **Success Attributes**. To determine examples of a *plan* for *success attribution*, we can look across these five categories of **Success Attributes**. With each, consider your product or service, its differentiating traits, and the potential value realization impact that would apply to your customers.

One common type of *success attribute* is a **Primary Capability**. We see these in any type of tangible product or services provider. Everything we sell is essentially made up by a set of *capabilities*. A business may find its path to reach its *purpose* through a single or very powerful grouping of *primary capabilities*. These are the distinct and foremost traits of a solution which could be a functional capability of a product or a unique service ability.

A *primary capability* is telling a Champion that this is the most impactful and differentiating attribution from our solution that you can count on to deliver the level of *value realization* you need to feel inspired to make this commitment. With comprehensive solutions in particular, the caution that a seller should have is to avoid positioning a *commitment plan* that's cluttered with every capability that they consider strong or differentiating. This message is like a garden that's been overplanted. With no space to breathe and grow, the strength of each plant won't be appreciated. It won't take root and will never get exposed aboveground.

Success attributes can also be found in a **Credible Process.** We could justify this in a core services methodology. Maybe it's a highly customer-centric process that's been developed and proven to ease the complexity, speed of delivery, or reduce risk to the customer. For the millions of us who love shopping on Amazon, it's their *credible process* of shipping our package in days, if not hours, with confidence that it will arrive on time.

I've worked for and competed against consulting services firms where both teams confidently proclaimed differentiation based on their *services methodology*. Conversely, I've witnessed technology companies who fail to implement or emphasize unique processes such as solution delivery, implementation, migration, or assessments that would have immediately disarmed and reassured the prospective buyer. Unfortunately, this is where many of their previously built Champion connections fell apart. What I learned, and what applies to any *credible process*, is that its components have to directly correlate to the biggest risks, needs, scope, and context of our buyer's greatest concerns for success. If they don't, those methodologies and intensive customer-centric processes will simply fail to inspire our Champion's commitment.

Related, a *success attribute* can be a **Premium Service**. This is any ongoing service that a provider offers which can be viewed above and beyond the standard of what most providers can deliver. In a career full of startups, while we were always quite proud of our product's disruptive differentiation, many startups actually find the most success inspiring Champion commitment from a more white-glove and higher expertise level of service.

In the effort to combat the rising cost of doing business at scale, many large companies tend to stray from their higher cost, lower margin services. Maybe you've experienced this. But if you asked their buyers, common perceptions are that those companies have become complacent in the established reputation of their products.

Many buyers, whether they share it or not with their salesperson, feel a strong hesitancy toward committing to a new solution due to their lack of resources. Buyers are understaffed or lack the expertise needed to ensure operational success. In the *commitment plan* of our greatest *success attributes*, a *premium service* can be seen as an extremely valuable differentiating attribute to deliver customer success and *value realization*.

Commercially, in the legal, financial, and business agreements that are structured between buyers and sellers, there are almost always **Special Terms** which, if identified and proposed, will serve as a calming *success attribute* or protective reassurance for a Champion. *Special terms* might take the shape of price incentives, payment structure, legal language, or service guarantees.

Two predominant missteps are made here from many sellers. First, we wait too long to consider and then introduce these *special terms*. Once again, we've failed to recognize that we were at a *commitment milestone*. We missed a potential opportunity to earn our Champion's loyalty and commitment to us by addressing something that they might be very concerned about. The reasons are that maybe we lacked *business empathy*, or we were scared that we might negatively impact our Champion's connection. It could be that we didn't consider or disregarded that a Champion would find the terms between our companies, or specific to this transaction, a substantial consideration of risk and success.

The second misstep is that when we do choose to propose *special terms*, we throw out and offer terms that don't solve a problem or address an issue that our Champion cares about. More specific to a *commitment plan*, those terms we offer don't correlate to the *success attribution* concerns of our Champion. So, while they may feel like an aggressive example of how badly we want their business, they make no impact on a Champion's commitment level. Have you or your teams ever proactively conceded a term or offered an incentive, such as a price discount or an additive product or service at no extra charge, only to be met with little to know action of response? Were you misaligned in the proposal and your buyer's path to commitment? Perhaps the term wasn't even your original gap. You just might not have had a Champion.

Special terms are most certainly an inspirational *success attribute* in our *Plan* to ensure positive outcomes for our buyers. However, they must align to the biggest obstacles, concerns, and risks that are preventing our buyer from placing their ultimate commitment with us.

The fifth *success attribute* that's one of the most common with the people who are trying to discern their level of commitment to us, are **Internal Qualities.** These are the more holistic characteristics and traits of the company or the people that we represent. *Internal* to our company, if there are *qualities* that our Champions would value toward their comfort and assurance that they will be more likely to succeed, then we can't minimize or hide those. Often, our Champions are the ones who convince us. Some examples you might have experienced:

Your company has a great reputation, and we really appreciate your partnership. We realize you're not perfect, but we believe that you'll always make things right and deliver for us.

Your subject matter expert has really impressed us. She makes us feel confident that we'll get the level of guidance and execution we need.

Our needs will be long-term, and your size and stability make us believe that you'll be able to scale and be around as long as we need you.

Or have you ever heard this from your Champion?

You've never seen an environment and needs like ours. We're different than any of your other customers; and we'll demand a partner like you who is willing to constantly innovate and enhance your solutions.

An *internal quality* tends to make more of an emotional influence on a buyer. Emotions, as you now know, are far more influential to the buyer's decision path than we think. However, these are more holistic and sometimes, less tangible in nature. So, the risk of *internal qualities*, if not paired with other more evident attributes in a customer's value realization journey, have the potential to be less empowering to a buyer's intellectual need for inspiration.

The success attribution of *plan* in the buyer's *commitment path* is all about *differentiating customer value realization*. As passionate and knowledgeable we sellers can often be about our products and services, we have to control those impulses to push a *commitment message* that comes from our own pride or self-righteousness. Our Champions need us to be disciplined in our prescription of what *success attributes* will make the most impact toward *their* unique desired value realization.

Those *success attributes* will most likely come from either our *primary capabilities, credible processes, premium services, special terms,* or *internal qualities.* So ask yourself, at the conclusion of one of your customer's journeys toward implementing, adopting, and ultimately realizing value, when they look back on that time, what primary and specific components or traits of your solution or your company will they be able to attribute their success the most?

When we're deliberate in strategically positioning a *plan* for success that encompasses differentiated value-causing attributes personalized for our buyer, we've now inspired our Champion by providing them *The Big How.* They now have two out of the three key components of a *commitment message* that will stimulate their inspiration and confidence toward sponsoring us.

The Conviction of PROMISE: *Legitimizing the Big How Much*

Purpose, plan, and now, **Promise**. Why would a human being need to understand a *promise* of value they should expect in return before committing to any investment? Trust me, it's certainly not because value metrics and proof points are what builds Champions and closes deals alone. We know this from our habits of *Emotional Connection* and *Leading Vision*. But we've also learned that for any of us to become *certain* in our beliefs, we need to have come as close as possible to experiencing *results*. *The Certainty Loop*.

To review, our perspectives of *potential* drive our *actions*. Those actions create our *results*. And the experience of those results is what forms our *beliefs*. When we reach this level of belief, we're in a state of *absolute certainty*. The very reason our Champion is at this *milestone of commitment* is that connection alone, which is really just a higher level of emotional interest, won't usually be enough to inspire someone to make a formal definitive purchase commitment.

Why is that? As their emotions and intellect have traveled down this *commitment path* of *purpose* and *plan*, without the clarity, validation, and belief in the *results* that they could achieve, our Champion will fall short of the *absolute certainty* that they need to become *convicted*. When we have **Conviction** in something, we possess a firmly held belief. It's that deep level of conviction that we should be working toward as we try to inspire this buyer's *commitment path*. But conviction doesn't come from merely an understanding of purpose and a plan of attribution. The certainty of *conviction* only forms when our confidence in the results that we should experience become clear. This is why our *commitment message* has to position a reasonable, relatable, and proven *promise* of the results that our Champion should expect. When we've effectively inspired this state of commitment in a Champion, they'll have **Conviction of Promise**.

Caution. Messaging and proposing our measurable value, or what some refer to as a *return on investment*, is a habit that salespeople all too often approach recklessly and ignorantly to how their message will be perceived. This creates unproductive distraction, distrust, and is completely unnecessary. The purpose that we should have served in patiently and thoughtfully leading our buyer's *vision* was that we built trust and connection to ourselves and the unique outcomes we could deliver, supported by our relatable differentiation and value points. The majority of selling should be done. This is about commitment. Our Champion needs intellectual *inspiration*, not more selling. We should have no reason to start desperately inflating and exaggerating our expected value return. Moreover, a *promise* of value doesn't necessarily have to be a carefully analyzed and calculated value metric that now exposes us to unnecessary risk and questioning of *our* credibility.

In order to internalize this aspect of your buyer's *commitment path* in the different products or services you sell, take a moment to really think about what promise of value and return does your buyer most need and expect from what you sell. What results would make the greatest impact on inspiring them to become committed? Where have you seen these levels of commitment in the past from your customers? The *commitment path* of *promise* is about our Champion being able to visualize themselves and thus, believe the most plausible results that they should get if they commit to us. Their conviction will grow when we can get them mentally *in the moment of value*. If we believe that we've truly built a Champion, this milestone now puts us at a point where this buyer will need to be tested as to how open they are to endorse a *promise of results*.

Commitment Promise

In communicating and gaining Champion alignment to our *promise*, we're trying to get to **The Big How Much** message. To reach a level of commitment to make an actual investment, our Champion needs to know and personalize how much value and results they should expect. To prevent or eliminate any misguided habits that you or your teams might be having in setting value expectations, consider these **Four Commitment Promise Criteria** to help you simplify an approach. In our *commitment message*, when our objective is to set a buyer's expectations of future results, their **Commitment Promise** should meet four criteria: **Relatability to the Purpose, Conviction of the Seller, Legitimacy in the Claim,** and **Validation from our Champion.**

Most companies can and will claim many different *promises* of results. Salespeople also won't be shy in making them as early and as often as possible. But our buyers would tell us that we're usually hurting our credibility, often detracting from the positives of our solutions, and not doing ourselves any favors. If a Champion can't connect to our value promises, then they're just noise blowing in the wind. This can easily become a turnoff, something that lessens a buyer's attraction to us.

To ask ourselves whether a *promised result* is the right one for our buyer, we simply need to look to *The Big Why*. For the different value results that we'll consider proposing to our Champion, what is each's **Relatability to the Purpose?** As we're discerning what promise of value would matter most, we need to ask ourselves how it aligns and can impact our Champion's core *purpose* for making this committed decision to buy us. Our *Champion's* purpose, not ours. No matter what we position and propose, our buyer's choice to commit to it will all revolve around that *Big Why* behind this decision.

The second *commitment promise* criterion is **Conviction of the Seller**. Simply, if we don't believe, we can't expect our buyers to believe. *Conviction* is a fixed or firm belief. Any results that we promise must carry the tone of our certainty, confidence, and conviction. This goes back to the *Law of Attraction*, positive thoughts bringing positive results. When we desire a particular behavior and response in another person, the *Law of Attraction* tells us that we must positively project it ourselves, from our energy, words, and body language. In sales, have you ever positioned what your solution could do for your customers, and yet a part of you was aware that you didn't totally know for sure? Or could you hear in your tone of voice that you didn't sound very believable? You were either in a state of your own uncertainty or you projected that state.

But it's not just about attraction. Our conviction when we position anything, is always going to be working against a very natural, powerful, and constant force of our buyer's survival emotions. Right or wrong, their mind will subconsciously question everything. Some buyer personalities don't like to be confrontational. So, rather than tell us that they don't believe us, make a smart argumentative objection, they'll smile and nod their head. Elite sellers don't leave Champion alignment to chance.

In order to fend against a buyer's suspicious survival brain, our *conviction* needs to support the *promise*.

Perhaps the most important criterion to maintaining the credibility and trust that we've built throughout this highly connected sales engagement is positioning a *promise of value* that has **Legitimacy in the Claim.** What is a promised result that has *legitimacy*? Something legitimate is *true*. It's based on established and proven facts. The claim that we're making isn't just to inspire our Champion's commitment. The ultimate mission of building a

Champion is because we know that we're going to need someone of power, influence, and access to effectively sell on our behalf to their peers and authority figures. So when we're proposing an expected result and that claim isn't valid or defendable with supported evidence, we're not only greatly risking the trust that we've earned with our Champion, but we're exposing them to potentially burn their own political capital, *their* reputation, and credibility.

The last criterion of a *promised result* goes to that mission of a Champion taking action for us with certainty. We would hope that as strong *vision leaders*, we already got our Champions intellectually connected to some level of expected value results during our sales engagement thus far. But this is a moment to challenge our buyer's *commitment*. Elite sellers have learned the hard way through surprises and letdowns that when the stakes get higher for our Champions, we have to reaffirm their connection to our value message. If we want our Champions committed to us with their own level of conviction, we can't assume that we have alignment and agreement on the relatability and legitimacy of our value promise until we have **Validation from our Champion**.

What does getting *validation* mean in sales? *Validation* is an act that we sellers lead and facilitate. In a direct collaborative discussion between us and our Champion, we have asked, and they have confirmed that they believe our projected results are acceptable and true. In some instances, our products and services have simple expectations of results and perhaps lower risk investments. Thus, those *promises* don't elicit as much controversy. In other selling situations, the results we *promise*, in order to support our higher value premium or because the buyer's environment is so complex, may need a concerted effort to gain our Champion's affirmation and alignment. Whatever amount of effort it takes, sellers should embrace and routinely exercise the habit of *validating* that a Champion is in agreement and feels totally willing and confident to support our expected value results.

If any of these four criteria of a *value promise* are missing, we'll fall short of providing our Champion *The Big How Much* message they need. We'll leave just enough doubt in our Champion's mind that their commitment will always have some level of hesitancy and question. But, when we gain alignment on those expected results correctly, there's nothing more powerful to inspiring the certainty that comes from a buyer who has seen themselves in and has conviction behind the results that we can deliver.

COMMITMENT STRATEGY

Identifying Commitment Gaps

When considering our Champion's *commitment path* across their different commitment challenges in an opportunity, this is where we sellers will clearly be able to find our **Commitment Strategy**. Simply, when the commitment of our buyer is lacking, we should first look no further than their *commitment path* to uncover any **Commitment Gaps**. How many times have you or your sales leadership gotten needlessly frustrated with your Champions, offering unnecessary and unproductive business concessions hoping to motivate their urgency? Or worse, have you ever escalated to higher authority and alienated your Champion, only to now firmly blow up your deal and your relationship?

Elite sellers are more pragmatic and considerate as to what exactly our Champions aren't getting from us. This mindset enables us to be in a constant state of investigation, trying to determine their *commitment gaps*. The *commitment path*, as I've laid out--*purpose, plan and promise*--has proven over the test of time to be the most common three sources of our Champion's unwillingness to fully commit on our behalf. When opportunities aren't moving, decisions of consensus aren't forming, and economic authority is still not in support, our instinct to qualify *why*, must directly go to the *commitment path*. Without emotional sway or bias, we have to be intellectually honest with ourselves in identifying a Champion's **Commitment Gap**.

This investigation starts first with their alignment for what greater *purpose* for the business or themselves our solution is addressing. If their commitment to *purpose* is evident, then we ask if they lack the clarity or confidence in our solution's *plan* to enable and ensure their success. If no *commitment gaps* exist yet, then we must seek to learn their level of validation and conviction in the *promise* of results that we can offer them. On many an opportunity, it was in one of these three *commitment gaps* where we gained a precision of deal strategy that empowered us to successfully take action on the *one thing* that was preventing our Champion from getting fully committed.

Even when opportunities appear complex in nature, wrapped within a complicated multi-stakeholder buying process, the truth is, especially when we've built a highly connected Champion, that there's usually one main thing blocking our business from moving forward. However, what happens all too often is that we sellers don't curiously seek out that *one thing*. We forget that we're selling to people. We lose sight of the mission that a properly built, informed, and empowered Champion will be our most effective path to close. That only happens when our Champions have no *commitment gaps*.

Testing Champions

Trying to inspire a Champion's commitment is an extremely positive and thoughtful habit. Our intention alone, when we're intuitively focused on connecting our solution with a purpose, plan, and promise that motivates them, will often be what grows our buyer's connection to us. They begin to form a deeper level of trust in us. However, have you ever had times in your opportunities where it seemed as though something just wasn't right in your Champion's behaviors or communication? While last month, they were boldly supportive and growing in their commitments, this month they'd become more detached, guarded, less inclined to sell on your behalf.

Or have you had opportunities where your buyer remained optimistic and claimed they were still in your corner, but you just weren't seeing any activity or movement? It's in these times, and especially during this G*o/No-go milestone of commitment,* where Elite Sellers consider a highly effective but delicate strategy. It's a tactical choice that Champion-based sellers have made for a long time called **Testing a Champion**.

When it comes to the commitment we need from our Champions, we don't always know if a *commitment gap* exists, or if we just don't have a Champion. Either because we've been witnessing a negative or neutral change in their behavior or because our opportunity's been trending toward a dormant state, this strategy is one that should be considered. What does it mean to "test" a Champion? In a sales opportunity, we ultimately define a Champion by their willingness to sell for us when we're not there. That's not something we observe. We're physically not there. So, we look for signs that we have a Champion. Are they getting us wider in the account? Elevating our access to higher executive and economic authority? Do they show willingness to change the decision criteria or process to better align to our differentiation and path to selection? Have they shared information with us that they haven't with our competition? It's in these buyer behaviors where we find our evidence that we in fact, have a true Champion. We believe it because they're proven.

Thus, as these are examples of what we mean when we say, a Champion has a *bias for action*, they're also some of the same ways in which we may *test* our Champion to gain some evidence during these less confident times in our opportunities. *Testing a Champion* means that we provide a challenge to them, typically in the form of a strategic ask or request. If they agree and follow through, then we've gained some recent proof that they are a Champion. What this tells us is that there may be some other reasons or potential problems forming that are affecting the movement of our deal. It could also mean that we're just in a season for this opportunity where it may be best for us to stand down, give our Champion a bit of space and grace. There may be some valid obstacles or priorities that our Champion needs to focus on.

So, how do we know if they don't pass the test? Well simply, they may just refuse to take action on our request. If so, our immediate response must be to ask them why. We deserve a reason. Then, by selling with a heart of empathy and patience, we should pay attention to what we hear. Their explanation could make total sense and even provide a bit of enlightenment on the qualification or upcoming challenges of winning this business. It may not necessarily mean that they're not our Champion. However, if their response is dismissive, obstinate, or even adversarial, they may have just failed their Champion test.

When we test them, always be direct, confident, and professional. Sometimes we'll be asking them to do something that feels a bit uncomfortable for them. So, my advice is to project how you want to be treated. Those sellers who sound like a subordinate will be treated like a subordinate. Leaders don't typically respond well to uncomfortable requests from their subordinates. But, if you want to be perceived as a peer, project yourself as a peer. From one professional leader to another, let them know what we'd like from them, the reason we're asking, and then offer any help they may need.

Why is it so important to begin testing a Champion during *this commitment milestone*? Well, if we truly believe that a buyer is at this all-important milestone in their decision process, the entire purpose of this *commitment milestone* is for them to choose whether to push us toward a close. Our buyer has gotten fully educated on our solution and all other options they have to solve their problems and reach their desired outcomes. The question is, are they committed to doing something about it, most importantly, committed to us? If we can find out soon enough that we don't have a Champion in an opportunity, then we can change our strategy, identify new targets, and get to work on them. If we wait too long, we either don't get commitment from a Champion at this stage, or they move us and all our competitors into a much higher risk *milestone of closing* business. Have you ever been in a closing stage of a deal all alone, in the dark, fighting for your survival with a blindfold on? That's not a place that any of us want to be. An elite *Champion-based seller* won't allow themselves to get to that state. *No Champion, No Deal.* So, this becomes our consideration for whether we choose to test our Champion.

While some tests can be subtle and pose little concern for us, testing a Champion can be dangerous. Growing up in a *hard knocks* school of sales, we were always reminded, "Never test a Champion too early and never expose your Champion." Why could *testing a Champion too early* be risky for a seller? First, we should always ensure that we've properly identified that this buyer is a viable Champion target. We may think they meet the profile, but it often takes some time to learn if someone truly has power and influence, access to economic authority. Then, we needed to have put the work in to actually build them. We've started to form connections. They've responded well to a unique *vision* that we've led with appreciation for our differentiation to get them there. In other words, we only test a Champion when we believe that we do have a Champion. We're just not certain. Testing a Champion *too early*, before their initial steps have played out, might send the message that we're not aligned or respectful of their process. Who wants to Champion someone who's misaligned and appears dismissive of the expectations they've laid out? Plus, there's a reason they call it *early-stage* in a buying process. There's just a lot of work that still has to get done in those initial steps of discovery and evaluation.

So, what does it mean to *expose* a Champion? We're there to have their back if we expect them to have ours. If we choose to do anything in a test of a Champion that alienates them, makes them look like they're not doing their job, or exposes any weakness or risk that they have in accomplishing their mission, especially to their management and peers, then we've just blown up any trust that we had. We could have now moved our buyer from Champion to *enemy*. So, in our craft of *Testing Champions*, and yes, we should be using this strategy in honing our Champion-sell craft, our success will be in the caution, thoughtfulness, and collaboration with others in discerning if and how we gain the evidence that we need. At this *Go/No-go milestone of commitment*, we must know if we have a Champion and if they are committed.

As you probably have already realized, while the *commitment path* sounds simple, there are so many dimensions of *purpose*, *plan, and promise* that could exist in the scope and scale of the business that our Champions try to achieve. In the effort to simplify the perceived intricacies of sales, those people who we're asking to sell on our behalf will feel confidently prepared to do so when they are void of any *commitment gaps*. Again, for a seller to lead with this level of investigation and problem-solving, we have to work in a mindset of *business empathy*, especially if we choose to *test* our Champions. If our deals are slowing and the path to move forward with any acceptable degree of urgency is unclear, then we should look no further than the *commitment path* of our Champions and any other key influencers in the buying process. This is where an unbiased level of intellectual curiosity can easily identify our buyer's *commitment gaps* across *purpose, plan, and promise.*

SUMMARY: *Inspiring Commitment*

How many times have you or your teams been in the heart of a sales engagement, still in a state of your own uncertainty if your supposed or intended Champion was fully committed to getting a deal done with you? The movement of a deal is a dangerous force to surrender to. In Newton's Laws of Motion, he makes it pretty clear that when the body is at rest, it will remain at rest. When we sellers ignore and choose not to act on the opportunistic and decisive *Milestone of Commitment,* we take a great risk that our Champion and our deal will remain at rest. It won't go anywhere. Elite sellers don't hope for deal movement.

Newton also tells us that if we apply a force to the body, then we will accelerate its momentum. This is the impact of our routinely and strategically discussing and aligning with our Champion on their *commitment message*. It's just like the *forcing function* of a compelling *purpose* behind what our solution can do for them. This is where we *test* our Champions. Even if the effort of this strategy exposes the fact that our buyer is not a committed Champion, then at least we've learned of our opportunity truth early enough. We've prevented ourselves from once again being at the end of a long sales engagement, uncertain of where we stand, likely to never close the business.

If we complacently assume that our Champion will drive this momentum without any involvement or effort from us, we're taking a fairly big gamble. Deal momentum can go any direction at any time. Any type of *competing* force on our Champion before they've made their mental commitment to sponsor us can create an adverse momentum that we won't like too much. Having a Champion who hasn't been inspired to a *state of commitment* is like owning a bank full of millions of dollars, but with the safe left wide open and exposed, absent of any protective armor to defend against the forces of a criminal coming to take what is ours.

In most sales opportunities, we'll be facing competitive threats, internal uncommitted and adversarial stakeholders, or even our Champion's own fears and survival impulses. They will all be forces working to change the momentum of our deal. In other words, whether we do anything or not, the deal's always going to *pivot*, change course and speed. An old manager of mine used to tell me, "All good deals will die three deaths." After two decades, I can't count how many times that's rang true. I call it *The Sales Pivot Principle*. Forces will always exist, both internal and external, to change the momentum and direction of a deal. For our own protection, we sellers need a *Committed Champion*.

By leading a highly convicted and Champion-aligned belief in a *commitment message* that inspires their motivations, we protect the connections we've built and ensure the loyalty and obligation that we've earned. We do so with a highly intuitive awareness of a mental *Commitment Path* which our Buyer Champions will need to traverse the *Purpose, Plan,* and *Promise* of making this commitment. When our deals aren't moving with the momentum or direction that we desire, our strategy must first look to these *buyer commitment paths* in order to identify our buyer's *Commitment Gaps.*

Then, in order to inspire that commitment where our Champions need it most, we partner with an awareness of the different types of commitments that they'll have to face, from commitments of *risk* to *advocacy, economic authority,* and *urgency.* Qualifying our Champion's level of *urgency* will come from uncovering the balance of *fear and desire* that exists in their perspective around our purchase. Here is where we seek to learn their *Urgency Threshold.*

Inspiring Commitment is an E.L.I.T.E. habit because every human buyer, every Champion we build, will eventually arrive at an inflection point. This will be where they must make a decision whether their interest and connection are meaningful enough for them to commit to the unique vision and value that we know we can provide. This decisive milestone in a buyer's decision process and the reaffirming information and assurance they need from us, are the motivations for why Elite Sellers will always prioritize and intentionally work toward *inspiring our Champion's commitment.*

CHAPTER 7

TRUST BUILDING

The Power of Trust

HEAVY METAL LESSON

Tom held the very utilitarian role as head of IT infrastructure for a ninety-one-year-old global steel and metal manufacturer. Tom was the kind of Champion customer whom I could always call on to be direct in asking if he had any growth needs, and in turn, he always knew he could come to me for any special needs like a pricing or commercial consideration, even a career reference. This was a buyer/seller relationship grounded in trust.

Yet, two years earlier? Pretty rocky start, because of me. When I started selling to Tom, I was at a place in my life where my finances and my career were still a bit "underdeveloped." They were not only my top priorities, understandably, they also ruled my mindset. The first several times that I had met Tom and his team were impressions that I would embarrassingly regret and eventually need to overcome.

After one brief introductory meet with Tom, I was set to meet with his entire team. I ensured that the meeting kicked off with no wasted time or unnecessary questions. I'd already learned all that I needed in my visit with their boss Tom several days earlier. I got there early and set up quick. Asking no questions, assuming I already knew what the team needed and cared about, I made my pitch and landed the plane as smooth as a top navy pilot. I was proud of that software I sold, and I acted like it. After talking with Tom, it was clear to me that they had all of the same priorities as my one other customer. Thus, I assumed the team probably wanted to spend more time on my core differentiators and how they could solve all their problems.

A bit of detail I should share. Tom's company was in global manufacturing and my one customer was a domestic clothing retailer. So, I probably could have used a bit more thoughtfulness and . . . some basic common sense. But at the time, I thought the meeting went great. I was really getting good at my spiel, if I had to say so myself. The next day revealed a different reality.

After a professional but direct phone call to my manager, Tom made two things clear. One, his team didn't like me very much. Two, he said that if we wanted to earn their business, our company better step up its game. His message was illuminating and uncomfortable. That was all the wake-up call that I needed.

I called Tom the next day, fell on my sword, and asked him to tell me directly what he needed from me that he wasn't getting.

"Empathy!" he barked. "Just stop being a jackass!"

He said, "With me, you were smart, respectful, and shared interesting information. With my team, not so much."

I'd never even heard the term "empathy" before. But, as he explained, there was no technology product that solves all problems for all people, and certainly not in the same way. So, he walked me through how his favorite sales rep with another tech company treated him, how he always tried to understand what his team was experiencing at the closest level he possibly could. He never proposed anything until he could really see the specific unique value for them. His words were always carefully chosen, and he never assumed he had any credibility with new people he'd meet. Over time, he said, this rep had figuratively moved from the sales side of the table to being one of them. He realized that no salesperson who had never done the IT job could ever fully comprehend the work. But Tom shared that often times, his rep would know their business better than some on his team. Why? Because he made it a priority for himself. He had taken the time to build *trust.*

With a sincere commitment to change my mindset and approach, Tom and his team allowed me back in the opportunity, on a very short leash no less. The only reason they let us continue to compete for their business was that our product had a really impressive reputation. They believed it was the only technology proven enough to help address their complex needs. Everything in my behavior changed from that point on, due to my painful attitude adjustment. Earned from months of reaffirming my integrity, rebuilding our credibility, and delivering the evidence they needed to see that our product and I had the competencies to help them survive their tough situations, I began to earn my own seat at their side of the table.

TRUST BUILDING: *The Closure Milestone*

So, we sell to people, huh? That's kind of a scary realization when you think about it. After all, the greatest conflicts of our world between tribes, nations, and reality TV stars have always been rooted in the judgements, differing ideologies, and rivalries between *people*. Recognizing that our sales livelihoods and future wealth is dependent on the high-risk stakes of doing business between strangers wouldn't elicit a ton of overconfidence in most of us. I understand that most sellers don't ever pause to think about this. If they did, I probably wouldn't even need to write this book. You ever heard the term, *ignorance is bliss*? Well, based on the devolving relationships between buyers and sellers that I've witnessed over time, ignorance isn't bliss. It just simply hides the truth in our business. Just how proficient are we in building *trust* with our buyers?

Just like the concept that lacking a real commitment from a Buyer Champion will usually come down to one thing across their *commitment path*, our inability to even attract those initial connections and move a deal to a state of closure will always come down to one thing more than any other in the business of selling to people. **Trust.** I'll talk about how *trust* starts building in our earliest of interactions and how it powerfully comes back into subconscious light as a Champion moves to their final buying stages.

I emphasize this fourth E.L.I.T.E. selling habit of **Trust Building** because before we're ready to *empower* a Champion to actually close an agreement between our two companies, we have to ensure that there are no **Trust Gaps** within our buyers and those who they share these decisions with. Remember, the human brain is dominated by its emotions. While there is no emotion more prevalent than *fear,* there is none more powerful than *trust.* What I learned the hard way, through years of confusion and frustration as to why we couldn't get certain Champions over the line, is that we had trust gaps that those Champions just couldn't overcome. *A buyer always starts a deal and finishes a deal with a need to feel trust.* I'll discuss the beginning of those revelations in a bit more detail as to how our path to *trust* begins and evolves. That should be fairly enlightening to some toward a level of self-awareness, and possibly validating to others that you're approaching the people you sell to in the right ways.

We say that we want to build Champions. Well, how does that relationship even begin evolving to that point? If *emotional connection* is the initial fire that drives a buyer toward becoming a Champion, *trust* is the starter fluid for that connection. Just think about the specific needs that both we and a Champion would have. We need them to give us the time to earn and build a connection. They need to relate to our message. We need to meet all decision-makers involved. They need us to listen, focus on value, and have their back. We need them to support our proposal and negotiation. They need to trust that they'll achieve the return they expect from our investment.

So, when you think about it, every need that either we or our Champions have all come down to *trust.* In this grinding battle we call *sales*, when we aren't aware that we don't have a buyer's trust, it can be that silent shot that comes out of nowhere, eliminating any chance we have of winning their business.

For Elite Sellers, building trust becomes intentional. This is where *trust building* becomes a *habit.* We need to humbly respect it, focus on it, and reinforce it from the initial moment of our first impressions throughout every ongoing interaction we lead in the buyer journey.

There's a reason that I'm choosing now to discuss this powerful habit of *Trust Building.* While *emotional* and *intellectual connections* have been made to what we sell, buyer *vision* has formed from us leading them toward positive future outcomes that we can enable, and a *commitment* to purchase and advocate for us has been *inspired,* the reality is that the emotions of our

Champions and other key influencers are about to resurrect in full force at the upcoming formal stages of purchase.

As a progression from very personal milestones of *connection* and *commitment*, we'll call this far more public stage in the buying journey, the **Closure Milestone**. As with the generic term *purchase* that I'll use, for simplicity, consider whatever method or structure that your unique sell takes on to execute a business agreement between both companies, to be a *milestone of* **Closure**. If a medical treatment has been prescribed or delivered, consider that to be your *closure.* If a purchase order has been executed or a services agreement has been signed, consider that your *closure.* Reaching the *closure milestone* is that point when the deal turns from a committed decision to move forward to starting a process toward closure. For some types of sales, that process is a simple few steps. In others, this can be one of the longest and most intense stages of a sale.

As I'll share in detail, when the gravity of the closing stage arrives, there is no more powerful force on the outcome of that milestone than the buyer's absolute and subconscious need for *trust.* In our fifth and final E.L.I.T.E. habit of *Empowering Champions*, we'll get into some tactical and strategic detail for how our Champions need to be *empowered* to execute those purchases, how to get the win we want in a predictable way, and on time. But we've got to get there first.

Consider your business over the years and the journeys you experienced to build and win with your Buyer Champions. From those initial meetings and all the efforts that followed to build strong Champions, how often did you feel that there was a huge mental wedge in those buyers between their mindset and either you or the solution you were trying to sell? In the opportunities where you were beginning that final stage of closure, think of the many times when that *emotional claw* resurfaced from the back of your buyer's mind, aggressively questioning its own intellectual justification, and halted any attempt to finalize those agreements.

Whether it was your Champion, another stakeholder, or some neutral sourcing agent, those emotions were always centered around the most important emotion in business, *trust.* While some may struggle to earn trust from the onset of our buyer engagements, it's in these later stage micro-selling situations where the needs for evidence, reminders, and unwavering confirmation of *trust* constantly appear. During a *milestone of closure*, the average seller rarely picks up on the fact that their buyer isn't looking to just satisfy a process or make a check in a box. They need to feel trust in *what* and *who* they're buying from. There's no time where that concern grows more than at this final and formal series of decisions.

Trust is what resisted your initial value claims. *Trust* is what stalled your deal at the end when all signs showed that it was coming in. *Trust* is what made your buyer ask for one more test, just one additional reference. And it was *trust* that caused different buyers in your consensus group to reopen the process, reconsider alternative solutions, and re-evaluate a few areas needing further clarity.

The weight of this official decision to make a purchase is what elevates *trust* to the top of the buyer's mind, **always, for everyone!** Their natural human need to reaffirm their trust in what we sell, our company, and even us as their business partner, is unavoidable. From the very initial moments of introduction and on through their *milestone of closure*, this selling habit that we need to prioritize and master is due to the *power of trust.*

As I've shared in multiple examples, the more we tend to learn and build confidence in this profession of sales, from how we sell to how buyers come to their decisions, experience teaches us that there's always more to the equation of winning business than we think. Don't ever let anybody try to convince you that sales is easy. Even in my leadership journey when I started making *Champion Building* the primary emphasis of our sales strategy, those buyers and their dynamic emotions would continue to challenge our pursuit of sales excellence. Where resolution would come for me was when we refocused our response to all the requested activities, questions, and negotiations into a conscious realization that our buyers were simply reaching out in need for *trust*.

You see, much like in the degree of difference between *connection* versus *commitment*, when there's progressively less on the line for the buyer, their *Thrive* emotions and logically *Thinking* intellect are more available to find reasons to overcome their fears and feel a commitment to buying. However, at the *milestone of closure*, our buyer is at their all-conclusive moment for making this decision. They have infinitely more on the line now.

If they choose to move forward and then resulting problems occur, if value fails to be realized, they will be accountable publicly. If they decide to pass or defer the decision and their current problems amplify, the microscope will be on them once again, but this time with far more intensity. At this buying milestone, much is on the line for our Champion, and it's rarely an easy decision. But, as we'll soon discuss, here lies our opportunity, through the *power of trust*.

THE 3 TRUTHS OF TRUST

So, to gain a deeper understanding of this *power of trust*, contemplate these **3 Truths of Trust**. You'll know each of these to be true, as they have most likely affected your business at some point. For each one, try to apply them to your unique sales situations.

Trust is a Force

As a sales opportunity progresses, the first *truth* we face with this powerful emotion of *trust* is that **Trust is a Force**. In physics, *force* is a push or pull upon an object resulting from its interaction with another object. When the interaction is weaker, the *force* is less. When the interaction strengthens, the *force* increases.

So, think about the *physics of sales* and how it changes depending on the scope and scale of your buying opportunity for them. Is an exceptionally high investment on the line? Are they risking the security of their business? Could a human's personal life be impacted? Are they earlier or later in their buying process? Is this an organizationally high scrutiny decision? Putting yourself in the buyer's shoes, think about how that context would impact and challenge their willingness to *trust* others.

Consider all these potential *forces* that could work against a buyer's level of trust as *emotional tensions*. Earlier on, specifically for the buyer, they feel more control. It's their decision to meet with us, what information they share, and how much time and energy they spend. In their minds, the interactions they're having with us and perhaps their buying peers are passive and weaker in force. As they progress through their buying milestones, from an initial stage of *connection* to one of *commitment,* and now their *milestone of closure,* the *contact forces* of the buying opportunity progressively increase.

Think about *force* as a cause and effect. While we sellers are usually aware of what we're doing or asking, we're often oblivious to the effect those actions have on our buyer's trust levels, especially our Champions. How many times have you built a Champion and then got a bit complacent in concerning yourself with their needs and questions? The presence of these causes and effects make that too risky an approach.

There's the cause and effect of **Doubt**. When a purchase requires a large total investment, especially if it's greater than our Champion had initially planned, there's a forceful reaction of *doubt* that begins questioning whether this potential gain is truly worth the absolute cost. Will it truly do what it says it will? Have your Champions ever waivered with *doubts* in your value?

There's the force of **Stress**. If our Champion is being asked to carry a much heavier load in the job, feeling stretched, or if the pressure of the buying process is growing, they can be experiencing a force of *stressful tension* that starts to question if there's even a viable solution to their problem. They'll also allow *stress* to challenge the process itself and their own abilities to get the deal closed. Do you think your Champions ever experienced *stress* in leading all the proper steps, evaluations, and meeting the timelines asked of them?

A force that can then result is **Friction**. When multiple buyers in a group of *consensus* who hold different roles in the process start experiencing *friction* across their different agendas and conflicting priorities, our Champions are now battling interactions where each stakeholder is questioning if they can even *trust* each other. Further, any *friction-filled* resistance that they may receive from us sellers, their clients, or internal authorities, only elevates the *force of trust* that their decisions will be the right ones.

The buying milestones where more is on the line for our buyer is where we most witness the *physics of sales*, force on force affecting energy of the deal. When we sellers can identify the varying types and levels of *force* that our solutions, actions, and those of the buying process are placing on our Champions, we can be more responsive in our strategies toward building as much trust with and within our buyers as possible.

Consider where your buyers might have experienced these emotional tensions. Has a validation event, whether a technical proof of concept or reference call, exposed some concerns with your solution? Has a controversy between internal decision-makers in a buying consensus ever slowed your deal down? Has the way that you and your sales team approached and navigated your buyer's frustrating process ever created tensions of trust? Procurement and sourcing agents are professionally trained to fabricate and dramatize concerns of trust. Have you ever been on that receiving end? The likelihood for doubt, stress, and friction existing in a purchase decision grows milestone to milestone. At each stage, more becomes on the line for all parties.

Yet, how often do we sellers think about that journey from the perspective of our buyer's experiences and emotions? Do our overly challenging sales habits and behaviors routinely agitate a buyer's tensions and trust concerns? Anyone with real experience in consistently selling to and winning with Buyer Champions has learned that human beings need to overcome this powerful *force of trust.* In your type of sell and the situations that your buyers encounter at their *closure milestone*, consider these questions: *What are the most common sources of doubt, stress, or friction that they face? What are the interactions and choices that make their moments of buying more intensified, more complicated? What forces would make their path to trusting get harder?*

A stronger interaction causes a stronger force. *Trust* has enormous *force.* This is seen in the fact that it can be lost so quickly. This could stem from other people's opinions and doubts, company rumors, technical validation issues, challenges in the processes involved, or the sales team, even in the buyer themselves. No buying force, from fear to rational thought, can impact the direction and speed of any part of a buying process more than *trust*. Because when *trust* is in doubt, it impairs any level of certainty or commitment that our buyer had otherwise formed.

Trust Always Has a Tax

The second *truth of trust*, is that **Trust Always Has a Tax**. A **Trust Tax** is when we sellers not only have to conquer the new forces of trust that build in the moment of our sales engagement, but also overcome negative experiences and often unfair buyer perspectives that linger from their past. A *trust tax* is a type of *historical bias*, when some experience in our past greatly influences our current perspective. A *bias* is often a very partial and unbalanced view with a refusal to consider any alternative ones. While your sales approach may be a joy to experience, some before you, *not so much*.

Unlike your company's pristine level of integrity, not all parties in business are always looking out for each other. Certainly not with your amazing product or service, but many promises of solution value and competency aren't as credible as they're made to be. Simply, not all expectations between buyers and sellers were met and not all commitments were upheld before you showed up. Thus, it's not uncommon that in order to build trust with a buyer, we'll need to face a *trust tax* to pay for all those past sins.

In a buyer/seller relationship and across a buying engagement, there are many situational triggers that take a buyer's subconscious memory back to a negative experience they've had with a person or a thing, even in someone who we'd consider a Champion. The truth that I speak of in the *power of trust* is that all sellers will be confronted with having to pay a *trust tax* at some point. A *trust tax* might exist with the *type of solution* that we sell. Ask yourself, is there anything about your product or service that may have delivered a negative experience with your buyer? In technology, biases form around how much we let algorithms and other automations make decisions for us. In medicine, a tax can be formed in certain types of treatments. A buyer may have experienced that their risk wasn't worth the likelihood of a patient being healed.

Tax biases could be much simpler. They could be cultural or just related to the name of the company on your business card. If these biases exist, we sellers will need to identify those threats to our trust and respect the force that they can bring. We'll need a message and potentially, a sales game plan to own that trust objection proactively.

Any time we're getting resistance that doesn't make a lot of sense on the surface, we should be diagnosing whether we're dealing with a *trust tax*. A resistance could come from an **Experience Tax**. Has this buyer had any previous experience with you, your business, or perhaps your competition that could have formed a negative bias? Too many times, I've witnessed sellers who knew that there was a rough historical experience with their solution, and still they chose to ignore it, wish it away. Not only is this a futile strategy, but it's an even greater accelerant of losing trust. The buyer knows that you're aware of an issue and yet, you just move along like it doesn't exist? They immediately begin to question your integrity and overall concern for them.

We could also face a **Results Tax**. While our buyer may fully believe and have even validated their alignment to our proposed value, that *closure milestone* they're in plays funny tricks on a buyer's emotions. If our Champion has tried and failed to achieve the specific *results* that we're proposing with alternative solutions, even if they've connected to our better and stronger value proposition, they may have a bias in the *results* themselves. Their peers and other stakeholders in *the consensus* certainly may. Have you ever been told something like, "While I'm on board with your approach, I'm not a big believer that there's ever a real cost savings to be had." Or perhaps, "I believe your solution could give us the results that you're proposing, but I'm not convinced that the rest of our business won't suffer in order to achieve them."

Results in business are complicated. There are many factors that can go into achieving them. In any situation, when we fear that we might be paying an unfair tax, we need to break down the buyer's reasoning for their disbelief. Respect it and analyze it for what it is. Is it coming from a negative historical experience, or is it supported by a very rational concern? When we intellectually uncover whether they're making a logical argument that we need to address or if we're just paying an *emotional tax* from the past, we can begin our road to properly recovering and reinforcing their trust.

Trust is Disguised

This third *truth of trust* is in reference to its mystery. The truth is that **Trust is Disguised**. It has a hidden pretext in the situations, objections, and misalignments that we encounter. A *pretext* is when we humans put something forward to conceal our true purpose. The emotional energy, signal, or even the literal words that our buyer puts out are often misleading to their actual intent. During any of your opportunities at a closure milestone, have you ever had a buyer make a distrusting request that seemed out of sorts, a bit disconnected to what they had communicated were their biggest issues? Has a Champion made surprising or even contentious statements about you or what you were proposing? Have they ever told you a process would happen one way, but it seemed as though it was drifting into a completely different direction?

One of two things was probably happening. One, a completely different stakeholder in the decision process communicated their own distrust and uncertainty. Your Champion was most likely only representing their interests as a part of their job, serving as an internal buying advocate. Or two, your Champion's communications and actions were just a bit misguided at addressing the actual areas they were struggling with. As I've mentioned, not all Champions are the best or most experienced buyers. It's rarely their *day job*. Sometimes, while they know the question they're trying to ask, they don't always recommend or request the best path to get to the answer. In other instances, they challenge us sellers to read their minds. And of course, there are those situations where they just don't want to tell us the truth. In any case, the potentially time-consuming and stressful requests for information, demands of additional steps in process, or problematic challenges and asks of concession are often disguises to an area of trust that remains a gap in a buyer's mind.

Far more common is that we sellers allow ourselves to get comfortable with the one Champion who we're working with, and we lose sight of the fact that there are usually other people in the buying consensus. Never forget that just because our Champion has been identified to have power and influence in an organization, that doesn't necessarily mean that they have *all* the power and influence. They could be using their power to protect or represent another stakeholder's trust concerns. An experienced Champion may also intentionally build a disguise in order to prevent us sellers from going around them. Yet in truth, there could be a serious underlying *trust gap* present in that disguise.

So, what do we do when we believe there may be a trust issue that we haven't uncovered yet? This is one of the most critical reasons to have a Champion. We must be direct in our communication. If they're truly our Champion, we should expect them to help us help them. Confronting our Champion with a simple and fair question of *where there may be any trust concerns present in them or others* is the quickest and most productive path to resolution.

I've often coached buyers to just directly tell me what they lack trust in. "Just give me the answer that you're trying to get to, and I can help you find it out. Hey, you've got me curious too." If we've seen a very strange change in the buying process, we might just ask directly, "Hey, buyer. Is the reason that the process is slowing down because either you or someone on your team is struggling to trust something about this decision? I'm totally open to hearing anything out and respect your concerns. But just shoot me straight." When we get these questionable buyer responses, this can work well toward establishing a shared mindset of partnering and problem-solving. Just don't be fooled by the *disguise of trust.*

RESTORING TRUST: *Refiling the Trust Gaps*

THE DENVER BLUES

Kimberly had been a consistent Top 10 percent performer in her territory, representing a newcomer surgical device for an innovative medical procedure in the orthopedic space. While the

Midwest territory she'd built from the procedure's launch was tops in the nation, Kimberly was recently asked to take on an additional territory in the Denver, Colorado area. Colorado was an orthopedics' dream with all the year-round outdoor sports and activities that can be extremely hard on bones and joints, from skiing to mountain biking and hiking. Denver is the biggest and most populated city, so the fact that this was one of the lowest performing regions in the country was frustrating for the business. They were confident that if anyone could turn it around, it would be Kimberly.

When she first got into the territory, she had assumed that most docs probably hadn't heard of her device or weren't considering a specialty in this newer procedure yet. She had observed that the previous rep didn't have the strongest worth ethic, so she was convinced that this would be a project to work on from the ground up. As it turned out, nearly every physician she met with had not only heard of her device, but several had also started performing these procedures years ago. She learned that this had become a fairly standard region for the acceptance and adoption of the procedure. So, why no device sales?

There were two other device options on the market that had been around for a while, but neither had the performance numbers to come even close to Kimberly's product. What was most shocking to Kimberly was that the majority of these doctors had met her predecessor and remembered her as a nice enough salesperson, always brought treats to the office, and talked about family. Yet, what became the most startling and obvious gap in this territory's performance was *trust*. From office to office, themes had developed like, the patients didn't experience any improvement in early attempts. The surgeries involved too much of a complicated learning curve. Recovery saw far more issues than they cared to deal with. While Kimberly knew that there were some risk factors involved, the data behind patient improvement was an overwhelming factor in her Midwest territory. Sure, there was the occasional surgery or physical therapy challenge, but her region was number one in America. Many of the physician speakers who would talk about the device at patient and orthopedic programs across the country were from her business. So, nothing could make sense why this trust gap existed.

One week, Kimberly scheduled three different meetings where the agenda was not about selling. Each doctor had agreed to share their perspectives on what their issues were. In all those discussions, Kimberly avoided any defensiveness, listened intently, but also wasn't about to accept any excuses. She believed in her product because she had seen it transform people's lives. She was determined to get to the bottom of the broad disconnect.

Her first goal was to uncover the root causes of this distrust. In the case of every doctor, each fell into at least one of three reasons for why this treatment wouldn't work. In her territory, Kimberly had learned to share three success factors with every physician. First, *patient selection.* This device wasn't for every patient, and it was specifically designed to perform in people who met targeted criteria. Two, *procedure support.* For every orthopedic who would prescribe this approach, they would need to partner with a procedural specialist who was bought in and trained, completely prepared from the staff to the insurance, and delivery processes. This was usually the salesperson's job. And third, *expectation setting.* Because this case type had a very advanced profile, this wasn't a patient where you would expect them to be able to do all the same activities as they did before their diagnosis. But, for what it did in the right patient population, there were thousands of people in Denver and surrounding areas who could benefit greatly.

Once she helped her doctors understand the success factor misalignments, Kimberly got two of those docs to agree on a plan where they would give her and her device another chance. Criteria were discussed and expectations were set. More importantly, without being insensitive to their past experiences or the responsibilities to their business, she was able to connect those doctors to the potential life rewards for the right patients. They all committed that if she and her company would establish the procedural support, training, and hands-on assistance needed for the first two patients, they would offer her the opportunity to become their standard if successful.

When we learn that a buyer lacks trust in any way, we need to confidently believe in our ability to deliver value. We can't lose sight of our solution's proven greater purpose. Yet, with a genuinely curious and intentional mindset, we can **Restore Buyer Trust.** *Restoration* isn't just doing random acts of work. There are specific components of a house that make it strong and desired. We simply need to find out where the cracks in the foundation are, which parts are weak, so we can restore this house and get back to selling.

In the effort to *restore a buyer's trust*, if we remove our own emotions, personal agendas, and focus on a factual investigation of our trust gaps, our communication and visible impactful work can be the repeatable path to restoring trust. To simplify how to be consistently effective at *trust restoration*, here's some basic guidance of a process we should always follow.

In the most disciplined Champion-based sell where our mission is accomplished by building a Buyer Champion, we should realize that there are almost always multiple people involved in the most business-critical buying decisions. These people tend to come out of the woodworks in our buyer's *milestone of closure*.

It's from these stakeholders, either early in our engagements or in these late-stage surprise introductions, where we often find the *trust gaps* and taxes that pose a risk to our sell.

The best mindset to have here is to realize that any *trust conflict* that we encounter in a sales engagement can be an immense *opportunity* for us, as long as we're honest and accepting of the need to *restore trust* with these individual people. Have you ever walked into a sales opportunity, fiercely positive and prepared to win over the buyer, only to be greeted with a list of what are essentially the reasons that they'll never do business with you? How did you or your team react? The average seller will respond with either defensiveness or more likely, a rush to blindly continue the fight to overcome their concerns until they win their business. These responses end up feeling more like desperation or stubbornness, and they often have the same results.

Elite Sellers however, seek to learn the intention behind the position. The buyer's position may be, *We don't trust you and there's no way we'll do business with you.* But the question is what's behind it, the buyer's intention? Is there a hurt that can be healed?

Believe it or not, when there's real value to be had in business, people are more willing to participate in some healing than you think. What's usually resulted here is a *breach of trust*, a violation of some expectation that was promised. A person's faith was burned. These shouldn't be viewed as annoying complaints to be minimized or valid reasons that they'll never do business with us. Great sellers just see these as **Trust Gaps** that are often fair and well-earned by previous teams and their performances. When we're faced with paying the tax of a *trust breach*, our path to restoring that trust will come through an empathetic focus on the *trust gaps* that caused the breach, and less on the breach itself.

This is where we see our *opportunity to restore their trust*. A lack of trust is such a personal and strong state of mind. The resentment we initially get may feel insurmountable. The sentiment and maybe even anger behind the distrust may be intimidating. Just remember, trust is more emotional than it is rational. How many people have you trusted in your life that you shouldn't have? What does this emotional state say about us? It means that just as easily as negative emotions can be inflamed, positive ones can develop as well.

As we learn about restoring buyer trust, let's get the right mindset. Through some patience, curiosity, and creative thinking, we can fill that *trust bucket* back up. In fact, the greatest opportunity here is that because we have the buyer's attention and we're starting at such a negative baseline, it's often the most basic and thoughtful actions that can turn those negative emotions around. Those low-trust buyers can become our most inspired and motivated Champions if we've worked to *restore their trust*. In this opportunity, we can become the emotional *hero*. In any sales engagement, all human buyers desire *trust* more than any other trait or intellectual understanding, because trust is personal. It's something that our buyer emotionally needs and subconsciously recognizes immediately when they don't have it.

To begin coping with any *trust gap*, we will first need *Self-Awareness* of any potentially problematic *trust forces* that exist in our sell. These could be related to buyer perspectives of salespeople or management, failed agreements, solution issues, or any relevant cause of distrust. In the least, we should then decide how we feel about those trust forces. Think of any time that you've felt burned or let down by someone. If you didn't immediately get a recognition of the issue you had, rather than disarming you, it actually made it worse for you.

When we choose to dive into the *trust restoration abyss*, we better get ready to disarm those buyers as our first objective. We need to get prepared. What is our position? Do we have a counter position, a priority, or mandate from our leadership to defend ourselves? My first sales mentor once gave me some good advice here. "Be careful to never be righteously wrong." Unless there's just some strong legal or business justification to defend ourselves, I'd guide most sellers to focus on the mission. Are we here to be right or to restore buyer trust and turn this conflict into revenue? Either way, it's time to calmly begin putting the plan together.

Some *trust gap* situations could be handled best with a *wait and see* approach. In these cases, although we know that an aspect of our sell may have a negative *trust bias*, we may think it's best to *wait and see* if our buyer shares or wants to act on that negative perspective. However, we should always be cautious that we're not avoiding the inevitable confrontation or surprise roadblock. Time is rarely our friend when it comes to trust. The more mature that a low-trust state of mind is allowed to grow, the more strengthened its force and harder it is to overcome. Here's where our awareness and acceptance of human nature really comes in. Once a person has developed a *trust gap*, the likelihood that we'll be able to say something charming or intelligent to convince them to just *let it go* and move on is very unlikely. Yet, never doubt the purpose and power of having a Buyer Champion. We just need to know how to support them as their buying peers are struggling with *trust issues*.

To simplify how to be consistently effective at *trust restoration*, here's some basic guidance of a process we should always follow.

The 4 Steps to Trust Restoration

Restoring Trust is a simple four-step process, where all four actions need to be done with devoted attention to our buyer, and ideally in order.

1. *Identify the Trust Gap Root Cause*

With a mindset of genuine curiosity and delivered in a sincere tone, directly ask the low-trust buyer and any other related parties just what specific trust has been lost. What expectations weren't met? What promises weren't kept? How exactly were they let down? If the buyer pushes back in sharing any detail, disarm them by relating, "I'm not sure I'd want to spend too much energy either if I was really let down. If you can just share five minutes here, you won't get any defensiveness or argument from me. Professional to professional, I need to understand how we failed you and determine if there is anything we can do to restore your trust. Because, if there's any way that we could get you to a better outcome on the other side, I'd hate for the past to get in the way of that." A buyer must know that there's a potential reason for them to participate in restoring trust.

2. *Gain a Shared Agreement on a Trust Restoration Plan*

If the root causes are within our control to fix and there is value for our buyer to do so, then both parties should be motivated to take some steps forward. If they're not, then that becomes our question. "So, help me understand. If the root causes that you've discussed are within our control, we fully commit to eliminate them, and we agree that those outcomes would give you the real value you need, then why wouldn't you support a shared plan for us to earn your trust back?" Ultimately, we want to gain an agreement on the specific criteria and steps that we sellers will take in order to regain their trust. Detail matters here. There's nothing worse than going through the work and then missing the mark. Those criteria could be related to anything from commercials to our quality of partnership, or our solution competencies. But the plan should be based on the specific actions that would matter to our buyer, and it must be shared.

3. *Ask for a Commitment of Action Upon Restored Trust*

There needs to be a reason for our effort here. That reason needs to serve a dual-value purpose for both our buyer and us. As we consider what commitment we need to ask for, always start with the ultimate positive outcome that we desire. Then, work our way back to where the buyer is in their process. This doesn't have to be one destination. Perhaps it makes sense for us to have more near-term trust milestones agreed upon, step-by-step working our way to a healthy state. Consider their natural buying process and decision milestones. With the actions that we request, ensure that we are de-risking our ability to win their business through that process.

4. *Hold Champions Accountable*

You've done your part. You've earned a restored trust. Don't forget that you've built a Champion for a purpose, to effectively sell on your behalf. We can't ask the buyer to forget the past. We can expect them to respect the present and recognize both the partner and solution we've proven ourselves to be. This is the time to test our Champions and reaffirm their *inspiration of commitment.*

Seller, there's no room for emotion or disbelief here. Have you or someone on your team ever made a statement like this: *This is hopeless. The buyer just doesn't trust us!* If we're going to be able to restore trust, we can't have limiting beliefs on the team. As far as your buyer goes, they don't need or want to hear an excuse or explanation. Eliminate the noise and focus on restoration as an *investigation of trust.* Trust can be restored. That's the mission. But we can't just make it about us. Our discovery must be genuine and thoughtful toward the true issues at play here. It's a simple two-part question for us. Is *trust restoration in our control and is there value for the buyer should we restore that trust?*

Realize that their distrust was formed from specific *trust gaps.* The more gaps that exist, and the more time that's gone by, the longer it will take to restore trust. However, while we'll need to be patient, we can also be confident that trust can and will be restored when we focus on *refilling* those trust gaps. What should leave us even more optimistic is that often, the mere behaviors and actions that our buyer sees changing in us begin to rebuild their *emotional connection* to us. Those connections can form in just the same way and path as they would have had trust never been damaged in the first place. Thus, the good news is that the time it takes to restore trust can often be much faster than we think. As I've shared, *Emotional Connection* is a foundational elite habit that can and must be applied to everything and everyone we encounter in sales. If there's a positive future vision that we can uniquely deliver for this buyer, both parties should want to work toward the outcome of *restored trust.*

THE SCALE OF TRUST

The last foundational understanding we need to have about *trust building* is what I'll call **The Scale of Trust**. As I explain it, you'll see how this is especially relevant in some newer more remote ways of selling to and building relationships with buyers, such as video conferences and remote meetings. This is also where we see the importance of our own personal communication approaches and how those can be far more important in our different types of sales.

I've never put too much emphasis on the idea of *relationship building* in sales as much as the critical outcome of *building trust* with our buyers. It's not that relationships aren't important, nor are they not the outcome of our efforts. However, if I asked ten different sellers to describe what a healthy buyer/seller relationship was, how many different answers would I get? More focused, if we were to define what a strong Champion-building relationship looks like, what would be its most important traits? The truth I hope that you can accept is that the very core of any strong and partnering relationship, especially one in which we sellers are asking a buyer to put their credibility on the line for us, is the existence of a *trust* held to a higher standard. As for any other traits that could exist in a relationship, certainly a business relationship, none will be able to sustain or override any level of distrust. Even further, our reality in sales is that trust must be built with our Champions and all their colleagues, despite the challenges that our unique sales situations may offer. For this critically important foundation to our Champion relationships, we must consider the scale to which we need to be considerate of and intentionally build buyer *trust.*

The **Scale of Trust** is simply a realization that all trust is formed by how we react to and adjust our approach based on two things, both the amount of **Time** that we or our solution directly gets with our buyer, in conjunction with the **Risk Factors** we're needing to overcome in an individual opportunity. *Time and Risk Factors.*

Examples of *risk factors* would be the number of buyers and stakeholders involved in the purchase process, the size of the investment, cost-benefit analysis, complexity of the solution, or any negative consequences that could be associated with it. Some products stand alone. Others need to be integrated into systems or applications. If an organization has to change their processes or do anything deemed disruptive, this adds more *risk factors* to the *scale of trust*. Many solutions have immense upside opportunity, yet associated risks to accept. Anything that factors in to putting a buyer's or a seller's success at greater risk should be acknowledged to be a *risk factor* in the *scale of trust*.

The second component to the *scale of trust* is **Time**. Now, *time* is straightforward to understand. We sell to people and lots of things happen and are said during a sales campaign. Technologies can have their own bugs and complexities. Other solutions have real concerns to overcome. Some may be so lacking in relevant differentiation that we sellers always want more time to build connections. The more time we spend with people, companies, and solutions, the more opportunity we have for them to get to know us, trust us. When obstacles arise and problems surface, even if caused by something we did as sellers, we're more likely to get the *benefit of the doubt* when we've previously spent more time with a buyer. The same could be true of our product. The longer they spend with it, perhaps the more they begin to trust it and consider the positives whenever a negative appears.

That scale of *time* in building trust is measured by the amount of *intimacy* or *familiarity* we're able to gain with a buyer. The relative combination of existing *risk factors* and *time* with the buyer that's involved in an opportunity will impact the *scale* of difficulty and importance in building buyer trust. If we're going to develop a deliberate habit of *trust building*, we'll need to always consider the *scale* of just what that will take. When we think of this *trust scale* as solution companies and providers of services, we can even implement proactive strategies to offset the *risks* our buyers will perceive from what we sell, *risks* for our sellers, as well as the *time* needed to build buyer familiarity and trust. To help make this personal, think of these four selling situations and identify which one, if not multiple, your type of sale involves.

Less Risk/More Time

The best situation we can be in for building trust is when we face a *lower* number of *risk factors* in our sales scope, and we also get a *significant* amount of direct *time* with our buyers. In this situation, something about our product or service is usually integral to their business or part of their business processes. So, it's not uncommon for us to get *time* with a buyer. Our lower risk may suggest that we're in a space where the price points and/or other risk factors are relatively low. Here, we have an opportunity for a very high level of intimacy or familiarity to be formed, while needing to focus on a fewer number of trust risk factors. If this is our ideal state, we should do everything in our power to get as many sales opportunities to this *scale of trust*, while not blowing the opportunity by doing something to damage buyer trust. Because little buyer *risk* is on the table, we should use the *time* asset we have to get wider in the account. Establish more affinity for us and our brand. Spread the awareness of value we're delivering. Maximize the time we have to build deep-rooted trust.

High Risk/More Time

We can't always control the *scale of trust* in front of us. When the *high-risk* nature of what we sell is unavoidable, and yet we do have an opportunity for *more* direct *time* with our buyers, we need to focus on how effective we are in spending that time to reduce the perceived risk to our buyers. In these situations, we're getting the time with a buyer *because* of the risk factors. The buyer wants to do anything they can to find the right solution and mitigate their own risk. And rest assured, they do believe they have some risk here.

Because these risk factors can't all be eliminated or minimized, they inherently will result in less intimacy overall with our buyers. In the time they spend with us, they'll typically be more guarded or cautious. This is where we should be optimizing the time we have, putting in place strategic *trust building* processes into our sales motion where we consistently address and build confidence around those risk factors with rigor and discipline. Examples could be *thought leadership* workshops, executive briefings and meetings, introducing *Subject Matter Experts*, building customized value realization plans, success playbooks, and facilitating customer interactions. Many salespeople find themselves in these types of selling situations, and yet they're the ones who get lazy. They'll send an email rather than insisting on a site visit. They accept a short phone call instead of a highly interactive video conference. They stay single-threaded with one buyer, even though multiple stakeholders are clearly involved. They'll handle a technical concern on their own rather than bringing in a credible trusted advisor. These sellers will obediently follow a low-touch buying process without challenging the additional value that a buyer could receive with more productive interactions. When risk factors are high, we have to look to the opportunity of time to build that trust.

Less Risk/Less Time

We might find ourselves in a third situation. While we may have a lower number of *risk factors* to address, you could argue a simpler sale, we also could be faced with a very limited amount of direct *time* to spend with our buyers. This is the sale where they just want a demo, a quote, or a sample, and they'll call us if they need us. In these situations, our biggest concern is being commoditized. Realizing that just because complicated risk factors don't exist to challenge a buyer's trust, we can't get complacent. We're also not getting much time to build their trust. This is why *Trust Building* is an elite sales habit.

Intentional *trust builders* realize that we still must overcome the fact that the opportunity to build a familiar level of intimacy with our buyer is less. So, we adjust in our approach. We insert high-trust strategies into our short engagements, differentiating content outreach and thought leadership touchpoints before and outside of our meetings. Our mindset also must change in how high we value the quality of these limited buyer interactions. As companies, we should hire a higher character, positive mindset, strong *emotional intelligence* sales profile. When trust factors are low risk, it's not uncommon that our solution is less differentiated or delivers less business impact. This is where the *high-trust* people we hire and elevate ourselves to be can often be the key difference that builds the Champion and wins the business. Our time is limited so we and our people need to be the *difference-makers*.

High Risk/Low Time

Now, the last type of sales situation is the most challenging to build trust in. When our *risk factors* are considerable, involving a high level of sales or solution complexity, and yet the buying process we've been offered is very limiting in direct interaction and *time* spent, our first step needs to be realizing and accepting that we have considerable trust risk. We'll need a smart game plan. Our *scale of trust* is as heavy as it gets. So, everything we plan for in our sales process, our messaging, meeting playbooks, engagement with our Champions, all must be centered around the mission of *trust building*. The risks that are perceived will need to be respected and addressed with succinct credible *risk mitigation* plans.

Those targets of trust should be both the highest of power Champions, as well as the broad spectrum of influencers. If we can maximize the small amount of time we're getting, but with a higher quantity of people, the power of their support and consensus can work wonders toward the confidence of our Champions. As companies, we need to realize that we're putting our sellers and our sales productivity investment in an awful high-risk state. We should be thinking about how our product roadmap, marketing approaches, pricing and differentiation strategies, and anything else that could de-risk these trust obstacles could be implemented.

Remember the premise of *The Champion Sell*. If we have nothing else, we must prioritize building Buyer Champions. In any high-risk complex sale with a formidable *scale of trust*, Champions and the trust they need in us should be at the core of our sales strategy. In the end, trust will need to be built, reinforced, and often restored with our Champions and all other buyers. So, we need to be intentional *trust builders*, considerate of the *scale of trust* that we will have to face.

THE TRUST PATH: *Character, Credibility, Competencies*

Think of the people in your life whom you most trust. They might be a family member, a life mentor, or a long-time friend. In business, who are you most willing to place your trust in? Why did these people come to mind? What about them makes them so trustworthy? Why should people trust you? What are your traits that justify that? Were your answers to the people you trust different than why others should trust you? Ultimately, do you think that others see you as you see yourself?

Whether our objective is to build trust in the very beginning of a buyer relationship, overcome a *trust tax* that we've inherited, or respond to a *trust gap* at a later stage milestone of an opportunity, like *commitment*, there is a mental path to how we humans form our trust. In that path, it's our habits that can often attract or deter that trust we desire. As I've said, we need to be *intentional trust builders*. Yet, as every person we sell to is unique, it's in the attention to our trust habits where we'll find the consistency of building buyer trust.

Trust is a state of mind, one which grows from far more automatic emotions than intellectual choice. However, *trust* shouldn't be a mystery. For many sellers, it often is. Gaining trust doesn't have to be an accident. If you've ever heard someone state, "Trust just happens." Well, they're wrong. You've also heard the saying, "Trust is earned." Yes, it is earned. But that shouldn't be a passive journey. Trust can and should be built deliberately.

In Stephen Covey's book, *The Speed of Trust*, he teaches the full breath of what makes up trust across the many dimensions of *credibility* and how our behaviors impact high-trust relationships. Covey helps us to become more aware of ourselves. Yet, what I've found in sales is that because the type of sale that we're in and the product or service that we sell doesn't often change, our path to building trust can be even simpler. It can be more repeatable if we think about it in a simple framework, from our buyer's point of view. From Covey and many others who have studied *trust*, based on how the human mind works, we've learned that we'll all go through a subconscious journey every single time to assess the level of trust that we should extend to someone or the opportunity in front of us. Now, this doesn't mean that there is some robotic order for how a buyer will assess any level of our *trustability*. There is a path, however, that all minds go through when we encounter new people or new opportunities, a path that determines our willingness to *trust*.

Based on the psychology of what we've learned, our **Trust Path** is essentially how our mind naturally perceives and develops a perspective of trust about someone or something, which I will directly apply to this fun profession of sales. When we engage in our communication and collaboration with a buyer, their subconscious mind is always paying attention to and measuring us against three important traits that make up this *trust path:* our **Character (or integrity)**, our **Credibility,** and our **Competencies**. All three work together, often having a common order of priority, depending on how a buyer comes to be introduced to us or what we sell. The best way to internalize this concept of *a trust path* is to think about your experiences in how you came to trust or distrust someone or something. Choose a person that you highly trust. In your first interaction, what was the first thought that crossed your mind when you encountered them? Was it your optimistic curiosity that they were probably awesome? Unlikely. Most of the time, did you find yourself struggling to pay too much attention to this person's agenda because you were trying to get a feel for just *who* they were?

THE TRUST PATH

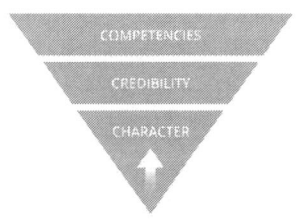

If this was your first impression, your mind's protective survival instincts were questioning the **_Character_** traits of that person before anything else mattered. _Character_ is the first observation of our _trust path_. If it's a person you came to know, on your behalf, your mind was observing them through how they were projecting themselves. Were they positive or negative, honest or deceptive, open or guarded? Were they humble or did they carry on, bragging of their greatness? Did they seem considerate and inclusive of others, or were they self-focused? Was the interaction all about them, or did they ask you questions? If seeing a product for the first time, did you ever find yourself questioning, _Does this product seem easy and focused, or complicated and confusing?_ That was you questioning the _character_ traits of the product. Just like in our buyers, this was your initial instinctual response, rather than immediately dissecting your intellectual understanding of its capabilities.

Consider a relationship you've had that, over time, faced more intense and consequential challenges. Did you remain in an unconditional all-trusting state, or did you find yourself subconsciously re-evaluating their _character?_ If so, your mind was probably asking a question like, _So, let's see how they'll handle themselves now._ As time goes on, we may learn more about someone or something's credibility or competency to deliver on a result. Yet, if we doubt in any way that their _character_ is up to our standard, then our mind simply won't give credence to those other credible traits and abilities. Have you ever experienced a buyer disallowing you to even compete or move forward in an opportunity due to character questions with you, someone on your team, your company, or the product you tried to present? If so, did it feel unfair and that it was out of your control?

In business, _character_ will always be the first subconscious assessment we make of the people we interact with, the products and services we encounter, and the companies we're introduced to. As sellers, our acceptance must be that no matter how credible or competent we believe we or our solutions are, if trust is questioned at all on the level of our *character*, this will be a tough emotional hurdle for us to overcome. As humans, *character* is the most foundational trait of our *trust path*.

The second mental journey in our *trust path* is **Credibility**. In sales, this is the most decisive trait that a buyer's emotions and intellect will anchor from. Their mind will never assume our *credibility*, as this is the most often over-sold and under-delivered aspect of what salespeople tout. So, what is *credibility*? Again, thinking of it in business terms and what you may have experienced yourself, *credibility* is having the proven ability to do what you say can. Now, in this world of buyers and sellers, I think we'd be better off to think of *credibility* for what it really is: a perception, an opinion.

In a *Champion-based* mindset, we're all about leading the connection and commitment of the most powerful and influential buyers. For that to turn into a purchase, they'll need to trust us. But it's *their* trust we need, not ours. Regardless of how believable we think we are, our buyers need to form the perception and opinion that we are *credible*. As they read our marketing and outreach, listen to our well-groomed sales pitches, their subconscious mind is really asking just one key question. Are we believable? Achieving *credibility* status, in those buyers' eyes, is all about them seeing reasonable evidence that we've done it before and we could do it again, for them.

Conversely, losing *credibility* with a buyer can come from anything that makes us less believable. When most sellers drift off into positioning how differentiated and high-value their competencies are, a buyer's natural reaction is to question the *credibility* behind the claims they're hearing, before they'll give them any credit. Many sellers veer away from communicating *credibility* to avoid sounding arrogant or boastful. Others ignore it all together, not realizing that the buyer needs that evidence in order to trust us. In a sales conversation, we'll go further and further into our message, professing our differentiation and promising great returns with the highest of expectations. But how many times have you found yourself facing a buyer's objection-littered response, questioning the *credibility* and legitimacy of all your claims?

Trust Builders have learned that establishing *credibility* is a prerequisite for bold aggressive selling. No matter how much conviction and knowledge we share, we just won't be trusted until *credibility* behind the message is formed. Everything that we and our solutions say and do needs to come across as believable. If we're going to consistently establish credibility with a buyer, we need to be listening to ourselves. If there's anything in the way that we or our team communicates or behaves to lessen our *believability*, the buyer will reject a willingness to trust in us. If our product, as amazing as it may be, shows poorly in a way or lacks any past evidence of its performance, its *credibility* drops.

Even with an amazing salesperson sitting face-to-face in a buyer's office, if anything that the company has done causes a question of *credibility*, that buyer will have some real *trust gaps* to overcome. At some point, the buyer can't take any more. So, they'll not only begin to distrust us, but some will also make it extremely challenging for us to begin to earn that *credibility* back. We can't assume that we'll have or stubbornly believe that we deserve *credibility*. We must establish it with every individual buyer we meet.

Now, we arrive at the last destination of a person's *trust path*. If, and only if, a buyer feels at least neutral about our *character* and reasonably trusts our *credibility,* we can't stop there. Eventually in a business purchase decision, we will need to prove that our **Competencies** are trustworthy. Are we *competent?* Can we actually do *the thing that our buyer needs us to do?* A good way to think about the difference between *competency* and *credibility* is that while *credibility* is another person's feeling of our believability, a *competency* is about our proof or evidence of believability. Without that proof, they simply fall short in their *trust path*.

When a buyer loses trust, they also lose any commitment they might have otherwise formed. Have you ever had a deal where the buyer showed that they were our biggest Champion, moving you along through a joy ride of a buying process, only to pump the brakes so hard that you got *sales whiplash?* They needed to see it work. They needed evidence. What you thought was a sufficient demonstration of your *capabilities* fell short of their trust criteria. What were the exact *competencies* that they needed to trust and how could you have proven them?

The sales world is full of shortcuts. Are we assuming that we know what the buyer needs and cares about most across our *character, credibility, and competencies?* Are we guessing what their *trust criteria* are? In sales, a loss of trust can happen in the earliest of meetings and on through the final steps of closure. And yes, that means that we can lose trust even when we've already built a Champion. Remember that mantra, *No Champion, No Deal?* Well, don't mistake that for, *Build a Champion, close a deal.* The subtitle of this book says, *building and _winning_ with Buyer Champions.* For them to actively support and sell for us, they will need to fully trust us all the way through the finish line.

Of the three dimensions of Trust, *character, credibility, competency,* some will get more of a spotlight later in their buying process as decisions get more scrutinized, such as a customer reference, proof of concept, or technical validation of our *competencies. Character* is usually more in question early on, but certainly can get exposed at any time, especially if others on our sales team project confrontation with our buyers. Our *credibility* is constantly being tested as scope and process matures, as risk factors surface, and the price tag materializes. All three traits are threatened more the greater the *scale of trust.* Think about your typical sales engagement. Where do those three trust dimensions get questioned and tested the most throughout your buyer's decision process? Based on a buyer's history or business situation, each trait can also have a different weight in their priorities. What's most important is how aware we sellers are across these three measurements of our trustworthiness.

So, you might ask. If every person is so uniquely different, how could *building trust* with them become a habit? Well, the better question is, how could it not? Here's why. While the final purchase decision to trust our *character, credibility, or competencies* will often require a thoughtful definitive choice, the mental path that every buyer goes through to arrive at their state of trust is primarily *subconscious.* When we sellers learn that any part of a buyer's decision path is emotional and automatic toward us, this should evoke a keen attentive energy to satisfy those emotions. That's where a sales *habit* comes in.

Think about this. Across any buying milestone that is predominantly led by subconscious emotions, such as forming *emotional connection* and *trust,* these will be where the specific actions we should take will be less clear and predictable. In other words, we can't solve those emotional challenges with process and methodology. To prepare and empower ourselves for those human unknowns, we should be intently developing the *habits* that will most often lead us to finding a way to connect and sell to individual people. Forming habits allows us to become routine and instinctual to ensure protection against these risk-averse automatic responses. And none is more automatic than *trust.*

In developing our *trust building* habits, we must also accept that all three dimensions of *character, credibility and competencies* work together. If any of these leave gaps in a buyer's *trust path*, a relationship may be blocked from developing. The *trust paths* of other stakeholders may be averted. Just one gap in a *trust path* will lead a buyer to choose *caution over commitment.* To be more direct—even if a buyer loves us, likes what we sell, and believes in our value, if they don't *trust* us, the deal will not happen.

Yet, when we achieve this state of Trust in a buyer, we can overcome just about anything the sales opportunity encounters. To drive this *power of trust* home, think of a diamond. It's the absolute strongest gemstone there is. Now, diamonds take on many different shapes, but there's a rare triangle shape called a *Trillion.* Like these three traits in the *trust path*, a trillion has three sides to it. It's a beautiful stone, but even stronger than it is beautiful. We should view those three dimensions of our *character, credibility, and competencies* as tightly connected as the sides of that trillion and as strong as any diamond.

Contrary to what many believe, in any environment—personal or business—trust is never built on just one thing. What I've learned over the years, either from my personal situations where I've broken trust with someone, or in sellers on my team that have been unable to build a trusting Buyer Champion, is that a lack of trust will always come down to a deficit in one of these three traits of *character, credibility, or competencies.* Test it yourself. List out the last five deals that you lost or pushed toward a *no decision*. In each one, honestly assess where your *trust gap* was. Get a second opinion. Discuss with your manager or a teammate. The chances are almost guaranteed that your buyer did not move forward with you because they had a *trust gap* in one of these three buckets that they could not fill.

The Trust Standard

For an individual buyer, I want you to think of these three traits in the *trust path* as the makeup of their **Trust Standard.** It's when we seek out and learn what specific trust criteria our buyer has for ours or our solution's *character, credibility,* and *competencies* that we get clarity as to their personal *trust standard.* This is an individual person's unique set of *Trust Criteria* that, if we expect to gain their complete trust and commitment to buy, we will have to meet or exceed.

It's in both the awareness of importance and determined curiosity to qualify a buyer's *trust standard* where we will find more consistency in getting aligned with the buyers we sell to. If in a Champion-based sell, we're maniacally trying to qualify and lead a buyer's decision criteria, there is no more powerful criteria than someone's *trust criteria.* Understanding a buyer's *trust standard* helps us avoid making general assumptions that derail our opportunities. We get fewer surprises. Our sales strategy becomes more intuitive toward driving a Champion's bias for action. By learning a buyer's *trust standard,* we get closer to this concept that companies don't buy from us, people do. A buyer may not always be consciously aware of their *trust standard.* Yet, they will show it if we pay attention and possibly even shed light on it if we ask. They'll respect our appreciation for their trust and certainly the thoughtfulness of discussing it on all three dimensions.

One thing we can guarantee is that their *trust standard* will always cross all three parts of their *trust path*. Like that trillion, if one of its three sides is broken off, it's no longer the beautiful strong diamond we'd like it to be.

And you see, trust is as fast as it is strong. In Covey's book, *The Speed of Trust,* he talks of the *speed* that trust can be built and restored, as well as the dividend that it can pay once it exists. He also warns us of the speed that trust can be lost and just how it can be lost. Trust has constant energy. *Trust Building* is a habit that never stops working. In fact, out of all five of your E.L.I.T.E. selling habits, *Trust Building* is the only habit that forms automatically. Meaning, all sellers have *trust building* habits today. The question is, are they positive, strong, and effective with most buyers? Do we consistently build trust with most people we sell to, or just those who match our personality? All sellers must ask themselves, *Are my natural habits diminishing a buyer's trust in me? What are my trust habits today, and how are those influencing the buyers whom I'm trying to build as Champions?*

Applying TRUST BUILDING in the Sales Process

THE 3 HIGH-TRUST HABITS: *Projection, Precision, Proving*

What I'm about to share are three habits that, when they routinely guide how we sell to people, will guarantee that we're doing everything within our control to build trust. These three trust-building habits must all be included in our comprehensive objective of *trust building* across *character, credibility, and competencies.* To prepare you for these trust habits, this would be a good time to embrace some self-awareness. Most people who struggle with *trust* think of it in their own terms. Those who master a habit of *trust building* care only about the perceptions and criteria of the people whom they are trying to build trust with. Too often in business, our belief of how people perceive our *character, credibility, or competencies* is based on our perceptions of ourselves. That's not *trust building.* We must shift our mindset to *how buyers perceive us.* Our priority and focus as *trust builders* should be based on understanding what a buyer's subconscious is paying attention to and just how we're being measured compared to their personal *trust standard.*

THE 3 HIGH-TRUST HABITS

PROVING .... COMPETENCIES

PRECISION .... CREDIBILITY

PROJECTING .... CHARACTER

PROJECTION of Character

I think I have strong character. I'm not too concerned that anyone would doubt that. Well, then why is it that they are? *Does something I do make people question my integrity? Do buyers not think I'm honest?* Could it be possible that many of us salespeople don't really know what level of *character* a buyer needs to see from us, our solutions, and the companies we work for? Worse, maybe we're completely clueless how buyers view us. *But how would someone who just met me be able to start trusting my character? They haven't taken the time to get to know me?* And. *How could they ever do that on Zoom, the wonderful video metaverse I seem to live in?*

A buyer's willingness to trust our character is more in our span of control than we think it is. Our first high-trust habit is our **PROJECTION of character.** How we *project* our characteristic makeup, our persona to a buyer, creates the immediate response of whether people begin to trust us or not. *Projection*, whether of us as humans or as with our products and companies, is how we show ourselves, mostly through our energy and behaviors. *Character projection* starts in the first fifteen seconds of our interaction with someone. Think about a strong respected person you know who, every time they walk into a room or join a video conference, projects this positive feeling, an energy that you're attracted to. Our initial reaction may be, *Well, I guess they must be having a good day.*

If this always seems like an act, we could begin questioning if they're faking it, being genuine. Yet, what if this positive and good energy you feel from them is consistent? There's nothing they say or do that contradicts it. The more they interact, they further reinforce our positive first response. As they speak, our subconscious forms opinions of them. *Geez, they're always so positive and confident. They must be really happy and successful.* You assume they must be in control. We admire this energy and want to be around those people. It doesn't take long for you to get more comfortable in the consideration to *trust them*.

The same would hold true with a product we demonstrate or begin implementing. In technology sales, there's nothing worse for a sales team, who feels they've done a solid job kicking off a meeting set up perfectly for this solution demonstration, only to have technical issues in the first several minutes. In this case, it was our product's *projection* of its character that came into question. As the audience watches our sales engineer troubleshoot in the silence of what feels like an eternity to the sales rep, the buyer's mind begins questioning, *Seems like the product's a bit immature. It's not fully baked.* Whether we like it or not, we've now just built some negative perception of our trustworthiness that we'll need to overcome.

Words also project trust and unfortunately, can even overrule the initial positive sense people got from our energy. I've even experienced this from my own behavior. I once accompanied one of my reps to a meeting with one of the largest global convenience stores. At their Dallas headquarters, all was cordial, and the energy was good. Later that night at dinner, after a few quick glasses of wine, I made a couple of joking remarks using words that were a bit unkind and came across rude. I learned about the distrust I'd built the next day. My lesson was that it was simply my choice of words that could damage some trust with an individual with whom I had previously established it. I then had to work on rebuilding trust with that person over the coming months.

The science of *projection* is a powerful human engineering. It can be turned on and off like a machine. But, when left on and ignored, the gamble we're taking in our effort to build trust is riskier than we think. I used to be a high school science teacher. Back in those mid-90s classrooms, things were a bit lower tech. Every room had what was called an "overhead projector." You might remember these. The teacher would take out a clear plastic sheet called a "transparency," and with their trusty colored markers, they would write whatever the class needed to see, could have been math equations, scientific formulas. And, I don't know about your school, but the first thing some jokester of a student would do when the teacher left the room was run up to the projector and draw some silly inappropriate picture.

The way the overhead projector worked was that a light would shine up through a clear box where you'd place a transparent plastic sheet down. The light would move through that sheet into a mirror sitting on top of a big metal arm. That light and mirror would basically work together to project the image that you wrote onto a big screen in front of the room.

You see, much like with this projector, in sales we project an image of our character through the light that we mirror to our audience. In other words, a buyer's perception of our trustworthiness is not really about what we think our true character is, or what it very well may be. Their perception is a reaction to what image we're sending out. What are we sellers writing down on our transparent plastic sheets? In sales, we are the *transparency*. If we were being ourselves in a natural agenda-free setting, our buyers would surely appreciate our good nature. However, if in that meeting our true character was a bit questionable, a buyer would see right through us, no different than anyone else would.

We would hope that the more common character projections we share in our personal lives are positive. This is why we have family and friends who love us and even like us. Yet, you might have observed that in a sales moment-of-truth, many sellers will believe that we need to take on a different sales identity. When the pressure of the moment, anxiety of anticipation, or career desperation kicks in, we'll often project a different image of our character, as if we're acting. This false identity ends up diminishing the trust our buyers should have in us. This character becomes our truth to our buyer. Have you ever felt like an actor when you've been on that sales stage? The same would hold true for products that don't show well in the demonstration or companies that form bad reputations and get negative social reviews. But let's just focus on us for a moment. How are we sellers projecting ourselves?

The 4 Sales Character Tendencies

In that intention to help you gain some self-awareness, or even awareness of the people who sell around you, consider these **4 Sales Character Tendencies** to determine which that you or your team members might find yourself resembling. As I lay these out, I'll help you simplify high-trust character off a scale that includes two dimensions a buyer might see us in.

For all the characteristics that a buyer would want and need out of a seller, think of a buyer trusting us on a scale of both an orientation to be **Value-Focused**, paired with the dimension of being **Service-Focused**. On one dimension, picture a vertical *Y-axis* labelled **"Buyer Value-Focused."** Here, a buyer would need to trust that we are ***Buyer Value-Oriented***. This is when we tend to think and drive toward our buyer understanding and achieving business value. Those sellers who are strong here care more about just what it is that our products and services do. They actually take the time to think through the impact that matters most to a buyer. They have an intellectual curiosity and mindset that the product or service they sell should actually deliver value. This character tendency creates a strong feeling of credibility with a buyer.

On the second dimension, picture the horizontal *X-axis* of a graph labelled **"Buyer Service-Focused."** Here, they want a seller who is ***Buyer Service-Oriented***. Meaning, a buyer needs to trust that we will actually work for them, be in service to them. This seller tendency will show the integrity to do what they say they will. They're not just all talk. In *service-oriented* sellers, a buyer trusts that there's actions behind our words and that we're competent enough to do the job well. Simplifying high-trust character to these two dimensions, let's get to know these ***4 Sales Characters***.

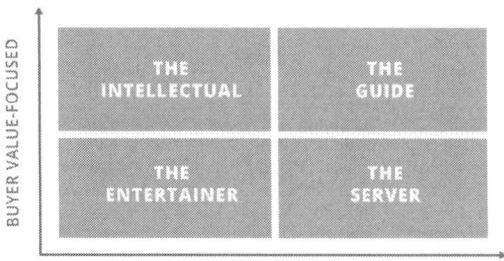

THE 4 SALES CHARACTERS

The Server

When a buyer meets a *Server* as a sales character type, they generally like them. Who wouldn't? A *Server* makes you feel good with a kind and cheery greeting. They ask where you're from, what kind of day you've been having. Their humility is off-the-chart and people rarely question their intentions. Yet ultimately, a *Server* is here to take your order, refill your coffee, and bring the check. In these sales interactions, there's rarely a focus on the business value that really matters to the buyer. Oh yeah, they'll send that quote over as fast a buyer makes the request. They'll take whatever shortcut is needed in an otherwise strong sales process, in order to accommodate the *Let's just keep it simple* preferences of their buyer.

If you've been a *Server*, you might have found yourself going to many meetings with little return. You've replied to multiple requests for more information and jumped through hoops to get internal approvals for pricing and business exceptions. However, after much time and effort exerted, working hard to win the deal with your buyer, it wasn't uncommon that they still went with your competitor, or just did nothing at all. This seller has heard that lamenting breakup lyric far too many times from a buyer: "Hey, we really appreciate how hard you worked for our business, and we'd love to work with you some time in the future."

What's most important with *The Server*, is that they're not building any value credibility with their buyer. Too often, a buyer lets *The Server* stay in the game as long as they'll keep showing up. As a deal might have progressed through the *connection* and *commitment* milestones of a buying process, that was usually because the Buyer Champion was optimistic and was driving the *value train* themselves. They emotionally started to believe in the possibility of your value because they wanted it to be true. Yet, while they might have had optimism and really enjoyed your company, they never built up real trust. Being *low buyer value-focused* and *high buyer service-focused*, The Server doesn't provide enough substance for a buyer to see and believe that they can be successful because of us and what we sell, no matter how hard they work for them.

The Intellectual

Everyone wants to be smart. But it's true that some of you sellers are just smarter than others. If you're aware of your high intelligence birthright, you might choose to use it for a greater good, applying it to thoughtful solutioning, strategic problem solving, and finding creative ways to get your buyer to a state of high-trust certainty and belief. Unfortunately, this is not how **The Intellectual** uses their superpower.

Their mind is their identity and working hard for you will not feed that highbrow ego. *The Intellectual* wants to be the smartest person in the room. Often, that savvy mind will be first to jump to the notions of quantifiable value, return on investment, and your inspiring opportunity for the business. While that level of intelligent discussion may offer an impressive moment or even many moments of credibility for the buyer, just how much can they trust that we'll actually do something for them, be in service of them? This *high buyer value-focused, low buyer service-focused Intellectual* may have grand ideas, but they just won't go the extra mile. They'll rely on their brains to bring you to the well, but it's up to you to take a drink.

To *The Intellectual's* subconscious, that working hard thing, *Well isn't that the buyer's job? I mean, I did my part. My explanations were profound. And I must admit, my competition probably looks dumb compared to me.* Ah, now you're starting to get nervous. You think you're pretty smart. So, you're wondering if your buyers perceive you to be *The Intellectual.* Well, most of you can rest easy. Our buyers do need us to be intelligent. This is how we're able to understand and lead them to a state of trusting in the value that we can deliver for them.

However, complete trust in our character must come from both dimensions. Do your buyers just hear you or do they see you working hard and smart for them? Do you have examples of when you've taken the initiative to lead them to a specific outcome in their buying journey? Are you often solving problems for your buyer as a sales athlete on the playing field, or are you typically the expert commentator up in the booth?

The Entertainer

Ah, my favorite seller on the team . . . to put on a performance plan. We've all seen *The Entertainer,* which frankly might be you. With a bold confidence built from a lifetime of affirmation of their charismatic charm, *The Entertainer* is a performer who loves to be on stage and be heard. They truly believe that the buyer would love nothing more than for them to sing their song, a sales pitch that's been rehearsed and perfected in rhythm and time. Yes, *the dog and pony show* is their moment, and they do love the spotlight. When the microphone is on, *The Entertainer* will blow your mind with their braggadocios claims, marketing jargon, and self-promoting speeches. *Where's the value,* the buyer wonders.

There's usually very little emphasis on buyer value and impact from *The Entertainer,* especially later in a buying process where discernment becomes more serious. This is when a Champion needs us the most to work hard at proving our value. And yet, *The Entertainer's* also not willing to do the work either. They're either incapable or unwilling to customize the message or tailor a strategic solution to a buyer's problem. Because *The Entertainer* is *low buyer value-focused* and *low buyer service-focused,* the buyer may be impressed with the product, but they'll lack a seller who can really build their trust in it. So, in spite of how impactful their solution could be and how hard the company might work to make that buyer successful, *The Entertainer* will often be the character roadblock for that prospect to build any level of trust in the solution.

The Guide

Have you ever gotten in a taxi or rideshare, and the driver didn't seem to know where they were going? They lacked the knowledge to navigate you to the right destination in a reasonable amount of time. You might have also ridden with plenty of drivers who knew the route, but many just didn't seem to care about you, some outright rude. But of course, there's that amazing unforgettable ride where, not only did the car smell like new and freshly vacuumed, stocked with free water and snacks, but the driver knew the shortest way to get you home, all while asking you how you felt and complementing your outfit. They wanted you to know that you were at their service. Every time you called for a car in that neighborhood again, you hoped that it was Chuck in that fresh white Tesla.

The ultimate character that a buyer wants and needs from us is one for whom they will see evidence of thinking and driving toward value for them, as well as putting the hard work in to ensure that they're successful. If you're looking to take on an identity of sales character that most defines this *high buyer value-focused, high buyer service-focused* trust builder, then consider **The Guide**. This is the seller who has both the credibility to understand and empathetically focus on buyer impact, while also being the one who *leads from the front* to get them there. A true *Guide* is the character who knows what a successful destination could look like. Their credibility and high-value character shows because they've done their homework. They know their stuff. No one wants to be led by a guide who doesn't know where they're going. When you're selling, do you work to understand the personal and specific value that your solution could deliver? Do you seek to understand before you're understood? Are you able to then gain and convey that shared alignment of expected value with the buyers you work with?

Now, while all buyers want to understand the value of a solution for them personally, they also need a *Guide* who will lead them to that value. As opposed to merely being an academic intellectual thought leader, are you also someone who actively leads a buyer's vision? Do you get on the muddy trail and lead them to the desired destination? Are you a *selfless seller*? The *Guide* brings the perfect balance of hard work and servant attitude to deliver for their buyer, while focusing all of that energy into a specific path toward buyer value. This *Guide* provides proof to a buyer, evidence of their character, credibility, and competencies to create the ultimate feeling of buyer trust.

We can think of trust from our point of view or a buyer's. Only one choice leads us to an individual buyer's *trust standard*. We've already outlined that there's a *trust path* that the mind subconsciously navigates from a person's *character, credibility, and competencies*. When we categorize sales character tendencies, we can consider the dimensions of being *value-oriented* and *service-oriented*. But again, buyers are diverse in personality and experience. So, we need to think about *trust building* as a habit where we want to be always as healthy as possible, for anyone we meet. Like with that *trillion* diamond, while it has three distinct sides, its uniqueness is crafted from the dozens of facets on those three sides. At its core, the identification of high-trust *character* can be projected and witnessed on multiple facets of our character.

So, here's some examples of different facets of high-trust *character projections* for you to consider and compare to how you or your sellers might be being perceived in your sales situations

Sales Projections of Character

Sales Integrity

Character projection starts with our **Integrity**. Some people think that integrity is just being a good person. It means more than that. Just what is a good person? How would we know if we saw one? Is our definition the same as our buyer's? *Integrity* is what starts to define the *Standard of Character* in every buyer/seller relationship. For you to consider your buyer's definition of *integrity*, think about why they would need to trust you, your solution, or your company in the first place. Based on what you sell and its different risk factors, there's some specific things that your buyers want you to have some *integrity* about. Having *integrity* as salespeople and as providers of solutions for our customers means that we're ethical. We do the right thing to a standard of basic morale principles. In business specifically, we believe that there are certain rules of conduct and behavior that are acceptable. We show that by how we act accordingly, how we *project our integrity*. So again, to understand how we can project a strong sense of our *integrity*, we should know what ethics and moral principles our buyers would most desire from us.

Consider that there are several facets to our *integrity*. One is **Honesty**. Buyers want to believe the words that we say, but how are our behaviors and words projecting themselves in an honest way? Even though we may think that we and our companies are honest people, how are we being perceived? And, if the sellers or company before us broke a buyer's trust with dishonesty, ours will definitely be in question. So, how are we projecting the consistency and depth of our *honesty*? Have there been things that we've said or claimed that weren't entirely true? Have any of our actions or behaviors been *incongruent*? Meaning, do we communicate the same message, act like the same person and company all the time, or are we inconsistent? Are the positions we state and claims we make authentically and consistently honest? Or are we often silently hoping that the buyer doesn't dig too deep into validating what we said? When we're incongruent in our behaviors or promises, buyers see those deviations as *dishonesty*. The more experienced and wiser they've become working with sellers and/or the solutions we sell, the clearer they can detect the truthfulness of our projections.

Reliability is another *integrity* facet. Buyers need to trust that we're going to do what we say we will. They're not only emotionally counting on us, but they'll also have other decisions and plans that are dependent on our commitments. *Reliability* would be especially important if what you sell is seen as more complex to deliver, implement, or support. *Reliability* is key when supporting a business-critical service, if the negative consequences of your solution not performing will be detrimental to their business. Perhaps your product or service is tightly connected to other major initiatives and business objectives. This is where *reliability* is everything. Projecting high-integrity *reliability* means always being and doing who and what you say you are and will.

Sales Positivity

Another major facet of our sales character is our level of **Positivity**, and certainly how we *project* it. Why would anyone trust someone in business if they were negative? Think of sellers or sales managers who you've worked with that always seemed to have a negative point of view, communication approach, or just negative energy in general. How often do you or your teammates speak poorly of your competitors or alternative solutions? How many of your sales conversations are negative commentaries versus positive thoughts and opportunities? When sellers and their teams project any of these pessimistic or unfavorable perspectives, it creates a subconscious cause for concern in a buyer. Maybe their fear becomes that your company culture won't be to the level of partner they'd prefer. They think, *perhaps this team and business won't be solutions-oriented.* When a buyer hears us emphasizing much of our message on competitors, throwing out *FUD* (*fear, uncertainty, and doubt*), how do you think this makes a buyer feel? *Why do they talk about their competitor so much? They must be pretty intimidated and not have much positive to say about themselves.*

The biggest distrusting concern a buyer will form from these projections of negativity is that a seller or their solution has not been successful enough to warrant being positive. It's ok to be educated and participate in thoughtful discussions about yours and alternative approaches. We should all have a point of view for the domains we sell in. But is it intelligent thoughtful discussion we're exchanging, or negative projections that we want our buyers to share? These have the opposite effect.

Negative projections build a buyer's distrust of the beliefs we communicate. It's healthy and credible for us to be pragmatic toward potential risks and solutions to mitigate them. However, negative disruptive beliefs projected to our buyer diminish our character, a fundamental step in a buyers' *trust path*. The mindset, energy, and behavior of a seller who always projects as *positive* will attract the same level of optimism from their buyer, optimism in potentially trusting them.

Would a positive projection of **Adaptability** be important to your buyers? What is the need for *adaptability*? Well, would your buyer need you to have a positive mindset of flexibility and always *finding a way* in how you service them? Needing to see *adaptability* means that a buyer already realizes that a solution won't be all sunshine and rainbows. This *adaptability* facet of *positivity* often relates if your buyer's environments are complicated, troublesome, or in a state of change.

Positivity also projects greatly through our **Confidence**. While the idea of a sales team being *confident* can often come with an arrogant connotation, that's more about their level of humility. Just how much does projecting *confidence* mean to a buyer? Think of an experience you've had with someone who you needed to trust in the moment. What if, when asked a hard question or challenged, they didn't waver in their confident ability to deliver. Regardless of the logical credibility of that belief, how did it make you initially feel? When that confidence is paired with serious, mature professionalism, backed up by a logical supporting position of why they're confident, the natural emotional reaction of a buyer is to assume trust in that seller. What buyer would want to do business with anyone who's not confident in the solution or themselves? I've always told my sellers, "If we don't believe, how could we expect a buyer to believe?" This is especially critical to *trust-building* if what we sell is a newer or more innovative solution.

Yet, the question is, how are we *projecting confidence?* Are we direct or meandering in our communication? Do our words drift and volume fade? Or do they project clarity and conviction? How do we respond to challenges or tough questions? Do we defer our answers to the realm of uncertainty? Or do we ensure that our buyer will get a *confident* response, whether we need to follow up or not? How does our body language and energy state change? Do we begin to flinch and fidget, look away and cower down? Or do we calmly stand in the moment of discussion, eye to eye?

Business isn't about being perfect, having the right answer for everything. It's about maintaining a level of trust from our buyers that we will be able to ensure the value that they expect. When we're confident, they're more likely to be confident. A buyer needs to trust that our *confidence* in their value realization will not wane.

Sales Kindness

Perhaps the most important, yet sometimes minimized high-trust projection in sales is **Kindness**. For some reason, when we think of this word in business, we associate it with weakness or having a lower impact on buyers. Well, let's think about this projection of *kindness*. If the most important aspect of our sales profession is the buyer we sell to, then in their consideration of our trustworthiness, why would any person want to work with someone who's not kind? In fact, this virtue of our character is what provokes us to do the very things that our buyers appreciate the most. Just how trustworthy would sales teams be if they were all honorable and kind? However, are we allowing ourselves to project that kindness?

In business, it often takes a while for buyers to get to know their sellers. So, how we consistently project ourselves to be kind both early and often will be vital to building that trust. What are some examples of these *kindness* facets to our character that we could project? When we show genuine **Interest** in our buyers, we create the feeling that it's about them, that we're paying attention and we care. We do this in the initial moments of our introductions and in the more individual interactions. In those earliest dialogues, do we ask genuinely curious and considerate questions? Are we projecting that we've researched them and done our homework? When the deal's not moving as fast, do we lower our conversational rhetoric and genuinely ask what's causing the problem behind the delay? Or do we use our one-on-one time to pounce on insisting that our buyer is accountable and follow through? When any less-than-ideal problem arises in our opportunities, do we show selfishness, ignoring their challenges, or show empathy and interest in helping?

There doesn't have to be a problem to project *interest.* There is such a power of attraction when we use those rare moments of personal time with a buyer to take just a few minutes to learn something about the person, find some relatability and middle ground where we can trust each other more naturally. Another facet of *kindness* is to **Give**. When we're **Giving**, such as personalized gifts, simple complements, offers to bring in subject matter experts, or networking introductions, buyers tend to reciprocate. In fact, the psychological *Law of Reciprocity* tells us that when someone does something for us, we feel obligated to reciprocate or do something in return for them.

While *giving* is a strong projection of high-trust character, our buyers also need to see and experience our **Grace**. *Grace*, or what some may refer to as compassion, doesn't mean that we're compromising our objectives. Compassion is a feeling, and *grace* is something that we extend to someone that could be based on that compassion. *Grace* is a behavior we project that comes from our business empathy, having sensitivity and consideration for our buyer's situation. Regardless of the circumstance and how it may affect us, we allow them some *grace*, which is the space to be who and where they are. It's a projection of humanity. We all deserve *grace*. So, why in business do we get so self-righteous? It's because we get selfish, desperate, or self-focused. We project our problems onto our buyer.

What many sellers don't realize is that our buyers know how serious this all is and that we both have something on the line. Yet, their priority will always be themselves. That doesn't make them selfish. This is business. Value can and should be bidirectional. But, if the confidence or the path to that value for the buyer has some real blockers, then perhaps the decision isn't ready to be made. Maybe this isn't the right time. If they're not getting to a high-trust state with us or not moving the deal along as fast as we had hoped, there's often complicated and challenging reasons behind it on their end. These are usually things that we sellers could never truly understand. We just simply haven't been there and done their job. Now, this doesn't have to mean that we absolve ourselves from our own sales objectives, lose our aggressiveness.

Yet, it does support another key lesson I've tried to pass on to my sellers in that we should never make our pipeline problem our buyer's problem. The two should be mutually exclusive. We need to take care of our own business, with nothing more important than having enough of it. Build enough pipeline in order to do the right things in the deals we work. This way, we free ourselves up to show the *grace* that our buyers may truly need from us. While in the moment, projecting *kindness* may not feel that productive. But in fact, we'll be attracting high-trust emotions from our buyer. This attraction of trust in our character will play a large part in their milestone decisions of *closure*. In those opportunities where we can project our compassionate examples of *kindness*, whether in just human interactions or showing our understanding and patience to their situations, our buyers will respond to the high-trust goodness in that.

It's in these dimensions and facets of our energy and behaviors that we *project* the transparency of our *character*. This is where we attract trust and build Champions. Too many sellers don't even think about a *standard of character* for what they sell. For them, *trust building* is not intentional. Average sellers don't put time and thought into how they're being perceived through their own *projections of character*. They think, *I'm a good person. There's nothing wrong with me. My company's reputation is fine.* Well, a state of neutrality is not a state of trust. In leading a *trust building* sales habit, we're trying to ensure that our buyer will form their own trusting state of mind in us. It's from those initial moments of introduction and on through the latest stages of the buying process where *trust* will start to build from how we're *projecting* our *character*.

PRECISION of Credibility

There's a difference between having credibility and being perceived as having credibility. Sure, anyone could research us, our product, or our company. Our references, known history, or reputation could help a buyer intellectually determine that we probably have some credibility they should trust. Yet, we're talking about sales communication, real-time interactions, sales meetings. Moreover, this chapter is about ensuring that we build the trust a Buyer Champion needs at such a deep level that they put their own credibility on the line to move forward with our purchase agreement. How, in our discussions and sales engagements, are we attracting a buyer's perception that we are credible?

When we think about our identity of how credible or believable, we are, do our expectations lean toward being credible *to* a buyer or being credible *for* a buyer? Have you ever been so passionate and sure of your product or service's credibility that you could have lost touch with helping your buyer make the same connection? Were you, in turn, frustrated that they didn't trust what you so strongly did? At the time, you felt that they just weren't understanding you. They didn't get it. Maybe they weren't smart enough or just didn't have the funds to make the purchase. Walking away satisfied with that deal diagnosis, did you later find out that they in fact bought something from someone else? Could it have been that they clearly saw and understood your solution's credibility in principle, yet they just didn't feel the credibility from you and the way you sold? Perhaps they saw your product's credibility in the market in general, but they just couldn't trust it for their needs. Maybe, for the price that you were trying to charge, they couldn't trust the claims that you were making in order to justify that high of a premium.

You see, the longer we sell in this career, the closer we get to an acceptance that there's a difference between who we are—as a partner, product, or service—and who our buyer needs us to be. If our objective in our *trust building* mission is to establish a buyer's belief in our credibility, we need to be very *precise* in those expectations and in how we attract that belief. Mastering this second *high-trust habit* of the **PRECISION of credibility** is about paying attention to the trust building details. The only way to be a consistent *credibility builder* is to have the mindset and discipline to always be in self-awareness mode, intentionally paying attention to what our buyers need from us, what they are distrusting, and how we're being perceived.

Gaining that credibility, that we are believable for our unique buyer, comes down to the ***precision*** of how we're establishing that credibility. Leading a routine habit of being *precise*, almost surgical in how we form credibility with a buyer, means that we have *precision* in three areas of our *credibility* habits. A buyer developing the belief that we are credible for them will stem from the *precision* of how we **Communicate**, the **Capabilities** that we position, and in the **Claims** that we make about those capabilities and their value.

I'll expand on each of these: the *precision* of *communication, capabilities, and claims*. And I'll share some situational sales examples for you to consider. But first, let's talk about what *precision* even means in the first place. When anything that we say, show, or do in the sales engagement appears *imprecise*, we lessen our credibility. As we've covered, those emotional reactions can go downhill as fast as an avalanche. In the game of *trust building*, we rarely get the chance to defend our credibility with a buyer. In fact, most of the time we don't have a clue how they feel about our credibility until it's come into question. That's often too late.

A habit of building credibility with *precision* is key in both building on the initial attraction we gain for a buyer's trust, as well as in qualifying whether this is even a *precise enough* buyer for us. Business credibility is like an *identity* or a brand. Like a retailer selling its products to its consumers, we must consider our credibility from the point of view of how *precise* our buyer is a match for us. The more we accept that, the easier it will be for us to remove our own emotions and see how credible both we and this buyer are for each other. We can now be honest about how qualified this buyer might be for our unique value proposition. Maybe our level of credibility doesn't align with what they're looking for. So, maybe we're wasting our time and we'll never gain their trust. We could also realize that it may be us who's missing the mark in being *precise* in our own credibility. Quite simply, we can't assume that our own view of our credibility is *precise* enough of a fit in the eyes of a buyer. They'll form their perspective of our identity by measuring the credibility of our **Communication**, the **Capabilities** we position, and the **Claims** that we make.

Precision of COMMUNICATION

How does our **Communication** affect our credibility? Well, since the buyer's first and last interaction is usually with the seller, credibility starts and ends with us. So, if in the way that we *communicate*, we lack believability, it's we who often become the *trust blocker*. Our *communication* can deter our buyer's emotional willingness to invest any more energy into hearing the message or in finding solutions to problems that come up in the deal. Being *precise* in how we *communicate* means that our words, body language, and the way we express ourselves is accurate, exact, and clear.

Think back to early in your sales career. Although I'm sure you were a *Rock Star*, in those first buyer/seller conversations, how precise would your buyers and customers say that you were? How precise is yours or your team's *communication* today? Consider these examples of *communication* precision. As I ask these questions of you, think back to any of the most typical sales conversations you've been experiencing either individually or with others. Was your **Knowledge** strong enough to react and respond to all the directions that those discussions would take you? Or do you remember your buyer wishing you knew more than you did? How many of those sales interactions you experienced lacked **Clarity**? Although we may think the words we're using make sense, do we ever find our buyer giving us that perplexed stare? You know the one, when both of their eyebrows are pinching together in a stressful strain of confusion. When our communication lacks precision in our *clarity* of message, that lazy buyer brain is more apt to give up and make a fast judgement on us and our solution's credibility.

How often have we found ourselves *imprecise* in the **Accuracy** of what we've said? Have you or your sellers been immediately called out on the lack of validity in your statements, aggressively counterattacked with argumentative corrections? How much trust do you think we sellers build in that moment when we're imprecise in our *accuracy*? In these, and far many more examples, is where we see the crucial importance of being *precise* in our *communication*. Our Champions don't want to search for the message, the positions they need to hear, and the answers to their questions. We gain and lose credibility in how easy or hard we make it for our buyers to get to those conclusions.

Have you ever gone into the mid to later stages of an opportunity believing that you had a Champion who trusted you, but then trust fell apart? Even after weeks of a Buyer Champion growing for us, we can shatter their trust in how *imprecise* we address some of their more serious buying considerations, such as product efficacy, technical validation, pricing and packaging, implementation, or commercial terms. Have you ever lost trust from a bad reference call? Thinking back, did you or someone on your team lack *precision* in finding just the right reference who had alignment in scope, relatability, and a willingness to actually sell for you? Have you, a partner, or a manager ever said or promised anything inaccurately during a sales milestone or negotiation, only to lose credibility when that blunder got exposed?

Like with any habit, developing our *precision of communication* takes a mindset change. We sellers are not only the messengers of what we sell. A buyer actually sees us as a representation of what we sell. If the communication isn't credible, we and our solutions won't be credible. Every seller has been given a sales *message.* However, it's *us,* the seller, who is the carrier of that message. You're the embodiment of what you sell and its credibility. Yes, we can lead a buyer's vision, but not without credibility. Our *communication* establishes the identity of what we sell. In our communication, whether verbal, non-verbal, or written, if any of that depiction comes across unknowledgeable, lacking confidence, vague, or inaccurate, our buyers mentally transfer that lack of understanding into a lack of believability.

Precision of CAPABILITIES

The solutions we sell have many different **Capabilities.** *Capability* and *Competency* work together and thus complete our *trust building* with a buyer. A *capability* of a solution is its ability to do something. However, how credible is a *capability* for a buyer, even what could be our most proud and differentiating *capability,* if it doesn't precisely align to that Champion target's needs and decision criteria?

Let's see if this relates. How many times in your career have you found yourself weeks or months into a deal or an account with growing positive vibes from a buyer? During that time, the buyers you worked with would continue to take your meetings and learn more about your solution. Some things they did made you think that they were most likely Champions. But eventually, they told you that your solution just wasn't the right fit for them. This was a bit of a shock for you, certainly disappointing.

If this has happened to you, looking back, how precise were you in qualifying that the very specific differentiating capability or set of capabilities you offered was what they believed they needed the most? Did you find yourself focused on presenting, demonstrating, and trying to provide credibility to a *capability* that turns out, wasn't even the most important toward the buyer's decision criteria? Again, was credibility being established from your point of view or theirs? What seems to happen too often is that, with all the time and energy investments that we sellers make, our buyers continue to fall short of trusting that our solutions align to and meet their greatest requirements and trust criteria.

So, in thinking about *trust building* as a habit, and more specifically establishing *high-trust credibility*, we need to be consistently *precise* in trying to build credibility in the right *capabilities* of the solutions that we sell.

What makes a capability credible? A buyer wants to know that a capability is relevant to solving their problem, delivering toward their desired outcomes, and that it will work for them in their environment or existing business processes. But *credibility* is always going to be in question until that agreement is closed. So, as a buying process progresses, we need to re-qualify this alignment. As new stakeholders show up to the decision, we must lead the same level of *capability* alignment with each one. Always remember, elite sales is all about *The Champion or Champions*. To be precise in the right capabilities we should be positioning to establish credibility, we must align and realign to the decision criteria of every single one of our buyers, both early and often.

We also need precision in *how* we communicate about our capabilities. Credibility is believability. Have you ever poorly explained specific capabilities of what you sell, only to see an actual negative reaction from your buyer? Not neutral, but negative? If in our words and actions, a buyer struggles to understand a capability and how it would be a fitting solution to their needs, then our solution loses credibility for them. So, why the negative reaction? They expect us sellers to actively make that connection of credibility for them. They expect us to listen, learn, and then align. They want to understand us. If explanations of capabilities are imprecise and complicated, perception of the capability will be that it's complicated. But what do we sellers do? We conclude that we've already earned credibility. We walk in believing that we know with certainty what a buyer needs: *our product or service*! We assume that *how* we're positioning that capability makes perfect sense, and so we move on to the rest of the show.

I completely understand that we all get into deals where the buyers we're selling to just don't seem to share our point of view or philosophy of what their required capabilities should be. This happens more times than not in tech startups or in the launch of new products to market. This is precisely why we need to develop our habit of being a strong *Vision Leader*. However, we're talking about credibility that will motivate a buyer to be our Champion and move forward in a purchase process. If we cannot lead a buyer toward a precise understanding of our key capabilities, those that are clearly aligned to the requirements that they're prioritizing, then we will lack credibility no matter how strong our capabilities are.

A good friend and mentor John Kaplan always tells sellers, "We have to be equal before we're different." Otherwise, we lose credibility. We waste everyone's time and gradually lose any credibility that we've been building. In these situations, it's not a disinterested, inexperienced, or unintelligent buyer at fault, as we often like to believe. Many times, it's our imprecise listening, capability alignment, and explanations that burn trust with a buyer. Thus, their feelings grow more negative. They think, *This seller is wasting my time, not listening, and they clearly don't care about us.* As elite Champion Builders, we shouldn't be expecting a buyer to prioritize our differentiating capabilities. Buyers won't become trusting of our solution until we align their priorities with *the precision of our capabilities.*

Precision of CLAIMS

Boy, we sellers can make some claims. Buyers have been burned for centuries by our random, misleading, and purely false claims. A *claim*, in the context of credibility, is something we say that our product or service can do for a customer, the impact we should be able to make, an outcome we can deliver. Whether we intended to or not, every seller reading or listening to this book, myself included, has made a claim that lacked credibility at least once in their career. Many sellers make a habit of making non-credible claims. Some do so out of inexperience or *value ignorance.* Have you ever stated a firm claim that your buyer should expect a minimum *return on investment,* achieve payback within a period, improve a key indicator by a certain percentage? There are many reasons you could have been wrong and only a few for why you might have been right. If there truly was credibility in those claims, it could have been from a deep and thoughtful analysis done in total partnership and collaboration with your buyer. In those situations, maybe our claims were credible. Perhaps they were just so small and reasonable that it was easy to have credibility. Or maybe you sold the most amazing unicorn your industry has ever seen.

However, to a buyer, the person we want to become our committed Champion, they often take our claims at best, with a grain of salt. What drives this immediate lack of believability? Their response doesn't always occur because their personality is necessarily skeptical. Often, they've heard this claim before to no level of success. Truth is, in business, there's usually multiple factors that go into the level of return or impact that a customer can achieve from the products and services that we sell. What buyers taught me, through some pretty tough conversations, is that most of those factors that make our claims sound so ridiculous to a buyer have very little to do with us. There are often situational factors, technical or business process interdependencies that are outside of our control. There could be a list of variables that all must play together in just the right tune for a buyer to achieve the claims that we'd hope.

And yet, we sellers march along oblivious, with our *value megaphones* screaming out our claims like some sidewalk preacher. This doesn't mean that our claims can't be true for our buyer. We just need to have the thoughtful awareness to learn the unique applications of our solutions with buyers and position our claims with as much precise credibility as we can.

Unfortunately, there are sellers who make a habit out of making *False Claims*. A *false claim* is an intentionally misleading suggestion of expected results. Engrained in their sales character, there can certainly be those who just don't care. Either their arrogance or disdain for buyers causes them to believe that most won't follow up and try to validate the claim, or even question it.

They're convinced that if they just make their claims with conviction and passion, most buyers are easy to sway. Slice it any way you want. Those tactics are what buyers would call *manipulation*.

While these sellers could be decent character folks at home, those claims they make lack integrity. No words I could write about credibility and trust building will ever change those habits. That's a personal decision. Now, if this sounds a bit like you or someone on your team, I'll offer two reasons for changing this mindset and habit of making *false claims*. One, when we have incongruence between the level of character we show in our business life compared to our personal life, we end up building these low-integrity habits as a person. We won't be able to help it. Our mindset drives our behaviors. Maybe it's a *make money at all cost* mindset. Perhaps some believe that all buyers lie and disrespect us, so they're just playing the game. Whatever the mindset, those behaviors become routines, involuntary ways that we act. So, we should ask ourselves how important success and people are in our personal life.

But the second reason to avoid *false claims* is all about buyer credibility. By skating the responsibility of making accurate credible claims, we also miss an opportunity to build real credibility with a buyer. If our claims consistently lack credibility, we just won't be able to build high-trust Champions. It's as simple as that.

On the flip side, let's talk about why having *precision* in the *claims* we make can support such a big opportunity we have with a Champion we're trying to build. At the end of the day, the reason that a buyer would be interested in any purchase agreement and certainly, why they'd want to sign up for the role of Buyer Champion, is because they trust in their own mental claim of the value we could deliver. Whether they got that claim from us or their own hopefulness, any purchase decision has some expectation of value results. *Vision leading* sellers are always trying to inspire a buyer's vision to go from outcomes to actual measurable value from those outcomes.

So, where's the opportunity? In the opportunity of *collaboration*, working with a buyer to agree on claims that we both believe to be reasonable, we form a *trust bond*. We did this together. When we sellers project ourselves as humble, yet very confident that there's a good chance a buyer can achieve these claims we've aligned on, we disarm them, and they begin trusting our character even more. They get loyal. Just remember, we should always position our claims with a *precision* of caution and responsibility. The minute we begin leading those discussions on value, measurable outcomes, or return on the investment, any *claims* we make will either build or break our credibility. This will be a very simple outcome. When our claims lack credibility in either their content or in the way we present them, we've just lost trust with our buyer. We now have a mental *trust tax* that we've created for ourselves. For us to get this person turned around with a level of trust that will drive a *bias for action* on our behalf, we'll now be required to take more time to restore their trust in us, that is if they even give us that chance. However, if we collaborate in the journey to high-trust credibility claims with our buyers, Champions build and become more committed toward their *milestone of closure*.

When we think about our level of *precision* in making *claims*, there's really three dimensions of precision that a buyer's trust instincts will react to. One is that we must show precision in the **Relatability** of the claim. How many times have you made or observed another seller making a claim that wasn't even related to the buyer's desired solution or outcomes? One of the biggest causes of this is the companies that we work for. Have you ever witnessed sellers get so caught up in the hype of the *super claim* that their company makes? *Any customer of ours will achieve 90 percent reduction in time and cost!* Everyone says it. Everyone believes it.

Have you or others fallen into a *recency bias*, where a value metric or measurable outcome was recently proven out in one of your customers or in a different deal that someone else closed? Then, in each of your meetings the rest of that year, all your buyers got the same value claim pitched to them over and over again. The precision of a claim that we make loses its credibility when it's not *relatable* to the buyer who we're selling to.

The second dimension of precision is in the **Projection** of the claim. We've already talked about how we can lose credibility in the way that we *project* our character. Think of a time when you or another seller had recently joined a company, changed roles, or just weren't very sure of yourself. Was the way in which the claims of credibility were made not so convincing? Did your projection lack confidence or a smooth delivery? Have you ever positioned a claim with that question mark tone at the end of the statement? *I'm fairly confident that you'll get 20 percent improvement?* Credibility is believability. When we don't believe, they won't believe.

The third area of precision is in the **Legitimacy** of the claim itself. How credible is the actual claim that we are making? Is the level or content associated with the claim legit, or is it a bit misguided? Can we say and should we honestly expect our buyer to believe that our claim will absolutely be true for them? If you've experienced this, why did you lack *legitimacy* in your claims? Were you trying too hard in your message? Did you not believe that your capabilities were differentiated enough against the competition?

Were you misled internally by someone at your company? When we make claims that lack *legitimacy*, we prevent trust from being able to be built. There's nothing more important to someone's credibility than the truth of what they say. Just as there's nothing more opportunistic, there's also nothing more dangerous than the *power of trust*. If a claim seems untruthful, the seller will seem untruthful. If the seller appears untruthful, the solution and their company will appear untruthful.

The *buyer brain* is emotionally driven, even that of a proven Champion. Despite all the intellectual connections and logical support that a buyer may have developed for a solution, even after months of evaluation, a Champion will not put their reputation and political capital on the line for us if they can't believe us. Can we still win that deal? Yes, for sure. But will we have a Champion? Will competitors gain leverage and consideration? Will the timing of the decision be delayed so that the buyer can prove out these trust concerns? Making low-credibility claims, whether in the *relatability, projection, or legitimacy* of the claim, will absolutely break the trust of any Buyer Champion who was otherwise growing in their conviction to trust us and the solutions that we sell.

PROVING of Competencies

Our third and final high-trust habit is seen in the **PROVING of our Competencies**. Is a *competency* the same as a *capability*? Let's start by looking back at our buyer's *trust path* thus far. We paid attention to how we *project* ourselves. So, our *character* is not in question with this buyer. In the effort to build real *credibility*, we didn't take a point of view for why we think we're credible. We established credibility with *precision* in our focus on what would be credible for them personally, their own situation and needs. We were precise in everything considered and planned in order to get to this point of the buyer's *trust path*. While they've spent the time intellectually learning about our capabilities, at least what we say we're capable of, they'll now be expecting to see some *proof of our competencies*. You see, lots of products and services possess the skills, knowledge, or processes that enable them to say that they are capable of delivering on a specific solution. It's not unreasonable or even that hard for a buyer to believe that a solution has the proposed *capabilities* that it says it does.

So, why do they then slow the deal down, beginning to question what we sell? How would they choose one solution over the other if both seemed to possess the same capabilities? You see, capabilities aren't usually what a human being's trust instincts are most concerned with. In any critical buying decision, a person's question of trust is whether those capabilities are *competent enough* to deliver for their unique needs. *Buying* is personal. While *capabilities* are traits that can affect an outcome, our *competencies* are a measurement of how we can perform those capabilities, proof that we can deliver the right outcome in the right way.

A *capability* can do something. A *competency* is how a capability can make an impact. Thus, *capabilities* are about us. *Competencies* are about what we can do for our buyer. How many times have you had a buyer tell you, "We're not like your other customers"? Or "I think the situation has to be just right for a solution like yours to work." Their concern wasn't our capabilities. It was our *competencies*.

Let's think of some examples. A services firm may have a team who has the capabilities to implement a specific business application. Some are engineers, others architects, all led by a project manager. However, if I were the buyer working in a large multinational enterprise with several interdependent systems and process challenges, I'd be looking for a service partner who has proven that they have the competencies to implement this application in an environment like mine.

A business owner is considering several different construction companies. Each firm has the same capabilities, the same equipment, roles, and resources. However, this business owner has an urgent deadline. They need their new site up and running by a specific date and with certain unique parameters being met.

A technology buyer needs a software platform that automates how they secure their data. If we asked five different buyers at five different companies, all five would require the same security capabilities. But each has a totally different mix of platforms and business processes. Worse, this buyer has lost two experts on their staff to attrition with a compliance deadline to hit.

Another example, a physician meeting with a medical salesperson quickly understands and believes that their treatment is capable of reducing the main side effects of a disease they specialize in. However, for a large group of their patients, their big concern is being able to trust that those capabilities won't create new problems, problems that they won't be able to treat.

These are all examples where our *competencies* are about the unique needs of our buyers. A buyer trusting our *competencies* is rarely as simple as we sellers would prefer it to be. Competencies are not capabilities. They are the impact and value characteristic of our capabilities. Trusting in a specific necessary level of impact within a buyer's context will come from a *competency* that will need to be proven.

What is *proof* and why is it important? How many times has your buyer confirmed a belief that your capabilities were strong and could even help them, so you or your seller convinced yourselves that you had a Champion? Yet, that decision never moved forward. Perhaps, even with the direct fear, uncertainty, and doubt that you positioned about your competitor, your supposed Champion went with them anyway? You told yourself that it must have been price! *Ah boss, I guarantee they dropped their price and bought the business.* Only later, you learned the truth. There was something about your solution that the buyer just couldn't overcome. They didn't get to a state of trust that your capabilities would be *competent enough* for them. How could they believe this? Because you never proved it.

Remember *Attribution Theory* I introduced to you? We humans just naturally need to explain how some outcome will be caused, how we'll be able to attribute our success. Our subconscious is ruled by our protective survival instincts. For a human buyer to place their complete faith and trust in making this final purchase agreement, they'll need to see some evidence that our capabilities will be capable enough for them, *competencies*.

Think of all the biggest or most profound sales opportunities you've worked over the years. Remember those buyers who supported you and made a purchase decision for you? They became your customers. How? What process of discernment did they go through? Because they became a customer, we can assume that they trusted your character and that your solution had credibility with them. But was being *credible* enough for them? Is it typically enough for you? How did other buyers in their consensus group react when they were asked to support your purchase? What was the buying process they went through? What extra steps did they put you through? Specifically, how did they gain proof that your solution would be *competent enough* for them?

If we think about buying decisions going through milestones for a buyer, even those who are trying to *champion* what we sell, there's going to be a stage where the buyer will need to address their questions of trust in the *competencies* of what we can do for them. This will need to happen before they complete any *milestone of closure*. Because a *competency* is so much more than a *capability*, there's no way to really trust how much impact or degree of success something can have without proving it. A *competency* isn't just the existence of an ability, it's the measurement of an ability.

The only way to trust this measurement is to have it proven. Without that evidence, a buyer won't form the trust they need. If they can't get it, they'll simply have to make a choice as to how risky this purchase is, considering that they don't really have proof yet. So, as you're listening or reading this challenge, ask yourself, *How much risk does what you sell place on your buyers?* Are your competencies not that hard to prove, not too complicated or unreasonable to believe? If that's the case, then perhaps actively proving out your competencies won't be as critical a habit as some of your others.

But, what if you're wrong? What if the lack of seeing and believing in the evidence of competency is one of the biggest reasons that your so-called Champions have not been able to move from commitment to closure? What if you've been selling in a single-threaded manner, usually with just one key buyer stakeholder? While the Champion who always took your calls and met with you was totally on board and trusting, who were the other buyers in *the consensus* group? What reasons would they doubt your competencies? Could they have had a different perspective based on what responsibilities, systems, or processes they own? Were some of them just more experienced and wiser in decision-making?

The fact is, in what I've witnessed in thousands of deals, from small ones with small companies to huge multimillion-dollar transactions in the largest enterprises, is that the number one factor in a buyer's decision not to close business in the final stages of a decision is a lack of *trust*. That trust is rarely lacking in our capabilities, especially after all the effort we've put into *leading their vision* and presenting our solutions.

Elite sellers know that making a final and formal decision to purchase a specific solution is about the buyer, not about us. If our price is relatively high, then can we prove that we'll be competent enough to deliver a return that justifies it? If the capabilities that our solution offers aren't yet a fully known commodity to the world with a standard of accepted trust, then how could our buyer just believe that we'd be competent enough for them? If the core problems that our business typically solves are viewed as complex and remain common challenges in industry, then why would our buyer easily assume that we could uniquely solve them when others have failed? After all our selling in these deals, how is it that our buyers still come to the conclusion where they tell us, "Look, you and your competitor basically have the same capabilities." *How dare they?*

What they're trying to tell us is that, in order to trust our solution, our buyers need proof of our *competencies for them*. Notice that I didn't say that in order to trust our solution, they need us to prove how differentiated or better than our competition we think we are. This is a great example of where we begin to change our mindset toward a habit of *trust building* within a Buyer Champion. *Proof of competency* is about *their* trust criteria and *their* solution requirements.

The first acceptance we need is that we will almost always need to be able to show proof of a Champion's desired competencies before we earn their complete trust. And I mean *acceptance*. For years, I've observed sellers who've tried to avoid this requirement of proving out a solution. Yes, most eventually accept it once a buyer escalates their tone, telling them that they don't have a choice. "If you want our business, then you'll need to prove yourself!"

So, why do sellers try to avoid providing solution proof? Have you ever been elusive and delaying in offering up a reference call? Did your team or company try to convince you to avoid a solution test at all costs? It's *fear*. We have fear of being exposed, fear of failing before we close the deal. We might even lack confidence that we can prove our competencies. All these fears may be completely justified. The more ambitious our solutions, the higher the investment, and the more that's on the line for our buyers, the bigger the risks exist for the both of us.

Yet understand, it's not usually that we fear that our solutions are capable of doing the things we say they can. We fear that we'll be *competent* enough for our unique buyer and to the standards that they're expecting. However, just because we have fear doesn't mean that the buyer's own fears will disappear or are less important. It's human nature. We all need to see proof of how our success will be attributed.

So, we sellers must accept the need and habit of *proving our competencies* to the people we sell to. If you're not confident that you can prove your competencies, then you might be selling the wrong solution. But realize, earning trust is rarely an easy thing in most situations in life. What is true for all of us is that in business, we sellers can't be ignorant of the reality of how trust will play a non-negotiable role in how buyers will make their decisions. Where a large *trust gap* lies in the sales universe is that many sellers aren't intentional and proactive enough in proving our competencies. No matter how impressive our product demonstrations or analyst write-ups are, the human buyer is going to need to see *proof* of those competencies before they can fully trust.

Now, if we identify that our buyer needs to see solution proof, then our question should quickly move to, *Then what are your decision criteria to fully trust this purchase?* What this chapter is trying to drive home is that we need to expand our view of merely aligning to a Champion's decision criteria for what a solution can do and go deeper toward what it would take to earn a buyer's *trust* in what we can do for them. Leading with this precise trust-minded level of qualification is when the ranking and prioritizing of decision criteria become clear. We now get focused on a mission to build their trust by proving it.

But you can't prove what you don't know to be important. To help you think about what would make certain criteria or competencies more significant to a buyer's *trust standard* than others, try putting competencies into two buckets. In one bucket, these are the competencies that a buyer just expects that we would have. I call these the **Assumed Competencies**. *I just assume that these would work in any solution like yours. If not, then your company's got bigger problems.*

But in this other bucket, these are the **Success Competencies**. For these a buyer thinks, *If these competencies don't work, then I am certain that I won't be successful.* It's this *success competencies* bucket where our Champion will absolutely need to see proof as evidence that these competencies will exist. If they don't get proven, then our buyer, even if they've become a Champion up to this point, will lose or question their belief that our solution will be able to make them successful. Most often, they won't move forward until their need for some evidence can be satisfied.

So, what's one conclusion with Buyer Champions? Sellers shouldn't just be striving for Champions who are really impressed with their solutions and love hanging out on their expense account. Elite sellers are looking to build Buyer Champions who are committed to *buy* what we sell. The final step they'll need in their *trust path* toward making that commitment to buy our solution is to see reasonable *proof in the competencies* of what we're selling. Here are some **Competency Proof** examples that might relate to your sales situations.

Solution Requirements

The *competencies* of the actual products and services we sell will often be the predominant set of *proof* that a Champion will need to see in order for us to meet their *trust standard*. It's in this profile of a *trust standard* where a buyer needs to see some type of validation or test that proves their **Solution Requirements**. We especially see this in sales where our technical, product, or service competencies are most associated with the buyer's *trust standard*.

Unlike the other *competency proof situations* I'll share below, *solution proof* is how most sellers will typically think about gaining a buyer's trust of our competencies. This could be a technical validation like a Proof of Concept, a workshop, or a customer reference discussing their experience with our competencies. The mechanisms that buyers are now getting proof of solution competencies are changing in some ways. Earlier in my career selling for software companies, we always created our standard test plan and implemented a validation event into the later stage of our sales process. Why did we do this? We knew that before a buyer could make their final *high-trust* decision to move to close, they would need to see *proof* of our *competencies*. Often, there were even formal stages of their buying process where they needed to see both our proof and that of our competitors through a technical benchmark or *bake-off*.

Yet, in more recent years we're seeing modern technologies get into the hands of the buyers much earlier, sometimes before they ever meet a salesperson. Some in the industry refer to this as *PLG, product-led growth*. The pharmaceutical industry has been doing this for decades with the use of free samples. Have your patients try before they buy to get some personal evidence of our drug's effectiveness. The pharmaceutical seller's challenge was that they were one step removed from the end buyer, the patient.

However, this type of product-led strategy proved successful at building multiple influencers toward a physician's credibility for the competencies of the treatment. As time has gone by and free technology accessibility has become more common, those conversion rates of moving from a *competency validation* to a closed deal have decreased. In other words, there's a lot of testing going on, but not necessarily a lot of buying. This paradigm should be a reminder that until we fully understand what specific proof of our solution competencies will satisfy a buyer's need to fully trust, we won't be in control of moving to closure. Roadblocks, stalls, and time extensions will continue to burden our sales pipeline because we will still have a *trust gap* to overcome.

So, for those who are experiencing less ownership of buyers testing and piloting their solutions, consider a process that's focused on qualifying and satisfying those *trust criteria* with your buyers while they're in proof mode. Rather than trying to sell them or prematurely incentivizing them to make the order, find out what's in their *success competencies* bucket. Be direct, intellectually curious, and make it about them. If you find that there's one main proof point that will take your buyer's trust over the top, focus there and you will find yourself making closure so much easier. Proving our solution competencies is where we strategically and carefully fight to win. The more we know, the more we can then confidently move mountains to ensure we've satisfied our Champion's trust concerns.

Trusted Advisor/Subject Matter Expert

If you're in a sale where a buyer truly desires a sales team or a company function to be more of a **Trusted Advisor** or **Subject Matter Expert**, then how well are you *proving* your competencies? Are you even aware of how important this type of competency is in your typical buyer's trust criteria? If it is, how have you or your team shown buyers that they can trust you to help them think through and plan for the critical decisions associated with your solution?

If you're personally not qualified to be the *Trust Advisor* or *Subject Matter Expert* they need, how regularly do you use the resources you have at your disposal? We see this *trust standard* in very technical buying scenarios or those in which we're asking buyers to commit to a complicated transformative solution. The solutions themselves aren't so easy to just prove out. So, the buyer needs to see proof of competency in other ways. Financial services, medical treatments, industrial services, business consulting, and broad enterprise technologies are some examples—really any solution that's seen as a transformation that solves a complex problem.

Let's say a physician is considering two different complicated disease treatments whereas each has a similar efficacy, cost model, and pros and cons that offset one another. Gaining validation from a *subject matter expert,* either internally or a peer in the field, can be a trust differentiator. In enterprise IT, two cloud technology providers might seem similar. All the buyer knows is that their business will need to primarily commit to one, and that it's going to be an expensive, hard road to transform. Of the two comparable but equally transformational cloud solutions, the one where a *trusted advisor* or *subject matter expert* exists to support that the technical competencies are highly valuable and risk-mitigating will usually become the winner.

In a financial services decision where an institution is considering their next partner to support a major project, it's the firm with the *trusted advisor* who walks them through their proven experience for how they've successfully delivered these similar business endeavors who creates the mental evidence of competency. In these and similar sales situations, how do we build differentiating trust? Most buyers will quickly realize that they could find success or failure in multiple solution offerings. The *trust standard* that they're often looking for is *proof* for which company or seller has the experience and credibility to guide them toward success. With these criteria, if we're not the success *experts* who can prove that we have what our buyers need to achieve success, then we won't earn the necessary trust of our buyers.

Business Advocate/Partner

Many buyers feel the stress or complexity of their buying process or program they're operating. In a seller or company they can trust, they seek out more of a **Business Advocate** or **Partner.** Some sellers believe that this is what all buyers need in order to trust them. Yes, in spirit, who wouldn't want a company to act like an advocate or partner? But we're talking about *trust building* criteria. These buyers need *proof* of our advocacy or support for a reason.

Typically, when a buyer puts a big emphasis on their sales or customer teams having strong competencies in *advocacy* or *partnership*, it's because they believe that their buying or solution adoption situations need more support. Maybe these buyers are commonly understaffed, lack expertise, lower in maturity, and have more basic needs. They won't usually believe that some magic product is going to mitigate their risks. In fact, these buyers will often view a new innovative solution as something that would add risk to their operation and them personally. We can't build high-trust Champions if we're disconnected to this buyer mindset.

It's those companies and sales teams who build these competencies up and make them known to the market who win the trust game. Several times in my career, we sold to business functions who were relatively immature in their systems, staff, and processes associated with the innovation we brought to the table. Because most of our prospects were afraid to take too many risks and just wanted to focus on getting started, we had to change our sales approach. These are the buyers that slow you down and say things like, "We're basically looking to crawl, walk, run." The competencies that those buyers needed to trust were far more related to providing simple playbooks for getting started and assigning program advocate-type resources. We'd seen these moves be made by competitors who were winning the market. So, in our attention to the *trust standard* that our buyers needed to meet, we had to adjust. Unlike your simple transaction-based sell, in these more complex and programmatic buying situations, the competencies of our people and processes drive the buyer's believability and can override the capabilities of the product itself.

Customer Services and Support Levels

Perhaps the set of competencies that sellers are frequently unaware of, and yet most common to buyers, are in a company's ability and strengths toward **Customer Services** and **Support Levels**. We see this in solution implementations, delivery of service, customer support, or high-volume business processes. We sellers often develop our mindsets from the companies we work for. If you've ever been in an organization that put all the emphasis on their product and yet minimized or ignored the buyer-crucial competencies of the associated customer services, then you may know what I'm talking about. Elite sellers can't allow their company's lack of awareness and empathy toward buyers to influence their Champion-building strategies. Other companies go above and beyond their customer requirements for services and yet, sellers get so narrow-minded on their product that they actually undersell those supportive offerings.

I once encountered a business who had launched a game-changing treatment for a complicated and life-altering neurological disease. The unique and new approach this treatment took could make a massive impact on the daily quality of life of its patients. While about 20 percent of the sales team was hitting their number, the majority was truly struggling. At first, I thought it was just their messaging. For many, it was. However, when I interviewed those top sellers, they painted a much harder path to establishing trust and building Champions. What I learned was that the adoption of the medicine required an intrusive surgery versus the simple daily pills of its competitor. With much of their population elderly, this was a serious consideration of risk versus reward. The bigger problem was for the physicians who needed a much higher level of training and support than the alternatives. But their company hadn't mastered these services.

Another example of *customer service* competency was seen in a technology that replaced old, antiquated hardware-based telecommunications systems. This newer tech was modern software-based communication. It delivered a strong value proposition because it could save a company millions of dollars by taking one of their highest costs and most complicated business services off their plate. It did it for them as a service. Yet, because it involved centralizing all management of convoluted carrier charges and usage, getting all the billing and cost centers accurate and on time was a business nightmare. Of the three top providers in this new space, it was the one with the service and support models that could scale that would most often win the larger accounts.

Whether emotional or completely rational, there will be many buyers who just can't get over the great concern for how what we sell could hurt their mission or their business bottom line. These Champions will need operational support through our competencies of customer services. When those decisions get broader across a consensus group, even more risk-averting voices come to the table. If the assurances of our *customer service or support level competencies* are a priority, then we sellers must learn and respect that *trust standard* and come prepared with a plan that we can prove.

SUMMARY: *Trust Building*

Trust Building truly does form along a buyer's *Trust Path*. If our buyer sees an acceptable level of *Character* in us, then they're willing to consider our *Credibility* for them. If that's established, they'll need to see proof of our *Competencies*. If all these three dimensions of their very personal *Trust Standard* are in place, we should have no problem earning and benefiting from the *trust* of our Buyer Champions. There's no time in a buyer's decision process where this is more critical than the *Milestone of Closure*, where everything gets more serious and real. *Trust* is a zero-sum game. We either have it or we don't. But the learning I want you to gain is that *trust* forms and can be restored through our *Trust Habits*.

Most high-trust sellers are unconsciously competent in *building trust*. And most buyers are not consciously aware of their *trust standard*. Here lies the opportunity to separate ourselves from the rest, to become *intentional Trust Builders*. Mastery of this habit can become our greatest *superpower* in building and winning with Champions. Toward all the career and financial goals we have for ourselves, this E.L.I.T.E. habit of *Trust Building* is how the top sellers routinely and consistently get their Champions to a state of winning on their behalf.

For those sellers who often get opportunities to the final stages and then lose to competitors or see pushed after pushed decisions, a lack of *buyer trust* is the number one root cause. This is when a *Trust Gap* exists in one or more parts of the buyer's *trust path*. All deals start and end with *trust*. When *trust* is a gap, even for the most hopeful and optimistic Buyer Champions, they will feel like there is no way that they can move to closure.

While we may have truly connected to a level of trust with our Champions, there are often new people introduced into the buying process as part of a *consensus group*. We'll need to recognize this and work toward building trust in each stakeholder individually. If trust is missing, they'll become doubters and cynics, and will quickly be cemented as nonbelievers. We won't turn them around because our Champion would have lost any *trust leverage* they otherwise had. We sellers can't afford to wait and hope that our Champion will just take our word for it and appreciate the brilliance of what we sell. That's not how the human buyer brain works. Eventually, they will need to form a real trust in the message and claims that we make, but mostly in their personal *trust standard*. This may not be a conscious standard, but it will be our judge and jury.

How contrary is this to your selling habits, your team's? In the opportunities you see to grow as a *trust builder*, will it be from a self-aware evaluation of our *Sales Character Tendencies*? Or will you find those opportunities in being more intentional with *High-Trust Habits* across the human *Trust Path*, how we *Project our character*, establish *credibility with Precision*, and *Prove our competencies*?

CHAPTER 8

EMPOWERING CHAMPIONS

The Work we do to Win!

MY GUITAR HERO

As an up-and-coming sales rep, one of the first major deals that I closed was an extremely technical solution to a large set of serious business problems. One of the world's largest technology companies was under extreme pressure to address several compounding problems. In the early 2000s, Sarbanes-Oxley was a new law that was sweeping across all public companies to help protect their investors from fraudulent financial reporting. This was in response to scandals at Enron, Tyco, WorldCom, and several others. If companies didn't pass these new and technically complicated audits, they would be subject to millions of dollars in fines and public scrutiny. My tech company prospect had already been hit hard by these fines.

When the lawyers created Sarbanes-Oxley, they didn't care too much about how complex and diverse most Information Technology or IT systems and environments had become. A company like mine was so important because we were automating all the different new platforms for their management. We addressed security and compliance needs like Sarbanes, as well as other operational needs like remediating failed servers. This was another problem for my *prospect*. They'd been having outages that were impacting revenue loss. These were some of the smartest IT and security professionals that I'd ever worked with, and yet they just couldn't solve the problems fast enough with their existing technologies. The whole team, from the executives down, were extremely technical. After months of deep evaluation and testing of us and the absolute best competitors in the market, we were selected by the team. I forecasted the deal. My Champions felt confident. It seemed like a slam dunk. Never had I ever learned a lesson as powerful as I was about to regarding how much our Champions need a seller to help empower them to close a deal.

We all took a first pass in December of that year, but the deal was rejected. Can you believe that? Millions were being spent on compliance fines and the outages were still happening. Even worse, their problems had now become public. The market had learned about their lack of compliance. Although this was really a technology and process challenge they couldn't overcome, the perceptions in the public market were a concern for unethical practices. Their stock was suffering. By going into that first push to close without any formal business justification outside of a technology solution write-up, my Champion wasn't empowered for what would happen next. Because of their financial challenges, they laid off thousands of people. There was no way a large high-profile expense was going to pass through their finance and legal department without a tight and well-prepared business case.

So, what did we do? We played *Guitar Hero*, a popular video game that was taking over the US population of hoodie-wearing, beer-drinking IT professionals. Well first, my Champion Cole and I set a meeting up with the new IT vice president, and he walked us through a process, structure, and plan for a business justification that he believed would empower him to get the deal approved. Empower him? I didn't even know he existed. The process had changed and luckily, this new VP had some experience at getting high-cost investments pushed through at the company. Then, like any Champion-focused seller who worked at building trust and inspiring commitment, we brought both of our teams together at Cole's house one night. I bought the pizzas and beer while the teams traded off their heavy metal riffs. But we were there to work. We all collaborated until the early morning hours to build that business case around the very specific and targeted decision points that their upper management would need to consider, from business service availability to financial impact, and every negative consequence that they would need to think long and hard on not addressing now. In early February, the deal finally closed.

Of all the deals you've won in your career, have you ever experienced the *Surprise Deal*? This is the kind where, as you were entering the final *milestone of closure*, you had an optimistic hope, but no logical reason or any level of certainty that the deal would come in. Perhaps, as the deal slowly drifted into its final stages of whatever its buying process was, your supposed Champion went dark. You weren't hearing anything from them. When your manager would ask for regular updates, you always had something clever or satisfactory to say. But you knew that you didn't have any idea for what was truly going on. Maybe the deal even died a few deaths, resurrected through your buyer's political capital and business savvy. But you didn't see that. Even though you got the *win*, when you looked back, it felt like an awful scary ride, like you just never had any control.

I would guess that we've all had the *Surprise Deal* at least once in our career. Or maybe some of us have made a career out of them. If we asked our buyer what really happened, why we were kept out of the loop, they'd probably tell us something like, "Look, there was just a ton of work we had to get through. Just so you know, we would have been open to any help you could have provided . . . had you only asked." They say, "Look, in the end, we just liked your product more." *They just liked my product more? That sounds like it wasn't really anything that I did. Was there more that I could have done?* Across all the different types of sales opportunities that we sellers work, what is the expectation of what a salesperson can and should be doing for their Champion when the time comes for closure?

EMPOWERING CHAMPIONS: *The Winning Milestone*

The purpose of this entire sales journey we lead, one of failures, growth, and scars from the battles we wage, is *winning!* When we can elevate our mindset to believe that we are now in a **Milestone of Winning**, our higher standard of the gritty persistence and tenacious work that we will do to win will separate us from all common salespeople. With our Champion by our side, this is where we become elite, with a *will and the work to win*. Once we've identified and built our Buyer Champions, when those people of power and influence have made their emotional and intellectual connections to us, is it time for our work to stop? *Not even close.* That state of *connection* that came from us intuitively and thoughtfully *leading their vision* was merely our first sales *milestone*. This is where an average seller would often pause or decelerate the work. But this book isn't really about average selling, is it? Elite sellers know that, not only are we gambling to win any opportunity without first building a Champion, but they also know that the work it took to build the Champion only laid a foundation for them to do more work.

After our buyer gaining a connection with what we sell, reaching their next *milestone of commitment* won't be an accident. Our work will lead them through a path toward clearly understanding the *purpose, plan, and promise* of making this decision. Now, they're committed. Our job is done, right? *Forecast the deal! It's ours to lose.* Not done yet. We've learned that as a buyer enters into their *milestone of closure*, their strong emotional needs for *trust* will always kick in. Always! They, as well as all the other stakeholders, begin to question just how much this brilliantly painted sales masterpiece is something they should trust. That sneaky two-million-year-old *survival brain* shows its emotional dominance once again. Our elite sales instincts realize that our work just isn't over. Trust building, reinforcing trust, and sometimes, even restoring a trust that we or someone before us inadvertently lost, becomes the critical work that our Champion needs from us, now! We work hard for this business.

Trust is eventually built on all dimensions of our Champion's *trust path*. They believe that we're the most aligned solution to their *trust standard*. Are we finally in the clear? At this *winning milestone*, is it time to play that jam of a Foo Fighters song that goes by the same name, "In the Clear" in a joyous rock and roll celebration? Well, is the deal closed yet? I don't think so. That same awareness and empathy we possessed to inspire a Champion's high-trust commitment and build their trust will now be needed more than ever in the work to **Empower** our Champion to get this thing done. If our type of closure isn't the clean signature-based transaction we'd all prefer, if it's a decision that manifests over time like service adoption, product consumption, or medical treatments, this is where our level of intuitive and strategic work will distance us from all other common sellers.

The fifth and final E.L.I.T.E. habit of **Empowering Champions** is all about the real work that our Buyer Champions will need from our partnership to close our agreement and start delivering them the value that they so greatly desire. Has a buyer ever given you feedback that what set your solution apart was the effort that you and your team put in to ensuring that they had everything they needed? Maybe put into other words, *you just wanted it more.* Your work made this an easy decision and made it possible for them to close the purchase with you. You were fully aware and aligned to their buying process and you *empowered* your Champions where they needed it most. This is where we truly prove ourselves as that trusted partner.

But this is also where we avoid getting ***outsold***. I once had a manager tell me that I was outsold. In the moment, I was ticked. I didn't believe it. I knew I had positioned my product as good as anyone could, along with a business case that any CFO would respect. But did I even know what that meant, to be *outsold?* Elite sales professionals know that the sellers who work smart for a Champion will make them feel like we have their back, really care about their success. They'll be the ones who ensure that the differing opinions, intellectual questions, competitive threats, and internal processes are all addressed. These sellers will be the ones who will consistently standalone a *winner.* Working for the win at these and any other levels that our Champions and our opportunities can benefit from is where we avoid getting outsold.

In this final E.L.I.T.E. sales habit, we'll break down **The 3 Champion Empowerments**. The...

Empowerment of *Justification*

Empowerment of *Consensus*

Empowerment of *Negotiation*

As we do, I'll try to make these as general as possible to all types of sales. Remember, I'm using the word *purchase* as a common vocabulary that covers all different ways that a buyer formalizes their business agreements with us. In the end, if it's true that *we don't sell to companies, we sell to people*, then how could we ever expect those people to get our deals done with the level of transparency, predictability, and control that we desire, without our active *empowerment* of anything and everything that they need. As I walk through these empowerments and you try to relate them to your type of sell, just keep your focus on all the relevant work that your Champions need to do, the steps and obstacles that *they* need to traverse for them to make your purchase happen. It's in their buying journey, their path to closure, where you will find *the work we do to win*. In that work, you'll be able to identify your opportunities and elite expectations of **Empowering your Champions**.

THE 3 CHAMPION EMPOWERMENTS

The Empowerment of JUSTIFICATION: *The 5 Essential Justification Questions*

What is a business justification and why is it so important in the buying process? In medical or biotech sales, this could be the doctor or management team's informal discernment around their profitability, business standards, risk to practice credibility. Often, the real medical justification happens between a provider and patient, a series of discussions ensuring that they're aware of the risks and opportunities of a new therapy, surgery, or treatment. In this sales profession, it's as if the patient and their family is part of *the consensus* group for our health care provider Champions. So, if we put ourselves in that Champion-to-consensus sales conversation, what justification would be so strong that it would be worth it for the patients to take on the potential health or financial risks of this decision? As a seller, assuming that we even have a Champion, are we hoping that our buyer positions it right? We're confident that our sales process got them aligned, connected, and committed, but they're not the final decision maker here. In this sensitive moment of decision, are they going to position the right justification the right way? Or is just going to be, "Well, here's the pros and the cons. Totally your decision." That's not the positioning we want, is it? But what have we done to empower them to position it right?

In a small business who might be considering a large investment to support their growth, decisions like these can make or break the business itself. What information and assurances does our Champion need in order to make this impactful choice? What factors do those business operators need their sellers to realize and respect? They can't be minimized. This year's income or even personal life savings might be on the line. In the largest of enterprises and institutions with complex buying processes, multiple different decision makers, and rigid formal procurement processes, what does their justification look like? Is it a standard template? Or is it a complicated custom collection of financial or technical insights that will clarify the business case to move forward? Or is it just about answering one key question, a business mystery that each seller is desperate to solve?

Regardless of how formal, every buying decision involves a final business justification that, if not directly recognized and properly addressed, will have the power to bring even the strongest of locomotives to a halt.

When, not *if* it happens, depends on the varying purchase processes across unique companies and industries. Just remember, we and our buyer are at their buying *milestone of winning,* whatever that means for them. What we'll learn from the other *Champion Empowerments,* is that a justification isn't the final work to be done. However, the power in the justification lies in that it's the mental prerequisite for any buyer to consider moving to closure.

In relatively all types of sales, a Champion will need to answer these **5 Essential Justification Questions**, either for themselves or for others in the decision process.

1. **Purpose** – *What purpose are we addressing?*

Although our buyers have learned about our product or service, formed and communicated a commitment to the purpose, plan, and promise of our value proposition, this is the time of final decision. Is it possible that the commitment we received was, at least in their mind, preliminary or conditional? Have things changed, where it was a priority a month ago, but not now? Has the previously aligned purpose become less relevant, minimized? Has it expanded and become more complicated? Has the process and people changed? Is there an economic authority that we're just now learning about? The seller's first *justification* objective must start with *Why,* with an absolute certainty that everyone in the decision process is fully aligned and clear on the purpose of making this purchase.

2. **Solution** – *What exactly is the proposed solution?*

You would think that after all our selling and building of a strong, intelligent Buyer Champion that they would be crystal clear on what the solution is. They probably are. Yet, how effective is their positioning of what we do? Will some stakeholders lack the technical expertise that our Champion has? Will others be negatively triggered if they hear certain words or concepts? Is our messaging so complicated that our Champion only gets it because they spent a lot of time with us? Too often, justifications aren't approved simply out of confusion and the wrong perceptions of what they're buying. Realize that most buyers don't do this for a living. Even though they may not say it, they need our help. And, especially when our solutions are somewhat complex or nuanced, a Champion needs to be empowered as to how to position it in the most simplified and yet, non-minimizing way. We need to avoid sounding complicated or too risky for their business, and yet we can't be perceived to be a commodity. This drives the next *essential justification* question.

3. **Differentiation** – *How is this solution different or better?*

If we fail to clarify just how we're so different or better for our buyer, we're taking a massive risk that even our Champion may not be able to overcome. One, if we're trying to charge a premium for what we sell, our Champion will immediately lose all credibility if they can't clearly explain just why we're a premium solution. If the buying team has seen a lot of different solutions, their understanding of and belief in our distinct differentiation will need to be solid. As I've also shared, the concept of *differentiation* should be positioned with buyer context. What may be different or better for one customer may not be considered differentiation at all for our new buyer. In a business justification, often new stakeholders have joined the final decision process. While they may not be well educated in the competitive landscape and alternative solutions, they do know themselves, and they'll have a perspective on what would be different for them. To empower our Champion, our differentiation must be relevant enough that diverse buyers could easily relate and simple enough that you don't have to get a master's degree in our competition to appreciate it. Justifications are best when netted out, succinct. So, remember the concept of *Differentiating Big Ideas*, which are concise and tailored for our unique buyer. Our *differentiating big idea* should be framed as a tight *mantra* that can be repeated and consumed across the buying team. They don't care about how we're different. They care how we're different *for them*.

4. **Impact** – *What positive impact will this have on our business?*

Whether something as formal as a meticulously calculated "ROI" (Return On Investment), a collection of well qualified operational use cases, or simple anecdotal outcomes that should directly result from our purchase, every justification comes down to **Impact**. Often, a Champion is faced with their own internal objections and pushback. Maybe it would help some stakeholders feel better if they put off or delayed this purchase just a few months. Perhaps our Champion's urgency doesn't align to other leaders or business functions. The empowerment they need in those moments of opposition needs to be centered around both the timely *impact* that this decision will make on their business, as well as the *negative consequences* of not moving forward.

Sometimes, our purchase decision is in complete alignment amongst all involved, but not necessarily at the price we'd like to charge. If any part of our justification package, such as fees, our service scope, implementation, commercial, or legal terms are perceived as less ideal than alternative solutions, our Champion will need to be empowered as to how they can justify accepting these exceptions. They'll need to understand and believe in the *positive impact* of making those commitments. At its core, *The Champion Sell* recognizes the power of and expectation that our buyer will be willing and able to sell on our behalf. But, when any part of our proposal is challenged, our Champion will need to be empowered, perhaps more than for any other purpose, in order to clearly define and defend the *impact* that our investment will have on their business or end-customer.

5. **Risk** – *What's the risk mitigation or joint success plan?*

In over two decades working around and leading sellers, the most common flaw in a closing strategy I've observed is a complete disregard or sometimes intentional deception of just how risky or disruptive our solution could be for the buyer. It's as simple as this. If you really are a Champion-focused seller, you'll have the empathy and interest to recognize and appreciate that there might be some logical **Risk** associated with what you sell.

Our own business maturity should tell us that no matter how strong a justification appears to a set of decision makers, any amount of *risk* to their business that can't be explained or satisfied will expose our Champion and completely implode this deal that we had so close to the finish line. If you've ever had this experience, even one when you had all the best intentions for your Champion, you probably learned that if there's real *risk* involved, it will eventually need to be addressed. And trust me, emotions flair up far less aggressively when potential risks and issues are introduced upfront and with a confident plan.

In fact, honest shared ownership of risk can even differentiate us as a trusted partner. Why? Because risk is real. Most business operators accept that. They expect it. When sellers dismiss it, a buyer's instinctual assumption, especially if they haven't become our Champions yet, will always be slow to trust and quick to reconsider us and the solutions we sell. Elite sellers proactively empower their Champions to be aware of risk, while providing them with a plan to satisfy any concerns that risk will be mitigated to the fullest.

The Empowerment of CONSENSUS: *The 3 Alignments of Consensus*

A simple definition of a *buying consensus* is the need for multiple people to come to an alignment on moving forward with a purchase decision. Why do we have a need for consensus? The business justification should sell itself, right? We've talked about risk mitigation and the all-powerful protective survival instincts that people naturally tend to be led by. Thus, buying in a consensus, whether as part of an intentionally defined process or if less formal, is a natural outcome that any elite seller would expect and assume as something they will need to empower their Champion for.

Now, caution is to be had. There are three different ways a Champion approaches the topic of consensus. One, they're upfront that others will need to get aligned to finalizing this decision. They say things like, "While I'm optimistic, I don't want to mislead you that I'm the only one who has to get on board." The second approach usually comes with good intentions but a lack of experience in making these buying decisions. This is when they guide us down a specific decision process, leading toward a targeted purchase timeline, only to discover new and previously unknown buyers who will now need to participate in the evaluation. They may try to comfort us with statements like, "I know this is frustrating for you. But on the bright side, we're still moving forward in the process."

However, there is also a third way a Champion might try to handle this reality of consensus. This is when our buyer reminds us with an overconfident swagger of, "I'm the only one who will be in this decision. This is well within my budget, and I have full authority to make this purchase." If it's not true, then why would they do this? Could their ego or need for control be this bad? Well, yes. But also, that interest in being able to control their buying process is understandable. We should appreciate their intention if they're in fact our Champion. Gaining consensus can often feel just as risky for our buyers as it is for us. Think about it. Multiple people involved will mean multiple agendas, priorities, and an ultimate need for more work to gain their alignment and move this purchase to closure. Who would want to work harder and deal with more frustrating internal processes and politics if they've already made their mind up for what they want to do? Now, is it possible that the decision to close an agreement won't call for a consensus between multiple people? Possible, but not probable, even in the smallest of companies or size of investments.

What does it really mean to win over a *consensus* in a decision process? While it doesn't mean that the contract is signed and the deal is closed, gaining a consensus is when either we or our Buyer Champion has reached an agreement from all or most of the key people who needed to be involved in the decision to purchase. So, if we're to empower our Champions to reach that consensus in the most efficient and effective way possible, we need to plan for that agreement to involve these **3 Alignments of Consensus.**

1. **Prioritization of Purpose** – *Will all stakeholders align on the priority of addressing the purpose of this purchase?*

Commitment doesn't come from a company. It comes from a person. And in a state of consensus, it comes from *people*. Even though our Champion has worked through their own *commitment path*, which started with the *purpose* of choosing to move forward with us, now in the state of *consensus-building*, our Champion is

327

faced with a new mission. The objective of that mission is to help their fellow consensus mates align on why addressing this purpose should be a priority . . . now! We're talking about timing, urgency. Many folks in business can easily come to an understanding as to why doing something would be important. Reality is, no matter how proud and passionate we are for the purpose we solve for, there are always several valid initiatives and business needs to consider. The question we need to empower our Champion to sell is, *Why prioritize addressing the purpose of our solution now?* Much as in the justification of *impact*, there needs to be clarity of their *negative consequences* of not capturing the benefits of our value proposition. Because we're in a state of *consensus*, our work must start with discovering, validating, and documenting who's in *the consensus* group, what unique objectives, priorities, and concerns each member has, and how any negative consequences might affect them individually. Our Champion's message of prioritization must directly link to a purpose that aligns with every person in *the consensus* group, or else some just won't feel the personal motivation to support moving forward.

2. **Personal Decision Criteria** – *What unique decision criteria will each stakeholder need to feel alignment to?*

If our Champion is successful in their effort to align *the consensus* on the prioritization of the purpose that we serve, then their fellow consensus mates are now going to start choosing the specific criteria that they need a solution to meet. Have you ever had a deal poised to close and yet within days, maybe hours, it flipped and went to the competition? All systems were *GO* on the prioritization of purpose. Our Champion told us that we were selected. So, what happened?

In a consensus group, some people just have *more* than

others, more than our Champion. *More of what,* you ask? Just, more of everything! Power, influence, leverage, louder voice, political capital. This is why we always need *more* Champions. Sellers often think of getting *outsold* as having to do with our competition's salesperson or team. It's possible. But any time that we're getting outsold, it's absolutely because someone else's Champion is selling better than ours. Some competitor was able to connect to their personal decision criteria for a solution, and we weren't. We should assume that each person in the *circle of consensus* has their own unique set of decision criteria. Depending on their role or function, some could care about a financial term, a specific service, while others a solution competency.

Where sellers miss the mark in the later-stage *milestone of winning* is that we assume that all the decision criteria for their product or service have been addressed. They've checked those boxes already. Time to move on. Remember *Elite Seller,* the work never stops until the deal is done. We can't get outsold. A consensus means that multiple people, sometimes brand-new people to the process, need to agree, or at least respect each other's decision criteria. Earlier in our sales process, those criteria discussed held less weight. Now, this wasn't because they weren't important or relevant to the success of their business. It was simply the timing of those decisions. Thus, their communication of their decision criteria held less weight. This is the actual *Go / No-go* time, and there are new sheriffs in town. Our Champion needs to be empowered to understand and position a solution tailored to the unique individual decision criteria of every single decision maker in that *consensus group.*

3. **Ownership of Decision Process** – *Who will own the different roles and responsibilities of the purchase process?*

It's one thing to have a general idea of the process that this consensus will lead us through for us to get to the closure we know we deserve. But every time we stop at gaining that general idea to a decision process, it's the same as saying, *It's no big deal. Our solution is so differentiated. It's going to make such a huge impact on this customer!* Deal pushed! *I gotta tell my manager this isn't happening. It's not going to be fun.* The specific people who are in this *circle of consensus* have been chosen for a reason. They all play a role in this action thriller ride we call a *deal.* If we and our Champion are not aligned on who is responsible for doing what in the **Decision Process**, not only do we risk some step going sideways or poor information flow bringing up red flags, that misalignment could also push our deal out longer. Far worse, any dysfunction in the process could create so much fear or negative justification for our solution that our Champion loses momentum and support. Yet, empowering our Champion to be ready for the process and minimize any potential surprises is not at all complicated. Once we learn it, there's no excuse for us to ever take any shortcuts again.

Our last empowerment for our Champion to succeed with *the consensus* group all comes down to us curiously qualifying a clear understanding of **The 3 Parts of a Decision Process**. Anything less than learning all three is incomplete qualification and a weak empowerment of the *Decision Process.* What are the **Steps**? What is the expected **Timeline** for each step? And what **People** will be involved in each step? **Steps, Timeline, People**.

We first need our Champion to walk us through every *step* that stands between where we are and when this agreement closes. Because we owe it to our management and our own mental health to know when an opportunity will close, we need to find out the *timing* of each step. If there's three main steps remaining in the purchase process and step three takes four weeks on average, then we would need to know that if we only had two weeks left in the quarter to get the deal done. The timing of closing a deal should always be important for setting our own and our management's expectations.

However, no qualifier of a *decision process* is more important than learning who the *people* are involved in each step. Not knowing people is where we can get outsold and where deals can completely fall apart. Yet, this knowledge fails to be identified so often by both sellers and their Buying Champions.

JOE PA MEETS CAROLYN

About to close my first deal with a unicorn tech startup I was at, I asked one of my Champions, Joe, the IT director of one of America's largest luxury retailers, to meet me in his office. Everyone called him Joe Pa because he was like a grandpa to everyone. After over thirty years at this same company, Joe was nearing his retirement. But still, he had a lot on his plate from technology transformation in the stores to growing the online business and addressing some new credit card compliance requirement called PCI. These three business drivers were the core of why this opportunity for us was even being funded.

Early on, I wasn't so sure because all our interactions seemed so informal and were with the same three people, Joe and two on his team. I was conflicted if this was a sign that there wasn't a serious deal here, or if we just had some down-to-earth buyers who didn't bring much drama to the table. My strategy to win this deal was a bit primitive. Find a way to get on site, walk the halls as much as possible, and the path to a deal would eventually appear. Sure enough, one day in the bathroom I ran into Phil, the CIO, *Chief Information Officer*. He asked how everyone was treating me. I told him the three key initiatives that we were working on and asked if he was aware. He said, "Of course! That's what we're all focused on."

That's all I needed to hear to believe that there was a justification that an executive was supporting. For the next month, my team mapped out and formally documented how we aligned to not only all three initiatives, but to each stakeholder who was owning them. These were all great guys, but very different in personality and priority criteria for each of their own objectives.

When Joe and I got together, I explained how hard we had both worked and that his team deserved to reap the benefits of our automation. I then delegated the selling a bit and said, "But you know, I've had a few customers who really got frustrated at the end with their final purchase process. Several steps and timelines changed, and some surprising new people got involved. My management got on my nerves. So, I don't want that to happen to us. Could we just take a few minutes to write out what you at least think the decision process will be?"

Joe actually appreciated the request as he was already overworked, burned out, and a bit frustrated with his own company's politics. So, I grabbed a marker standing at his white board and we listed out each step, the longest amount of time he thought each step should take, and we named the people involved along the way. While Joe wasn't a hundred percent certain of the process, and he told me as much, that exercise exposed that there was another pretty important director named Carolyn who hadn't even been introduced yet.

That week, rumors had spread that she might be taking over for Joe in preparation for his impending retirement later that year. Carolyn came from a different part of the organization and Joe hadn't even met her yet. She worked in a separate building you had to drive to. So, Carolyn was next on both of our lists. In that new but very positive connection, we discovered alignments that even further justified this purchase of our solution. We closed that deal with complete transparency and predictability. But most importantly, it closed with Joe having a real feeling of empowerment to get our solution in time for him to pass his compliance audit and replace his current spend.

For all the alignments on *purpose* and *decision criteria* across *the consensus group*, not to mention the *steps, timelines,* and *people* involved in the *decision process*, our Champions need to be empowered to both learn and organize amongst *the consensus*. Whether the consensus dynamics involve a reselling of purpose and urgency, a recalibration of priority criteria, or a clarification on who will own what in the *decision process*, our job as Elite Sellers will be to empower alignment between our Champion, *the consensus*, and ourselves.

The Empowerment of NEGOTIATION: *The Champion-Based Negotiation*

Some of you have had different levels of experience and even formal training in sales **Negotiation**. There are types of sales where it seems that there isn't an actual negotiation stage to the deal. Two things to consider here. One, there's always a negotiation, even though we salespeople may not be in the middle of it. This mindset shift is all about Champions selling for us and our E.L.I.T.E. habit of determining anything and everything they need for us to *empower* them to do so.

All buyers in significant purchase decisions need to get through some level of internal negotiations. Quite often, this stage also includes external negotiations with vendors and solution providers. Champions will have to internally negotiate several different decisions, from prioritization to price. Especially in our recognition of the consensus-driven purchase, there will always be something and someone to negotiate with. The second consideration in a Champion-based sell is that of all the calls-to-action that we'll want and need from our Champions, none is more important than them working with us in a negotiation.

In the more traditional negotiations, many buyers and even sellers find it acceptable that a Champion would turn adversarial for the negotiation. Bottom line. This isn't acceptable and it could be a sign that we don't have a Champion. While we should be consistently leading a habit *of empowering our Champions* for those sometimes controversial and tense negotiations, that also goes with the expectation that we're still in this together. You're either a Champion or you're not. If we don't find ourselves able to get to the state of a healthy *Champion-based negotiation*, then we may only be selling with a coach, a sponsor, or maybe just a cheerleader.

We've all worked hard to get to this *milestone of winning*. We've built trust, commitments, and connections that justify us working covertly around a formal negotiation process, because it's the right thing to do between business partners. We'd never want to get our Champions exposed or ask them to do anything unethical.

However, we sellers need to realize that when a buyer leaves *us* exposed with no support or even a semblance of guidance during a negotiation, we simply don't have a Champion by the very disciplined standards of an elite seller. A *Champion-based negotiation* means that we will rely on the open communication, guidance, problem-solving, and continuous selling on our behalf until the deal is closed. A collaborative highly aligned *Champion-*

based negotiation shouldn't be the exception or a nice-to-have in business. This needs to be our default expectation.

Ok. So, anything we expect out of another human being, we should expect out of ourselves, right? That's a partnership. To further motivate our Champion to continue having our back during a negotiation, we need to first have theirs. This is the **Empowerment of Negotiation**. In leading this habit, we will do everything we can to ensure that our Champion is empowered to answer all the questions they'll face, solve any problems that arise, and move the process to close. Of all the situations when we need our Champion selling on our behalf, none can be more challenging and stressful for both of us as during this final stage we call a **Negotiation**.

A true Champion, even if part of their job is to play the role of negotiator, will be on our team in *help mode* the best they are able. Our powerful and influential business partner, the one we've intently worked toward building connection, commitment, and trust with, has now reached their Super Bowl of sales battles. Seller, this is no time to disappear. It's time to step up! This is *the work we do to win*.

Now, determining just what our Champion will need from us to feel empowered during their negotiations starts with a direct question, "Hey Champion, tell me what you think you'll need from us through this upcoming negotiation." There's nothing like directness. What then follows in their guidance will usually fall into three buckets: **Communication, Messaging and Information**, and **Negotiation Guides**. While certainly every type of sell is different and negotiations can have as many flavors as those old-fashioned candy shops in the airport, consider this framework for a well-empowered *Champion-based Negotiation*.

Communication

Our first step toward empowering the *Champion-based Negotiation* starts with setting the expectation at the onset that we will need an open and agreeable way to communicate with one another. Both of us should feel empowered here. This could be a simple arrangement with an open invitation to visit the office, exchange email, have a regularly scheduled touchpoint call, or something as personal as a special pass to text message whenever necessary.

Also, *Elite Champion Seller*, this communication agreement is completely acceptable to ask for if in a formal, otherwise locked down procurement process. You know those. This is when the sweet and partnering vendor email states emphatically, "All communication outside of procurement should cease immediately." While we should always be considerate of a buyer's internal processes, understand that the details aren't always our Champion's doing, nor are they necessarily a fan. In fact, breaking communication with the very people who understand the solutions and context most is often a very counterproductive and overcomplicated approach. It's a negotiation tactic to maintain control.

But it's also how otherwise logical decisions and information can get so disrupted that a purchase process adds weeks, heading in the wrong direction, simply because of poor communication. Just stay focused on the mission. The bottom line in our understanding and appreciation for the importance of building a Champion in the first place is that we realize that other people internally will need to be sold, resold, and reassured with ongoing concerns addressed. Things will change in our opportunity.

I've shared that, "All good deals die three deaths." Elite sellers know that it is no less our job as professional sellers to be in open and transparent communication with our Champions, as it is for our buyers to do their jobs. Again, our Champions need our empowerment far more than we realize. As those deal dynamics change or intended plans start going haywire, remember that our Champion has done their own work, invested their time, spent political capital, and they deserve to close this deal too. Champions owe it to themselves and for the dual-respect partnership that we've formed to openly and readily communicate with us throughout the ups and downs and twists and turns of the final negotiations.

Messaging and Information

For all we've covered to this point in the *winning milestone*, from the purpose we deliver to what our solution is for their business, its differentiation and expected business impact, we should consider this all the Champion's needed *Messaging* to win. With all the questions and requested details that will be asked to our Champion by the different stakeholders, from our delivery and risk-mitigation plan to pricing and billing detail, situational or customer-centric items, these and other examples could all be considered *Information*.

While it could work out fine if we relied on the assumption that our Champion is fully prepared and confident to communicate all relevant *messaging and information* about our solution, is this something that we really want to risk? Just think about what negotiation is, compared to something like gaining alignment amongst a *consensus group*. Negotiation is a final step and formal commitment to do business together. This is about the terms that will frame and define our relationship. Gaining alignment across a *consensus* is about ensuring that all necessary parties are *on the same page*. There are no general objections to moving forward.

However, when the negotiation hits our Champion, those verbal attacks could come as fast and furious as Conor McGregor in an MMA press conference! Elite Sellers ask themselves, in a worst-case negotiation conflict or debate, what is the level and quality of empowerment that my Champion would need? What netted out *messaging* is needed for the different relevant negotiation players? What's the standard *information* that the company usually requires? How responsive will I be to urgent information requests? This is another reason for us to gain that open communication agreement with our Champion. There's often just no way to know all the different informational directions the negotiators will try to pull our Champion. It could be our very Champion who's facilitating the negotiation, and they're trying to avoid any issues. Our on-call communication for them could reap just as much benefit for our Champion as us in a time of negotiation crisis management.

To avoid the very possible risk that our Champion could lack the empowerment they need to win this negotiation, consider proactively sending them some type of informational package. Because my teams would often use PowerPoint slide decks to summarize a Champions business justification, key messaging, and information, they often called this a "Champion Deck." Many great sellers practice a succinct but complete email summary, maybe a bulleted write-up. While we should avoid anything too verbose, where it's not easy for our Champion to get access to and comprehend the net information they need, the Elite Seller knows that a Champion deserves this level of thoughtful work done on their behalf. *Champion Empowerment* means going the extra mile and mitigating any potential risks for both of us in order to *win*.

Negotiation Guides

A **Negotiation Guide** can be thought of as any rule, objective, or parameter that both we and our Champion should be aware of before heading into the negotiation. Getting these clearly laid out empowers both of us. We sellers feel prepared and avoid any unnatural or counterproductive behaviors to our Champion's mission. Our Champion is armed with what they need to make this negotiation as seamless as possible.

What would be some examples of **negotiation guides**? Obviously, these would vary across the many different types of sales. Two fundamental guides to any negotiation are **Value Threshold** and **Leverage**. In the *empowerment of justification*, there was an expectation of *impact* to be made, the measure of *value* associated with the scope and price of our investment.

Our Champion needs to be empowered to understand at what point do we go below a **threshold of value**. Meaning, the lower they request the price, for example, there needs to be a distinct threshold we set where the reduction in what we are willing to deliver for that price now diminishes the value they are expecting out of this purchase. Our response to a hard negotiator, or even better done through proactive education, needs to be clear communication that if they try to reduce a certain amount of solution scope or the fee to pay for that scope, the value that we both share will be at risk. That *value threshold* needs to be clear to our Champion so they can decide whether to support the ask or not. If they're going to haggle on price or anything else, we'll certainly need to get something in return for every give that they get.

The *negotiation guide* of **Leverage** that either we or our buyer has in any negotiation is foundational to just how far each of us can push the other. In a B2B negotiation, leverage could be the opportunity to consolidate several providers and reduce the buyer's overall Total Cost of Ownership. It could be to eliminate a vendor who has a bad reputation from delivering subpar service and performance. Preceding a drop-dead date on a related contract renewal could be leverage. In a medical sell, the leverage could be the urgent and critical nature of the treatment for a group of patients. It could be an operational expense savings for one of the healthcare business units. A government contractor may have leverage in the multiple other contracts they already manage related to their new customer. For a marketing team, delivering on a new revenue initiative by a compelling date could be the leverage of time. Leverage could simply be that we have the only solution that has been proven to meet their needs.

However, we should never minimize or allow ourselves to be surprised by the power of a buyer's leverage over us. Our buyer could have leverage in a counter proposal from our competitor. It could be from their current incumbent solution, especially if our Champion isn't confident that they can defend our position and terms. Maybe the requirements have recently been reduced and we're less differentiated, less leverage. Perhaps we're a startup and the buyer knows that if we don't get this deal closed in the quarter, we'll have to delay our next funding round.

Every type of sale has its own different examples of buyer leverage. The point to understand is that in many negotiation scenarios, we sellers have less leverage than we think we do. This is another justification for our mission to be *Building and Winning with Champions*. Rather than emotionally dismissing the threats, Elite Sellers respect these legitimate leverage points. They see them as a possible reason to adjust strategy or proposal, but in alignment with our Champions. We should always be cautious to wait too long to react to leverage that our buyer has over us. People buy on emotions, and they'll walk away from us on emotions too. The list of a buyer's leverage over a seller is usually far more extensive than we sellers give credit to. Yet, this is a Champion-based sell. So, we communicate. We align. And we *win* together.

As we do, we'll find ourselves potentially needing to empower around other *negotiation guides* and parameters that can provide value and clarity for our Champion. An **Anchor Point**, in negotiation terms, is a deal point such as a price or a commercial term where any negotiator, buyer, or seller designates as a line in the sand. It's a *mental anchor*, no different than a boat that moves but doesn't drift away from its anchor in the sand. The mental strategy of using an *anchor point* is that our buyer, whether they choose to respect it, will need to hear it if we have some guiding parameters we want our deal to anchor around. *We can talk about further discounting, but this contract must close by the end of the month.* This could be a price point that we set. *Hey Champion, no matter what direction this negotiation goes, what I've been told is that this agreement's structure has only been approved if the price remains at least $1 million. Otherwise, finance says we can't make the math work unless we reduce scope.*

Buyer negotiators will also throw out their own anchors. *No matter what we do here, we are not paying for the first three months of service.* In these and any example of an anchor point, the key in a *Champion-based negotiation* is that both we and our Champions are empowered to know what each other's *anchor points* are as a guide to our negotiations.

Another *negotiation guide* example is a **Sacred Cow**. Attorneys, finance executives, and contract analysts like to use this term specially to protect their interests. Buyers and sellers can both have their own *sacred cows*. A *sacred cow* is any term in our agreements that just cannot and will not be compromised. In most cases, these are contractual commitments we're making here. Even though some deals feel great to close, they can include specific terms that have a negative impact or create business risk for one of the parties. It's in these terms where we typically find the *sacred cows*. Be careful here. If it might be negotiated by your company, then it's not really a *sacred cow*. Our Champions need to know this clearly and upfront. If they're truly a Champion, they will respect and prioritize representing our needs on those non-negotiables, if we empower them to. In that empowerment, they will tend to support us if they can understand the *intention behind any position*. We should share these intentions with a clean explanation. What does this *sacred cow* mean to the health and responsibility of our business? However, we can't lose our credibility by eventually accepting to *give* on a previously stated *sacred cow*. Afterall, a non-negotiable is a non-negotiable. This could be payment terms, a special clause for terminating the contract, passing through specific third-party costs.

At the heart of what makes a negotiation a craft into itself is that any of these *value thresholds, leverage, anchor points,* and *sacred cows* can often be confused with or merely disguised as **Negotiation Currencies**. These are the things that can be haggled back and forth. A seller and experienced Champion will communicate a list of both of their currencies. These could be final price, fee per unit, amount of service hours included, close date, payment terms, solution scope, essentially all the items that could be negotiated.

Then, as the negotiation goes on, a good seller tracks these as *gives* and *gets*. If our buyer has asked for and we've conceded five items, and yet we've only gotten one thing we asked for in return, then we have five Gives to our one Get. An Elite Seller then communicates those *gives and gets* openly with a Champion, empowering them to consider making this agreement more balanced. The communication and consideration of these *negotiation guides*, along with the alignment we have or haven't gained with our Champion, will define how strong our *Champion-based Negotiation* is.

In all these areas of *empowering a Champion through a negotiation*, it is fundamental in our relationship and shared trust with our Champions that we are open and honest with each other. A good *Champion-based Negotiation* is when both buyer and seller are communicating and aligned. As in any true business partnership, a seller and their Champion have earned the right to ask one another for this level of transparency and dual value across *communication, messaging and information*, and any important *negotiation guides*.

SUMMARY: *Empowering Champions*

The final E.L.I.T.E. habit of *Empowering Champions* is all about the *work we do to win*. Elite Sellers don't get to this final *Milestone of Winning* and get outsold by competitors or outmaneuvered by other stakeholders in the buying process. They know that our Champions need us far more than they'll admit or realize in order to avoid the frustrating sidetracks that justifications and negotiations can take. So, they work. They work on behalf of this business partner we call a *Champion*. There's way too much on the line for both partners. Too much can go wrong and too many people can sabotage what we and our Champions have worked so hard for. This is not our time to beg, chase, rest, or wait for the order. If a business justification is needed, we qualify every detail of what and who is needed to satisfy the case to buy us.

Armed with that detail, we empower our Champions with any information or messaging they need. If the negotiation is ramping up, stressing out on price discounts and uncertain negotiation tactics all alone without a Champion is not fun. We've worked to build a Champion. That earns us the right to have a highly aligned open-communication *Champion-based Negotiation*. The work that our Champions need from us at this final milestone is to be *empowered* to overcome any people or positions that are counter to us winning this business.

Think of the great uncommon sales work that we've done here. Our Champions have been built and tested over time from those initial *connections* to a positive future *vision* we could deliver for them to inspirations of *commitment*, and on through a trust-building journey toward *closure*. All of that's led to this final decision. They've communicated with us openly, redirected us with guidance and advice, all while forming a tightly aligned partnership. So, *justification* and *negotiation* are no time for this bond to breakdown. It's time for us to do the work needed to win together.

A purchase is rarely a unilateral decision. Even in the smallest of deals, a *consensus* will be needed, and the questions just get harder, needing answers that are rock-solid. All buyer risks will need to be mitigated, and it's our job to help win that trust.

It's in these challenges for our Champion where we find our opportunities to **empower them**!

They'll need empowerment in the final *justification* for this investment, where understanding will need to be shared in the *purpose, solution, differentiation, impact, and risk-mitigating plan.* The buying *consensus* will then place broad challenges on our Champion. For that decision circle, they will also need to be *empowered.* Those *consensus* stakeholders will all be faced with making a formal commitment to this purchase, so they'll need clarity and alignment to the *prioritization of the purpose* of making this decision now for a solution that meets their *personal decision criteria*, all with well-defined roles and *ownership of the decision process.*

Lastly, while the *negotiation* may be a simple discussion between clear-headed parties, it could also be a storm of chaos, ripe with egos and competing agendas. Our Champion will need us here more than ever. We'll need to facilitate a *Champion-based Negotiation* complete with our *empowerment* of an agreed *communication plan*, the necessary *messaging and information,* and all *negotiation guides* they'll need to be able to support us with confidence and effectiveness.

Empowering Champions is about *winning,* but *winning together.* Elite Sellers never back down from the *work it takes to win.* No work is more vital than supporting, inspiring, and motivating our Buyer Champions through the way that we go above and beyond what common sellers do. *We empower our Champions to win.* This separates us as Elite Sellers who consistently reach all our career, wealth, and fulfillment dreams in this crazy work life we call *Sales.*

CONCLUSION

THE GRIT, GRATITUDE, AND GRACE OF THE CHAMPION SELL

T here is nothing about the sales profession that is easy or predictable. While many of us sellers enjoy the thrill of the win or the security of the reward, far too many are still struggling with the journey. If you're already a strong sales athlete, good on you! I hope you were able to take at least one thing away that will help you perform consistently at the highest of levels. Every great athlete is always striving to win more while burning less calories. So, here's to your sales efficiency!

My purpose in writing **The Champion Sell** is to help anyone and everyone who's serious about their sales craft, sellers who are finding success but not enough to make life-changing money, managers working to become great high-productivity sales leaders, and those who are still trying to *crack the code* for this Central Intelligence Agency we call *Sales*.

All Elite Sellers struggled at one time. The difference with them? Great sellers have **GRIT!** It's how we get through the learning, how we maneuver across the tough buyer jungle, and how we survive and win the sales battles with our competition. It's our *grit*, our *resiliency!* If you're one of those sellers who are still suffering through the grind, just make a choice. Say, "I will not accept the struggle any longer." You've got the tools.

And I don't just mean this book. While my hope for *The Champion Sell* is that's it's given you all a unique insight into the people we sell to, clarity for what makes the greatest impact on those buyers, and enough detail for you to apply these concepts to winning, you already had the tools. Not only have you committed to honing your sales craft by investing your time and mental energy to learning, you also already know how to build Champions. People know people. You already have friends who love you with a sense of loyalty and support. How did that happen?

We've been experiencing people every day of our lives. Each year, we learn just a bit more about what makes us all tick. None of your friends or relationships ever expected you to be perfect. And, neither do your buyers. Yet, out of a lack of *grit* and belief in ourselves, we allow our fears, insecurities, and absence of leadership to cause us to change our mindsets and behaviors in business. We lose the determined intention to attract connections with people, forget the purpose of the relationships we serve, and abandon all empathy and concern for the people we sell to. Because we become uncertain about how and when we'll achieve our sales and career goals, we overcompensate. We stop paying attention to people. And yet, the secret to sales is PEOPLE! **Buyer Champions.** It's people who need to be connected and committed to what we sell. Those human buyers we get the opportunity to spend time with should be the maniacal focus of our sales resiliency.

A lot of us sellers allow our knowledge and passion for the products and services we sell to get in the way of the **GRATITUDE** we should have for our buyers and value that we can deliver for them. I'm not suggesting that all Elite Sellers have saintly levels of character and always have honorable motivations. But elite salespeople are pretty *grateful* for the opportunity to get a meeting, curiously learn about a buyer, and use their talents to see if they could actually make a difference. How do I know that they're *grateful?* Because they don't take shortcuts. They prepare and strategize with pride in every detail. And, because their greatest sales trait is that they routinely Build Champions, that means that they don't take the people they sell to for granted.

Don't make a lack of deal pipeline your buyer's problem. Desperate sellers don't make connections with people. Not everyone's the right buyer for us. But it also can't be us who gets in the way of what could be a really special opportunity for our buyer to realize the vision and value of the solutions that we sell. When we have a mindset of *gratitude*, it comes across, and buyers want to become our Champions. We walk out of their offices, and they wonder, *Wow, I sure hope we'll be able to do business together*. So, be *grateful* for the opportunity to attract **Emotional Connection, Lead Vision, Inspire Commitment, Build Trust, and Empower our Champions to win**.

How do we win in sales? Well, go on a sales call as soon as you can, and the answer will be right in front of you. **We don't sell to companies. We sell to people.** The greater an understanding we can learn about the human beings we sell to, why they would take a meeting and seek out solutions, what they're trying to accomplish for themselves, and how they make their decisions, the easier our job gets. The stronger our intuition becomes and the more empathy and awareness we gain for them, the more **GRACE** we'll naturally start showing them in all our interactions.

Buyers aren't robots and all companies and their situations are not the same. No matter how strongly we believe in our own value proposition, it may not always be the right buyer we're selling to with the right set of problems and desired outcomes that align to what we sell. Or it just might not be the right timing to make a change. Buyers are human and their internal processes and challenges are real. Our question for ourselves should be, *How strong and capable are we at leading their vision toward a positive future state that we can uniquely deliver?* If they just can't connect to that vision, we should have some *grace* for them and find our next Champion Target.

Most of the time, however, it's us who's failing to make those emotional and intellectual connections to a vision that they would care about. When we're making it all about us, we're not showing *grace*. As you battle through your own development as a seller, have some *grace* for yourself. If you're leading salespeople with a responsibility to develop them, have some *grace* for your team. You become the master for that which you lead and model what an *Elite Champion-based Seller* really looks like.

Sales isn't a destination; it's a journey. Imagine a long ultramarathon that's made up of hundreds of mini sprints. That's a *sales year*. We need to be strong enough for the sprints, because the windows of opportunities close fast, and the buyers are diverse. We survive the sprints because we work with a resilient *grit*. We emotionally and mentally last through the long marathon because we have *gratitude* for the experience and greater purpose of why we're even in the race. But make no mistake. We win that race because of the *grace* we show to our buyers, which allows us to build the Champions who will always carry us through the finish line a *Winner!*

Thank you for investing in *The Champion Sell*. Enjoy your sales journey. But always remember: **Normal is Overrated. Be Elite!**

ACKNOWLEDGEMENTS

"We make a living by what we get, but we make a life by what we give."

- *Winston Churchill*

One can't teach with any level of confidence or credibility without the wisdom and investment from their own teachers. While the concepts and disciplines I've shared in this book have been influenced by so many whom I've both worked with and certainly sellers I've led, I'd like to at least acknowledge the leaders who have and continue to serve as my teachers.

All my gratitude to Brad Clark, John McMahon, John Kaplan, Scott Davis, Richard Duggan, Kelly Connery, Geoff Lochausen, Luca Lazzaron, Dan Fougere, Andy Byron, John Byrne, and Kimberly Rivera.

- R2

Printed in Great Britain
by Amazon

28786899R00201